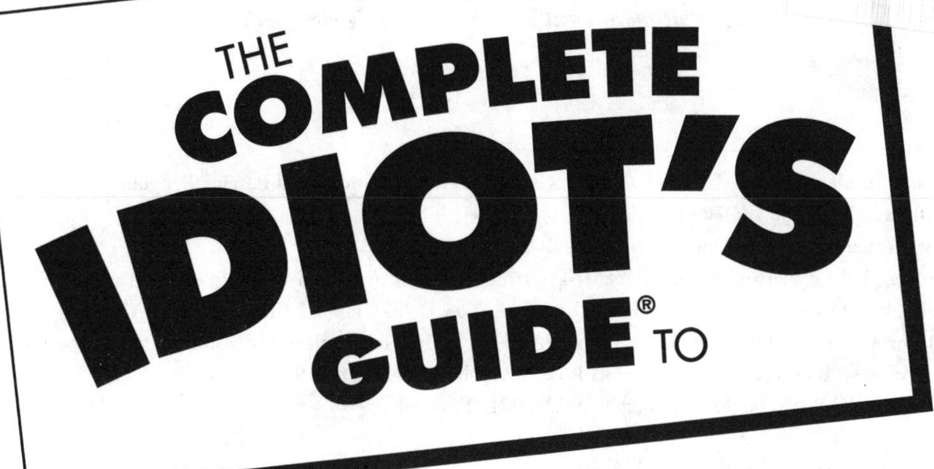

Singing

by Phyllis Fulford and Michael Miller

ALPHA
A member of Penguin Group (USA) Inc.

This book is dedicated to my son Jim, who spent a lot of childhood years sharing me with other people's kids. His selfless acceptance and understanding of all that taught me more about love than anything else. —Phyllis

ALPHA BOOKS

Published by the Penguin Group

Penguin Group (USA) Inc., 375 Hudson Street, New York, New York 10014, U.S.A.

Penguin Group (Canada), 10 Alcorn Avenue, Toronto, Ontario, Canada M4V 3B2 (a division of Pearson Penguin Canada Inc.)

Penguin Books Ltd, 80 Strand, London WC2R 0RL, England

Penguin Ireland, 25 St Stephen's Green, Dublin 2, Ireland (a division of Penguin Books Ltd)

Penguin Group (Australia), 250 Camberwell Road, Camberwell, Victoria 3124, Australia (a division of Pearson Australia Group Pty Ltd)

Penguin Books India Pvt Ltd, 11 Community Centre, Panchsheel Park, New Delhi—110 017, India

Penguin Group (NZ), cnr Airborne and Rosedale Roads, Albany, Auckland 1310, New Zealand (a division of Pearson New Zealand Ltd)

Penguin Books (South Africa) (Pty) Ltd, 24 Sturdee Avenue, Rosebank, Johannesburg 2196, South Africa

Penguin Books Ltd, Registered Offices: 80 Strand, London WC2R 0RL, England

International Standard Book Number: 1-59257-086-0
Library of Congress Catalog Card Number: 2003106907

10 13

Interpretation of the printing code: The rightmost number of the first series of numbers is the year of the book's printing; the rightmost number of the second series of numbers is the number of the book's printing. For example, a printing code of 03-1 shows that the first printing occurred in 2003.

Printed in the United States of America

Publisher: *Marie Butler-Knight*
Product Manager: *Phil Kitchel*
Senior Managing Editor: *Jennifer Chisholm*
Senior Acquisitions Editor: *Renee Wilmeth*
Development Editor: *Nancy D. Lewis*
Senior Production Editor: *Billy Fields*
Copy Editor: *Cari Luna*
Illustrator: *Chris Eliopoulos*
Cover/Book Designer: *Trina Wurst*
Indexer: *Julie Bess*
Layout/Proofreading: *John Etchison, Karen A. Gill, Ayanna Lacey*

Contents at a Glance

Contents

Foreword

The teaching of voice may be one of the most elusive and careful art forms. In singing, one deals with *human* physiology, not *mechanical* engineering. A beginning singer cannot reach down inside the body and adjust this or that to produce a beautiful tone. It is here when the expertise of a good teacher must enter. The artful teacher knows just what to say and when to say it, and the results can be surprising, and enormously satisfying.

I have met few individuals who did not want to sing better. Some beginning singers, after only a few lessons, immediately began to grasp the mysteries of beautiful singing, later developing into artists who are pursuing careers as performers. Others may take more time, slowly absorbing the principals of healthy vocal technique. Every singer is different, and every physical makeup is unique, even down to the subtle distinctions of bone structure. Some singers are born to sing a Schubert *lied*, others may have a penchant toward more contemporary idioms, many are destined to be leaders in choral groups.

Regardless of disposition or ambition, there are some things that all singers need to know, and a considerable amount of that knowledge is found here in this book. *The Complete Idiot's Guide to Singing* exemplifies artful teaching and clearly illuminates the perils, pitfalls, joys, and extreme exuberance that singing can offer.

The authors state that there is no substitution for a gifted voice teacher, and they are right. What has been needed, though, is a clear guidebook, a reference to the many concepts inherent in the careful study of singing. This book offers that and more. Especially important is the emphasis on musicianship and the development of music reading skills. One of the great tragedies in music education in the last number of years has been the disintegration of a systematic teaching of basic skills, something that all students should and can learn. It is hoped that the strong emphasis on *musicianship*, not just singing, found in this book will inspire and provide substance for music students to extend their training to include music theory, ear training, and historical matters.

What has always struck me about singing is the fact that it is so personal, and that there is not one degree of separation between the singer and the instrument. Learning to sing places one in a vulnerable position, and this book helps the burgeoning singer to honestly understand what is involved. There are no shortcuts offered here, just clear, artful teaching.

James Bagwell

James Bagwell is Founder and Artistic Director of the New York Repertory Singers, Artistic Director for Cappella Festival Orchestra and Chorus in New York, Music Director for the May Festival Youth Chorus in Cincinnati, and Music Director for Light Opera Oklahoma in Tulsa. In addition, he is Director of Choruses for the Bard Music Festival and prepares the New York Concert Chorale for performances with the American Symphony Orchestra in Lincoln Center. Since 2000 he has served on the music faculty of Bard College, where he is director of orchestral and choral activities.

Introduction

Everybody can sing—but not everybody can sing well.

You know this. You hear some singers, and you hear the sound of angels. You hear other singers—whether on the stage or in the shower—and you hear the sound of wild animals being tortured over open flames. What makes some voices sound great and others sound grating?

It's all about technique.

Good singing isn't a secret, it's a skill—one almost anyone can learn. You just need to know the right way to do things, and then you need to practice them. Over time, you'll become a better singer. It isn't that hard. Really.

The Complete Idiot's Guide to Singing will teach you basic vocal technique, and then some. It doesn't matter what your background is or what kind of music you want to sing. All you need is your voice and a dedication to your goal; we'll help you with the rest.

Want to sing in a choir? Want to be a big-time pop singer or a country star? Want to sing jazz? How about gospel, musical theater, or opera? It doesn't matter what type of singer you want to be; *The Complete Idiot's Guide to Singing* will teach you the proper vocal technique you need to be successful. Singing isn't rocket science, after all; like we said, anybody can do it, especially if you have a good guide—like this book.

By the way, the "we" behind *The Complete Idiot's Guide to Singing* is a vocal teacher with 30 years of experience and tens of thousands of former students and a former musician who is now a successful nonfiction writer. If you're keeping tabs, Phyllis Fulford is the vocal expert; Michael Miller is the professional writer—and one of Phyllis' former students. We think the pairing makes for a useful and easy-to-read book.

In this collaboration, Phyllis definitely supplies the singing expertise. She draws on more than 30 years of teaching students at all levels, from junior high to adult. She knows what works and what doesn't and the mistakes beginning singers are most apt to make.

Michael's contribution is to put Phyllis' vocal coaching into words on the printed page and to help out with some of the theory and musical examples. So if you like the content of this book, thank Phyllis. If you like the way it's written, thank Michael. (And if you like the approach of the *Complete Idiot's Guide* series in general, thank the publisher!)

We hope you will like this book and, more important, find it useful. Our goal is to help beginning singers improve their technique and become better vocalists. That means learning proper posture, breathing, diction, placement, and phrasing. It also means learning how to sight sing, which requires a basic grounding in music theory. And it means learning how to adapt your technique for different musical styles and mastering the physical tools of the trade—including the microphone.

All of this—and more—is covered somewhere between here and the end of the book.

What You'll Find in This Book

We've arranged this material in such a way that even if you know *nothing* about singing, you can start on page one and progress through the book, moving from the basics to more advanced techniques. And, throughout much of the book, you can practice the techniques at hand by performing the accompanying exercises.

The Complete Idiot's Guide to Singing is composed of 24 chapters, each of which presents a different aspect of vocal technique. The chapters are organized into six general parts, as follows:

Part 1, "Finding Your Voice," provides you with your very first singing lesson. You'll learn how to employ vocal imagery, find your range, and develop basic vocal technique. (This is the place to start if you've never sung a note in your life—or never sung one well!)

Part 2, "Learning to Sing—Properly," presents you with the *right* way to sing. You'll learn how your voice works, how posture affects your singing voice, how to breathe properly, and how to perfect your vocal placement and develop what we call an even voice.

Part 3, "Sight Singing and Vocal Theory," is all about reading music. You'll learn just enough music theory to read basic notes and rhythms, then learn how to apply that theory through the Solfeggio technique. Finally, you'll get the opportunity to test your skills through a series of sight-singing exercises.

Part 4, "Taking It Further," helps you develop advanced vocal technique. You'll learn proper singing diction, phrasing, and dynamics; then you'll find out how to put it all together to learn and practice a song.

Part 5, "Singing in Style," is all about the different styles of music you can sing. You'll learn the specific vocal techniques required to sing choral music; classical and musical theater songs; pop, rock, and country music; jazz; and gospel and R&B. (We think you'll really like these chapters; each one includes a full-length song for you to practice!)

Part 6, "The Next Steps," gives you the last bits of information you need to become a successful singer. You'll learn how to take care of your voice, how to find a voice teacher, how to sing on stage and in the studio, and how to approach—and ace—an audition.

But that's not all. There are five appendixes at the end of the book, providing useful reference information—including a glossary of vocal music terms, a pronunciation reference, a guide to troubleshooting vocal problems, a listing of singing resources, and a practice checklist.

Still not enough? Then how about a free CD! That's right—that shiny little disc in the back of the book is all yours, and it includes performances of all the key exercises in the book. Practice an exercise, then listen to the CD to see if you got it right.

What You Need to Use This Book

Any practicing or aspiring singer can learn basic vocal techniques from *The Complete Idiot's Guide to Singing.* You don't need any initial knowledge to get started; you can use this book even if you've never sung in public or don't know how to read music.

However, it will help if you have access to a CD player (to listen to the audio CD) and to some sort of pitched instrument. This can be anything from a pitch pipe to a piano to one of those inexpensive consumer-grade music keyboards—anything to help you get your initial pitch.

Other than that, the only thing you need to work through the exercises in this book is your voice!

How to Get the Most Out of This Book

To get the most out of this book, you should know how it is designed. We've tried to put things together in such a way that makes practicing both rewarding and fun.

There's a lot of text in this book, as well as more than a few vocal exercises. When you come across an exercise, do it! Follow the instructions and practice the exercise until you get it right. And if you want to hear how a particular exercise is supposed to sound, listen to that exercise performed on the accompanying audio CD. (See Appendix E for a listing of exercises and songs on the CD.)

When you come to the songs in Chapters 16 through 20, note that these songs are presented on the CD—most of them twice. That is, you'll hear the song performed by a talented vocalist, and then you'll hear the song without lead vocals. This is kind of a "music minus one" or Karaoke approach to practicing; sing along with the instrumental-only track to practice your own lead vocals.

Throughout the entire book, you'll see a number of little boxes that present additional advice and information. These elements enhance your knowledge or point out important pitfalls to avoid. Here are the types of boxes you'll see scattered throughout the book:

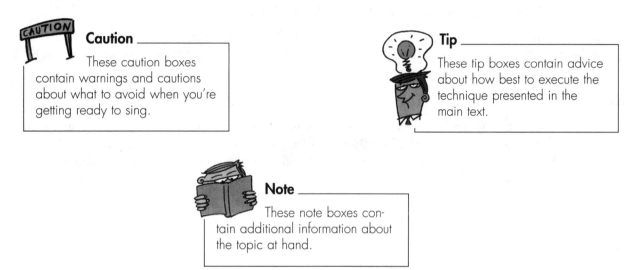

Caution

These caution boxes contain warnings and cautions about what to avoid when you're getting ready to sing.

Tip

These tip boxes contain advice about how best to execute the technique presented in the main text.

Note

These note boxes contain additional information about the topic at hand.

One last thing. This book is written by two people who speak with one voice. That said, when you see an "I" in the text, it's Phyllis' voice you're hearing. She's the one with the thirty-plus years of teaching experience—so when she speaks, you know it's with authority!

Let Us Know What You Think

We love to hear from our readers—especially when the readers are fellow singers! If you want to contact Phyllis or Michael, feel free to e-mail us at singing@molehillgroup.com. We can't promise that we'll answer every e-mail, but we will promise that we'll read each one!

While you're on the web, check out Michael's website at www.molehillgroup.com. Here you'll find any corrections or clarifications to this book, as well as notice of Michael's latest literary projects. Who knows—you might find some other books there that you'd like to read.

It's Time to Start Singing!

You know how important good technique is to becoming a better singer. (Or else you wouldn't be reading this book, right?) Now it's time to stop talking and start practicing—so turn the page and get ready to sing!

Acknowledgments

We had assistance from dozens of individuals in the creation of this book and would like to thank the following for their help:

Thanks to Mark Yount for his valuable contribution to the jazz chapter and for his insights on microphone technique.

Special thanks to Dr. Eric Stark, Assistant Professor of Music at Butler University and Artistic Director of the Indianapolis Symphonic Choir, for his thorough technical review of the book's content. We also appreciate Eric's continuing advice and his assistance in suggesting individuals to perform on the accompanying CD.

Many, many thanks to the talented individuals who participated in the recording sessions for the audio CD that comes with this book: William Barnhardt, Brad Brock, Joe Brown, Doug Henthorn, Ken Fary, Stephanie Mitchell, Mary Moss, and Dr. Mitzi Westra. Thanks as well to Michael Graham and Andy Symons of The Lodge Recording Studio—and to Damon Earlewine, for helping to haul the drums!

Additional thanks to the following individuals for their expert advice: Dr. Michael Barbara, Phil Kern, Karl Manders, Orson Mason, Stephen Moore, James Mulholland, and Travis Nesbitt.

Finally, thanks to the usual suspects at Alpha Books, including but not limited to Marie Butler-Knight, Renee Wilmeth, Billy Fields, Nancy Lewis, and Cari Luna, for helping to turn our manuscript into a printed book.

Trademarks

Part 1

Finding Your Voice

Want to be a singer? Then start singing! This part shows you how to find your vocal range, use vocal imagery, and start developing your singing technique. It's your first singing lesson!

Chapter 1

So You Want to Be a Singer ...

In This Chapter

- Discover the many different outlets for your singing talent
- Learn how singing developed through the ages
- Find out how twentieth-century technology changed the way we sing

So you want to be a singer.

Well, why not?

Everybody sings a little—in the shower, at least. But you want to be a *real* singer, a bona fide *vocalist*, someone whose voice carries far and wide with the most beautiful of melodies.

I think that's great!

This book is all about helping you become a better singer. Of course, it takes dedication on your part and a lot of practice. You can't become a world-class vocalist overnight. But if you put your mind to it and put in the requisite amount of hard work, you'll find your vocal skills improving as time goes by.

And that's what you want—right?

Why Do You Want to Sing?

There are many different types of singers, and many different reasons for becoming a singer. Maybe you just want to sing well enough to join the church choir. Maybe you want to go further than that and establish a professional singing career. Or maybe you want to hit the jackpot and become the next American idol.

There are many opportunities available for serious vocalists. Here's just a short list of what you can aim for as you develop your singing skills:

- Singing in an amateur vocal ensemble—community choir, school chorus, church choir, and so on.
- Taking a solo role in a local choir.

- Singing in community theater.
- Singing for hire in local recording studios—for commercials or backup on local artists' recordings.
- Singing backup in local bands or behind local artists.
- Becoming the lead singer for a local band.
- Becoming a jazz vocalist.
- Singing solo (or with your guitar) in local pubs and coffeehouses.
- Singing in a band or choir at a regional theme park.
- Participating in local, regional, or national talent shows.
- Singing in touring productions of Broadway musicals.
- Moving to New York and singing for the legitimate Broadway stage.
- Performing opera on the local or national stage.
- Winning the next round of *American Idol* or *Star Search*.
- Getting a record contract and becoming a big star.

It doesn't matter what type of singer you want to be; the basic technique is pretty much the same for all musical genres. You have to learn proper posture, proper breathing, proper pronunciation, and other proper vocal techniques. Unless you're naturally talented, you probably can't just stand in front of a microphone and sing to your maximum potential. You need to learn the right way to sing, and you need to train yourself—through lots and lots of practice—to integrate proper technique in your own singing style.

But if you love to sing—*really* love to sing—you'll find that even practicing can be fun.

A Short History of Singing

Before we start learning how to sing, let's stop for a moment and examine the role of singing through the ages. You see, since the beginnings of man, singing has been a basic means of human expression. The need to voice our deepest and most personal emotions is both ancient and universal.

Singing is all around us—but where did it start?

Where It All Began: 3500 B.C.E.

The exact origin of singing is unknown, although it's commonly thought to have emerged *before* the development of spoken language. The voice is, after all, our original musical instrument. Even the most primitive and isolated human cultures sing. Primitive man invoked his gods through incantations, celebrated rites of passage in song, and recanted his history in ballads and epics.

It is not known when or where *art music*—as distinct from *folk music*—began, but there is evidence that as early as 3500 B.C.E., various Mesopotamian cultures already considered music an art. In fact, the oldest notated music we know of is an ancient song, titled "Hymn to Creation," dated before 800 B.C.E.

> **Note**
>
> **Art music** is defined as music written by a trained composer and passed on in written form. **Folk music**, on the other hand, is music of the peasantry or common folk created by unknown or untrained composers, and typically passed on orally from person to person.

Singing in the Early Christian Church

Of course, singing has been integral to all cultures and religions. Singing was such an important part of early Christian worship that church ritual and music developed together and became almost inseparable, borrowing music from other religions and from existing secular tunes to develop a form of liturgical chant. Based on melodies of limited range, expressed in flowing rhythms, liturgical chants were typically sung as solos or in unison by unaccompanied male voices.

In the fourth century C.E., Christianity was established as the official religion of the Roman Empire and a *Schola Cantorum* (singing school) was established by Pope Sylvester. The Roman Catholic Church would control the development of Western music for the next thirteen centuries, during which time religious singing would evolve from simple one-line chants to complex *polyphony*.

Note

Polyphony means music with many interwoven parts.

Developing a Pedagogy

Throughout all ancient history, there was no formal method for documenting what was being sung. It wasn't until the tenth century that there developed a way to notate music, and thus preserve it for future generations.

Musical notation began with symbols being placed above or below a horizontal line, to suggest pitch variances. As both musical notation and polyphony evolved, the concept of high- and low-pitched vocal parts developed. It soon became necessary to distinguish and notate the different vocal parts—leading to the now-standard designation of soprano, alto, tenor, and bass parts.

As we move forward a few centuries, we find more and more singing instruction coming from books and other written tracts. The treatises of that time reflect the preoccupation with cultivating a powerful as well as an agile voice. They also show a more "scientific" approach to the voice as a musical instrument and to matters of voice production.

The most important and influential publication of that era was the *Traité complet de l'art du chant* (Complete treatise of the art of singing) (1840), by Manuel Garcia. Garcia's method was one of the first that was based upon a thorough understanding of the workings of the "instrument" (larynx, throat, palate, tongue, etc.), and covered such fundamental aspects as posture, breath control, enunciation, and the use of the three registers (chest, middle, and head). Numerous books on singing after 1850 took Garcia's as a model.

The Rise of Opera

Backtracking a bit, two very important developments in the history of singing occurred around the year 1600—the invention of opera and the rise in popularity of the *castrato*.

It was pretty much a man's world in those days, with women being barred from singing in church. The female voice was increasingly accepted in secular music, however, and the church hierarchy sought a way to incorporate higher parts in church music. The result was the practice of taking young boys with exceptionally beautiful voices and castrating them before their voices changed. This enabled men to sing the high parts in church—a fairly high price to pay for art, all things considered.

When the musical style known as opera emerged (around 1600), its composers made great use of the castrato voice. It proved to be the best of both worlds, as a typical castrato possessed the strength and endurance of a mature man with the purity and range of a woman. The castrati became the superstars of their day and were the first professional singers to tour and perform across Europe.

It wasn't until the second half of the sixteenth century that the female voice emerged as an important player in the vocal scene. It took a while, but by the dawn of the eighteenth century, the soprano had become the darling of the opera world. The flexibility and purity of the soprano voice provided the perfect vehicle for the popular virtuoso style of the day. This period saw the rise of the opera star—otherwise known as the *diva*.

The heyday of opera—and opera stars—continued through most of the nineteenth century, with composers creating more and more demanding roles for the singers. Opera houses were built to accommodate larger audiences, and singers were forced to consider new approaches to singing technique. The Italian *bel canto* style of singing, which emphasized tonal intensity and beauty over sheer volume, took a back seat to a more rigorous and flamboyant approach to singing. In short, everything about opera got bigger—the houses, the music, and the singing.

The Art Song

Parallel to the development of opera in the 1800s was the emergence of an artistic alternative—the solo art song. It's fair to say that the art song, also known as German *lieder*, was perfected by the composer Franz Schubert. Using the voice and piano as equal interpreters of a story, he was able to create the kind of drama and beauty that opera had provided, but on a much more intimate scale.

The art song was a form of vocal music that could be enjoyed in the comfort of private homes. It was also a much more voice-friendly kind of music, without the destructive bombast typical of the operas of the day. This new vocal style became so dominant that the majority of repertoire studied by voice majors in colleges and universities today is in the art song form.

Singing in the Twentieth Century

The twentieth century saw many cultural and technological developments that significantly changed vocal music as we know it. Tastes changed, and opera lost much of its mass appeal. Instead, "popular" music, derived from both the classical art form and from indigenous folk songs, enchanted the public as had no previous type of music.

Popular music emphasized the solo vocalist, and technology enabled the vocalist to be heard. The development of the microphone and other amplification technologies reduced the need for "big" voices that could be heard above a large orchestra. In addition, technology enabled live performances to be shared with those outside the concert hall (via radio and television) and stored for future listening (via the gramophone, tape recorder, and compact disc).

The singers who arrived after the advent of vocal amplification and recording learned how to use the technology to their personal benefit. In fact, this new technology (in the early years, at least) didn't work well with the loud, resonant voices of the past. For that reason, early radio performers tended to have light and intimate voices that would have been wholly out of place just 50 years earlier.

These lighter voices led to a more conversational style of singing that exploited the contours and cadences of normal speech. There was less of a focus on a classical vocal display with a sustained melodic line. Singers learned a different type of phrasing that matched the increasingly popular jazz and light orchestra music of the day.

Throughout the century, amplification and recording technology progressed to the point that even ordinary voices could be made to sound acceptable, using reverb and other forms of signal processing. The advent of rock and roll (especially after the invasion of the Beatles—and the subsequent groundswell of guitar-based garage bands) meant that vocal standards had been reduced; anybody and their brother could be a singer in a rock and roll band, as long as they had a microphone and an amplifier.

The Least You Need to Know

- Singing has been a part of our society since before man developed language.
- Popular types of singing throughout the ages have included hymns, opera, and the art song.
- In the twentieth century, amplification and recording technology changed the nature of singing.

Chapter 2

Your First Singing Lesson

In This Chapter

- Learn the tools you need to get started
- Find out how to prepare the breath
- Discover your "singing voice"
- Compare the speaking and singing voices
- Perform your first vocal exercises

You got all the vocal history you need (and maybe more than you wanted!) in the last chapter. There's no sense waiting around any longer—so let's get right to it and start your very first singing lesson!

What You Need to Get Started

If you've ever taken instrumental lessons of any kind, you've had a musical instrument in front of you, loaded with numerous keys or strings or "buttons" to push to produce musical notes. While the voice is also a musical instrument, it's a very different one.

We can't actually see how our instruments work when we sing, but we can and should observe the many physical aspects of good vocal technique. The best way to do this is to sing in front of a mirror. I recommend using a full-length mirror, if possible, to observe the whole body while practicing. (A hand-held mirror will most likely detract from good singing posture—and your arm will get tired, besides!) If you don't have a full-length mirror, use a smaller, wall-mounted one that lets you observe your entire upper body. You will also need to closely observe your mouth, jaw and tongue position as you practice.

The next tool you need to obtain is a tape recorder, so you can listen to yourself while you're not busy singing. I know that listening to yourself on tape can be a humbling experience (to say the least!), but it's something that you're going to have to do if you want to improve your singing voice.

You see, what we think we sound like inside our heads is not at all what others hear. This isn't to say that your internal voice is better or worse than your external voice, just different—and you need to know the differences.

I remember, when I was a young voice student, first hearing myself on tape. I was singing an Italian aria and feeling quite "operatic" with newfound resonance and support. Unfortunately, when I played back the tape, I sounded very much like a typical teen-aged girl—nice, but not even approaching operatic. It made me realize that hearing on the inside was an exaggerated version of what was being heard on the "outside" by others.

The exercises in this book are going to create some new sensations and sounds for you, and it's imperative that you be able to hear and evaluate the results—which means you must use a tape recorder when you practice. You don't need anything expensive (we're not talking a full-blown recording studio, here), just a low-priced cassette recorder, with a separate microphone if you can.

It's important to remember that while the limitations of this type of inexpensive recording equipment won't do your voice justice, you'll still have a means to evaluate your progress. Even small tonal shadings will be evident on playback. When you're in a private lesson or voice class your teacher can provide this second set of ears, but when you're practicing on your own, this type of independent feedback is invaluable.

Tip

Keep your tapes as an oral history of your vocal improvement. You'll be pleasantly surprised when you compare your beginning tapes with those made after several months of working with this book.

Finally, unless you're blessed with perfect pitch, it helps to have some sort of musical instrument handy that you can use to establish the starting pitch for each exercise. If you have a piano (and can play it, just a little), that's great. If not, a simple pitch pipe will do the trick. (Of course, when you're practicing the exercises in this book, you can get your starting pitch by listening to the accompanying CD.)

Preparing the Breath

In the Top Ten list of all human needs, oxygen is number one. This is definitely true when you're singing; you need your air.

You might not be aware of this, but when you speak, you use only a small portion of your total lung capacity. For this reason, preparing to sing is going to place some new demands on your concept of breathing.

Let's take a look at what "normal" breathing really is. Put down this book, sit quietly, and take a moment to feel yourself breathe normally. In and out, in and out. Now look at your watch and time the interval from a normal inhalation to a normal exhalation. If you're like most folks, it took about two seconds for you to take a breath and release it.

When you sing, you not only have to take in more air, you also have to control its release. You can practice this type of controlled breathing by following these steps:

1. Stand up and plant your feet firmly on the floor, about shoulder's width.
2. Hold your arms directly in front of you, palms down, parallel to the floor.
3. Inhale for four seconds.
4. Hold the breath for four seconds.
5. Release the breath over four seconds.

Caution

When you're trying to stand straight and tall, don't allow your back to become "swayed." This is a common mistake that you can correct by vertically aligning your spine so that you feel a slight tuck of the hips.

How did that feel? Very different, right?

Now repeat this exercise and pay attention to your belt line. Compared to normal breathing, what happens? It expands! That's because you involved the complex set of strong muscles of the upper abdomen called the *epigastria*. These muscles allow the diaphragm to relax and expand the capacity of the lungs, resulting in a deeper breath.

We'll delve further into proper breathing techniques in Chapter 8. For now, practice taking these four-second breaths, holding then releasing, until it feels more natural. And remember to check your posture in the mirror to make sure your body is relaxed, not rigid.

Speaking Versus Singing

Many voice teachers and most instruction books begin the study of singing with endless terms, charts, or vocalises designed to familiarize you with the workings of your vocal instrument. But if you think about it, this isn't how we learned to *speak*.

As children, we learned to speak by listening and mimicking. We heard the speech of others and, through the wonders of the human brain, we internalized it, imagined ourselves producing it and—voilà!—one day we mimicked what we heard. Through the years, in the course of your own personal development, you've actually become an expert at producing speech sounds; learning to transfer those sensations of speech into singing is really quite simple.

By practicing the exercises in this chapter, you'll learn how to make the distinction between speech sounds and singing sounds. Once you've done this, you're well on your way to understanding what the singing tone is all about—without having to endure a physiology course on the way!

In general, your speaking voice comes from your mouth and doesn't require a lot of breath. Your singing voice comes from your head (around your eyes) and requires more support (and more breath). In addition, if you're doing it right, your singing voice will create a kind of vibration or "tingle" in the areas above your lips.

You can use Table 2.1 to help you isolate and analyze the different sensations that will become apparent as you continue these exercises. The sensations in the right column refer to the higher pitched, elongated or "sing-song speech" productions I'm calling your "singing voice."

Table 2.1 Speaking Voice vs. Singing Voice

Speaking Voice	Singing Voice
Posture doesn't play a noticeable role during speaking.	Good posture plays a big role in deep breathing; more air is needed to produce higher pitched, elongated words.
Only shallow (chest) breathing is necessary to produce speech sounds.	Deeper breaths (involving expansion of the belt line and the back) are needed to produce singing sounds.
Spoken words feel as if they originate in the mouth; you feel vibrations in the mouth and the throat when speaking.	Words produced in your singing voice feel as if they originate in the area around your eyes, nose, or even forehead; you'll feel a sense of vibration in these areas more than in the throat.
Words seem to leave the mouth on a horizontal stream of air.	Words seem to float into the head on a vertical column of air.
There is no real sense of vibration or "tingle" above the upper lip when speaking.	There is a real sense of vibration or "tingle" in the areas above the lips—such as the nose, forehead, or around the eyes.
The roof of the mouth is uninvolved or feels low and "lazy"; the jaw is often quite rigid.	The roof of the mouth is arched and raised, as if you're beginning a yawn.

continues

Table 2.1 Speaking Voice vs. Singing Voice (continued)

Speaking Voice	Singing Voice
The lips are close together, forming a small horizontal opening when speaking.	The lips are farther apart, forming a more vertical opening when you produce words in your singing voice.
The space between the upper and lower teeth is small, as is the back of the throat.	There is a sensation of space between your upper and lower rows of teeth, particularly near the back of your throat.

As you produce and compare sensations in the following exercises, refer back to this chart to see how it holds true for each of the five basic vowel sounds.

Finding Your Singing Voice

Singing tones are sustained on five basic vowels—A, E, I, O, and U. But the vowels you use when singing are a little different than those you use when speaking, so you have to learn the proper way to pronounce each of these vowels. It's not difficult; examples for all five vowels can be found in Table 2.2.

Table 2.2 The Basic Vowel Sounds

Vowel	Sounds Like
Long U (o͞o)	Yoo-hoo
Modified ī (ah)	Ah-ha
Long E (ē)	We
Long O (ō)	Oh-no
Long A (ā)	Hey Ray

The following exercises help you find your singing voice through the reproduction of these five basic vowel sounds. So get out your tape recorder (to record your progress) and your CD player (to play the examples on this book's audio CD), and get ready for your first singing lesson!

Exercise 2.1: Yoo-Hoo!

Once you've prepared your breath (as described earlier in the chapter), you're ready to roll.

> **Tip**
>
> It might help to think of how your grandmother might sound saying these same words. It might sound funny—but it's an effective image for reproducing the proper sound.

Begin by speaking the words "yoo-hoo" in your *normal speaking voice.* You should sound the words the same way you might say "hello" when entering someone's office or home. Repeat the phrase and concentrate on what your mouth feels like. Focus on how much breath escapes your mouth. If you could take a picture of your mouth and throat, what would it look like? Try to sense the involvement (or noninvolvement) of the area around your waist or belt line.

Now repeat the same words ("yoo-hoo") using a much higher pitched, elongated sing-song voice—the type of voice that would have to travel through several rooms in order to reach someone's ears.

Can you feel the difference? What was the variance in the size and shape of your mouth? Your throat? To what degree was your belt line involved? Was there a sense of your head being more involved in the production of the tone than your chest or throat? Where did you feel any vibrations?

Tip

Use your tape recorder to record each of these exercises, in both your speaking and singing voices. You can then play back your performances so you can better hear the sounds you're producing.

It's easy to picture the differences between the first "yoo-hoo" (your speaking voice) and the second "yoo-hoo") your singing voice). This shows the imagined pathway of your voice as you raise the pitch and elongate the words in a sing-song fashion.

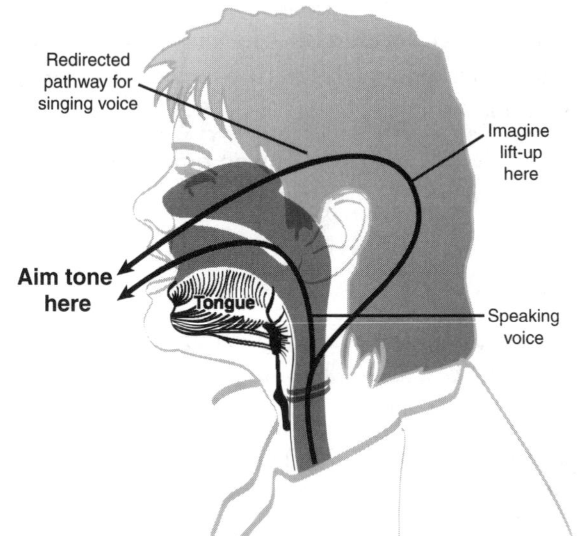

Figure 2.1

The vocal pathway.

Exercise 2.2: Ah-Ha!

The next exercise repeats the same process as in Exercise 2.1, but with another basic vowel: the ī, or modified "ah" sound. You make this sound by saying "ah-ha," as if you'd just made an important discovery.

Begin by speaking the words "ah-ha" in your normal speaking voice. Be aware of how much air escapes your mouth as you speak the words.

Now repeat the words ("ah-ha") in a much higher pitched, elongated version—as if you've just discovered electricity. Note the different sensations—and the difference in your breathing.

Repeat this exercise a few times, switching back and forth between the spoken words and the sing-song versions of the same words. You'll soon begin to feel and understand the differences in speaking and singing.

Caution

The long E is a particularly difficult vowel to reproduce properly. When sounding the "whee," don't allow the corners of your mouth to pull back into a squeezed grin. Your mouth should feel more like it did in the "ah-ha" exercise.

Exercise 2.3: Whee!

What we're going to do here is practice speaking and singing the long E sound.

Begin by speaking the word "we," as in "We the People." Think about each point in Table 2.1 as you repeat it. This is your speaking voice.

Now imagine that you are a small child going down a giant slide for the first time, then elongate and raise the pitch to an exuberant "whee!" The feelings are very different, aren't they?

Exercise 2.4: Oh, No!

Now we're up to the long O sound. Start by speaking a rather resigned "Oh, no." Then repeat the words in your high-pitched, sing-song voice. (This should sound a little like Mr. Bill when the little clay figure used to appear on *Saturday Night Live*.)

Exercise 2.5: Hey, Ray

We're on to the fifth and final basic vowel exercise—the long A. Start by speaking the words "Hey, Ray" as if coming into a room and seeing your old friend Ray. (If you don't have any friends named Ray, just pretend; if you don't have any friends, period—sorry!)

Now imagine that you have just seen Ray on a far canyon rim and you are calling out to him. Note the different sensations between the speaking and the singing approaches.

Exercise 2.6: Singing the Alphabet

There you have it! You have successfully investigated the differences in speech sensations and singing sensations as they apply to the five basic vowels—A, E, I (ah), O, and U. Pretty easy, wasn't it?

And here's what's really cool. You've been able to produce great singing sounds for as long as you've been able to speak—only you probably didn't realize it! There's just one more exercise left in this chapter, and this one is as easy as A-B-C—literally.

Note

In musical terms, smoothly connecting notes in this fashion is called *legato*, which is Italian for "bound" or "tied."

What I want you to do is to "say" the entire alphabet, A to Z, using your newfound singing voice. Run all the letters into one another, so that A slides smoothly into B, which slides smoothly into C, and so on. Continue until you run out of breath, then take another breath and continue to the end.

Even though you're (presumably) familiar with the alphabet, this exercise will make all the letters sound new and different. You'll want to remember how this feels, as it's very close to the sensations you'll feel as you start to vocalize and learn real songs.

The Least You Need to Know

- You should always practice in front of a mirror and with a tape recorder so you can hear what you really sound like.
- When you sing, you breathe deeper and longer than you do when speaking.
- You have two different voices—a speaking voice and a singing voice.
- The singing voice feels more elevated and elongated (and more "tingly") than the speaking voice.
- Singing tones are sustained on five basic vowels: A, E, I, O, and U.

Chapter 3

Employing Vocal Imagery

In This Chapter

- Understand what vocal imagery is and how it works
- Learn how to use imagination and imitation
- Pretend to be the singer you want to be
- Listen to and mimic other singers

As William Vennard said in his book, *Singing: The Mechanism and the Technique* (Carl Fischer Music, 1967):

> Learning to sing is a slow and patient undertaking, in which a good ear is the prerequisite, the imagery is an aid supplied by the teacher, and the experience is gradually accumulated until it is so powerful that merely calling up the memory will reproduce it.

What this means is that great singing is as simple as imagining it. What we hear in our "mind's ear" can be replicated in what and how we sing. If you can imagine yourself sounding like a great opera singer, you are well on your way to actually sounding like an opera singer.

Hard to believe? Then read on, and I'll explain.

Understanding Vocal Imagery

It's no secret that we are all born with different musical abilities. While some people are born with a highly developed ability to process aural stimuli—what we call a "good ear"—the rest of us have to develop our ears for music through ear training courses and lots and lots of practice. What we're trying to achieve is the ability to remember notes and to hear what we're going to sing in our heads—before we sing it.

You see, singers are arguably more dependent on aural discrimination skills (those "good ears") than other musicians. As singers, we don't have *external* devices to help us create our music, such as keys on a piano or strings on a guitar. Instead, we must use imagery and other *internal* sensations to guide our production of tones.

Vocal imagery is best described as the ability to imagine the various shadings of pitch or speech made by the human voice. It is the ability to hear sounds from memory, in your "mind's ear"—in other words, to imagine the sound *before* it is produced.

You see, *how* we hear determines *what* we produce, musically. Sounds that are stored in our aural memories are the "tapes" we play to help us sing in a certain style.

Think back to when you were a child. (Or remember your own children as they were learning to talk.) If we were blessed with good hearing and no vocal impediments, no one had to teach us how words were formed. Imagining speech was all that was needed.

Look at it another way. A person deaf from birth whose vocal apparatus is intact cannot produce normal speech sounds—because he cannot imagine them.

Note

William Vennard says that imagery is "an aid supplied by the teacher" but I think that's a little misleading. The teacher can guide the imagination through example or suggest a tonal image using descriptive terms, but the student must be able to actually imagine the tone and its quality in order to produce it. Teachers can provide vocal images and examples all day long, but if a student has no "ear" or cannot imagine himself producing the sound, he can't reproduce it.

Composers use a similar skill when composing away from an instrument like the piano. It is possible to "hear" (imagine) melodies in your head without ever playing them on an instrument. Remember that because he was going deaf, Beethoven never actually heard his last four great symphonies—except in his "mind's ear."

The same is true for entertainers who do impersonations of famous celebrities. Rich Little once explained that he had to *imagine* how it would feel to sound like someone else. Only then could he make the adjustments in his mouth and tongue that produced "Richard Nixon" or "John Wayne."

Using Your Imagination

This talent for composition or impersonation can be explained as an ability to imagine sounds before they are produced. They are both creative processes. Imagination is the seed of creativity; those learned or applied skills are the soil in which it develops.

Conversely, having an ear for music can also be thought of in terms of having an *imagination* for music. Most people recognize that the ability to sing varies widely from person to person—anywhere from "Boy can she sing!" to "He couldn't carry a tune in a bucket!" Few people realize that singing ability has more to do with a highly developed imagination than it has to do with highly developed vocal cords.

Here's an example of what I mean. After years of classroom experience and thousands of students, I came to tell which students were going to be the better singers by their nonsinging behavior, both in and out of class. You see, the most imaginative student is often not the best behaved one.

I remember one particular young man who drove me crazy with his constant talking and antics in class. He didn't sing particularly well and I was considering removing him from the choir. It was not until I had the opportunity to work with him in the school's drama production that I witnessed the unbelievable talent he had for acting and mimicking character voices—small glimpses of which I had unfortunately seen in rehearsal. I knew that he had the ability to become an outstanding singer if he could just apply all that vivid imagination and energy to the study of voice.

Happily, the result was just what I had hoped for. I encouraged him to turn his talents for mimicking other voices to his singing. He fearlessly experimented with new sounds and gladly "tried on" different vocal timbres. Because of his willingness to imagine and experiment with new sounds, he became a joy to teach—and quickly became one of the best voices in the choir.

This relationship between acting and singing ability (both dependent upon imagery skills) is seen over and over again on television, on stage, and in the movies. It is never a surprise to me that a fine actor is often a good singer, or vice versa. Frank Sinatra and Harry Connick Jr. are both wonderfully gifted singers who turned out to be fine actors. Glenn Close wasn't particularly thought of as a singer, but then she wowed us in *Sunset Boulevard* on Broadway and again in the television remake of *South Pacific*. Mandy Patinkin is as fine a singer as he is an actor. And the list goes on and on.

Applying Vocal Imagery

The idea that the vocal mechanism is controlled by the imagination was never made more clear to me than in my first few years of teaching junior high school chorus. Being young and inexperienced, I lacked a lot of know-how and hadn't yet developed a tried and true teaching technique. Consequently, I found myself frustrated by the results I was getting—or, more accurately, wasn't getting.

It's not that the kids weren't working hard. They'd learned their parts and were singing pretty well in tune, and their diction was even understandable. But their tone sounded thin and unfocused—and I didn't know what to do about it.

One day, out of sheer desperation (and lack of anything better to suggest), I made a crazy suggestion. "Just for fun," I said to them, "let's pretend that you are all opera stars!"

The result was amazing!

Their eyes widened and their jaws dropped in amazement as they found themselves producing a focused, supported, and resonant sound. The harmonies were much more in tune and their diction was even sharper and clearer than before.

Of course, they didn't *really* sound like opera stars, but they *did* sound like 75 well-trained young voices—like they had never sounded before. And, after all my previous head-banging and hand-wringing, it was incredibly easy to achieve.

Just imagine it—and do it!

We all laughed at the shocking results, but I know we all learned a valuable lesson—the importance of the imagination. For me as a teacher, it was a defining moment. All the undergraduate classes in Vocal Techniques with their endless charts, terms, and exercises suddenly seemed useless to me. All I had needed to say was "*Imagine* that you are ..."

Vocal Imagery Exercises

The key to using vocal imagery is to imagine a particular singer or type of singer and then try to mimic that voice. Think of yourself as an impressionist, like a Rich Little, and do your darndest to imitate that particular person. It's even okay to exaggerate a little—sometimes that's the best way to "nail" certain techniques. Just pick a singer, pick a song (this helps a lot), and start singing!

Exercise 3.1: Be Operatic

For your first exercise, let's repeat the experience I had with my junior high choir. Puff up your chest and, in your best imitation of a Pavarotti or a Beverley Sills, belt out a chorus of "Mary Had a Little Lamb."

(Yes, that's right—"Mary Had a Little Lamb.") The result will probably be comical, but you'll probably surprise yourself at how big a voice you really have.

Exercise 3.2: Be Soulful

Now let's try something a little softer, and with feeling. Conjure up images of your favorite smooth soul singer and take another stab at "Mary Had a Little Lamb." Imagine how a soul singer would approach the song—with smooth, dulcet tones, very clear, very soft, but not breathy. Notice how different this feels from your "opera voice" in Exercise 3.1. You're singing the same notes, but approaching them from two totally different perspectives.

Exercise 3.3: Be Your Favorite Singer

Let's finish up by letting you pick the singer or singing style. Pick a particular singer who you really like, and imagine that singer singing "Mary Had a Little Lamb." Now do your best Dana Carvey and imitate that singer singing the song. When you're done, take a minute and evaluate what you just did—and how. What are the distinctive features of that singer's voice? Is it loud or soft, brassy or breathy, clear or full of vibrato? What can you learn from listening to—and imitating—that singer?

Great Singers to Listen to—and Learn From

Some singers have vivid imaginations and already have in place a natural system of aural imagery and tone production. We call these gifted musicians *natural singers*. They most likely have done a great deal of listening to other singers or role models and have certainly experimented a lot with their own sounds.

The best of these singers integrate all their influences to create their own unique voices. Unfortunately, some singers do nothing more than mimic these other singers—often calling on several different singing voices in the course of a single song!

This is *not* the goal of imagery and imitation. Imitation can be a helpful learning tool in the journey to becoming a better singer, but finding your own unique voice is the ultimate destination.

Note

Discover more great singers in a variety of styles in Part 5 of this book.

To help you develop a database of singers to learn from, I've prepared a short list of great singers, in a variety of styles. You should be able to find a wealth of recordings by these artists, either in your local music store or on the Internet. Of course, there are easily a hundred equally fine singers for each one I've listed, but you have to start somewhere—and this is my starting point. I've tried to include a mix of well-known singers and those who haven't received as much exposure; view this list as an opportunity to expand your listening horizons.

Tip

You should listen to as many varied singing styles as you can—and not limit your listening to singers who match your own personal tastes. You may be surprised at how your taste changes as you continue to study and grow musically.

As you listen to singers from the list that follows, try to determine what you particularly like or dislike about their tone quality, their diction, or their style. I recommend keeping a listening journal as a point of reference as you're listening. By paying close attention to the technique of others, you'll become much more aware of your own.

Classical/Opera

Most vocal teachers coach their students to sing in a classical style. In many ways, this is the most demanding type of music you can sing. As you'll learn in Chapter 17, this type of music requires a purity of approach and a mastery of dynamics unlike any other genre.

When it comes to the great classical singers, here are some performers to seek out:

- **Sopranos:** Kathleen Battle, Maria Callas (for sheer emotional impact), and Renee Fleming
- **Altos:** Cecilia Bartoli and Frederica Von Stade
- **Tenors:** Ian Bostridge, Placido Domingo, Salvatore Licitra, and early Luciano Pavarotti
- **Baritones:** Deitrich Fischer-Dieskau, Thomas Hampson, and Bryn Terfel

Tip

If you're new to opera, where to start? I recommend you begin by listening to selections from Puccini's operas because they're so expressive and melodic—simply put, his music is very pretty and very accessible to the novice. Many of Puccini's arias have become pleasantly familiar due to their inclusion in movies and television shows—and even a few commercials!

Note

Salvatore Licitra made his name in May of 2002 by stepping in at the last minute for Pavarotti at the Metropolitan Opera. Since then, audiences have been asking, "Luciano who?"

Jazz

Jazz singing is a unique art form, as different from opera as it is from rock. As you'll learn in Chapter 19, not only do jazz singers utilize different vocal technique, they also have to be able to "play around with" a melody and even improvise their own melodies over a song's chord progression.

When you listen to the great jazz singers, you hear not only a purity of technique, but also the ability to "own" a song and make it theirs. Here are a few of the very best jazz singers you should be familiar with:

- **Women:** Karrin Allyson, Ella Fitzgerald, Jane Monheit, and Sarah Vaughn
- **Men:** early Tony Bennett, early Frank Sinatra, Mel Tormé, and Joe Williams

Musical Theater

The musical theater is still an important part of the musical landscape. The American musical has produced a wealth of great compositions that singers love to wrap their lips around. You can hear terrific singing in any Broadway musical, but when you want to learn from the best, check out these "singer's singers":

- **Women:** Audra McDonald and Marin Mazzie
- **Men:** Brent Barrett, Howard McGillan, and John Raitt

Popular Music

Popular music—whether rock, country, or soul—isn't always vocally demanding. In the world of popular music, the song and the production are often as important as the vocalist. That said, there are some terrific vocalists in the world of popular music, singers who eschew vocal gimmicks to focus on a purity of technique.

I talk about a lot of different pop singers in Chapter 18, but for now here are some of the best vocalists the genre has to offer:

- **Women:** Patsy Cline, Kathy Mattea, Linda Ronstadt, Barbra Streisand, Trisha Yearwood
- **Men:** Elton John, Kenny Loggins, James Taylor

And More ...

While you're listening, here are a few more personal favorites that deserve your attention, for a variety of reasons:

- k.d. lang, for sheer beauty and power and depth of tone in the middle and lower register.
- Nancy LaMott and Ann Hampton Calloway, for beautiful tone quality and dynamic expression in the upper register.
- Bobby McFerrin, as the ultimate example of using his "voice as an instrument."

I'm sure you have your personal favorite singers, as well. Here's a good exercise: Listen to your favorite singer and try to describe just what it is about his or her voice that you find unique and appealing. Evaluate that singer in terms of formal singing technique, and try to determine what you can learn from studying that person's voice. Whomever the singer is, there's always something about that person's voice that can help you improve or fine-tune your own vocal technique!

The Least You Need to Know

- Fine singing is initiated in the imagination and developed through technique.
- With training, you should be able to hear a melody in your "mind's ear."
- You can learn a great deal about singing by listening to other talented singers.
- You must be willing to experiment with new and different sounds—trust your imagination!

Chapter 4

Finding Your Range

In This Chapter

- Understand the different voice classifications
- Learn about each voice range
- Discover your vocal classification
- Manage age-specific issues—and the changing voice

If you've been around music at all, you've no doubt heard the terms *soprano*, *alto*, *tenor*, and *bass*—in vocal music, often referred to as SATB. You probably have a pretty good idea of what these names mean, that soprano and alto are female voices, and that tenor and bass are male voices. You might even know that the soprano and the tenor are the higher of the female and male voices, and the alto and bass are the lower voices.

But there's a lot more than that to know. For example, do you know the range of each voice? Do you know where *your* voice fits into all of this?

If you want to know more about these voice ranges, you've come to the right chapter. Read on to learn more!

Understanding Voice Classification

Every singer should know what type of voice he or she has. This chapter—and the accompanying audio CD—will help you identify your correct range and classification. Note, however, that it's not necessary to make this determination in order to use this book.

The general conception is that voice classifications are based on vocal range or pitch abilities—that is, how high or how low you can sing. While this is true, more factors need to be considered when classifying a particular voice type. For example, tone quality is equally important in making this determination; other factors—such as *tessitura*, *timbre*, and *passaggio*—can also come into play.

Note

Tessitura is the range within which most tones of a voice part fall. **Timbre** (pronounced "tamber") is the distinctive character of a voice—in other words, its tone quality. **Passaggio** is that point where your vocal quality switches from one register to another; this transition point is also called a lift or break.

You should also know that as your voice develops, your voice classification may change. After all, voice lessons are all about developing tone quality and extending your range. It takes time for the voice to emerge, and you shouldn't rush to simply "put a label" on it.

In addition, know that the voice "label" you were assigned back in junior high or high school choir most likely had very little to do with your true voice classification. You may have been placed in the alto section because you could read music or in the tenor section because the section needed filling up.

With all these caveats in mind, let's look at the basic classifications and characteristics of male and female singing voices.

Classifying the Adult Female Voice

There are two classifications typically assigned to the female voice—soprano and alto.

Soprano

The highest female voice is the *soprano*. The typical soprano range starts at middle C and goes up two octaves, to the first C above the treble clef staff.

Sopranos are further subdivided into types according to their differing timbres, ranges, and technical abilities. The highest, lightest and perhaps most "agile" soprano is called the *coloratura*. These are the gals who specialize in highly ornate songs and arias, sung mostly on one-syllable nonwords somewhere in the upper stratosphere. (Among the current crop of pop singers, Mariah Carey is a definite coloratura; she does a lot of warbling high above the staff!)

The most familiar or generally accepted soprano voice is the *lyric soprano*; this is the "standard" soprano voice. Another subdivision of soprano is the *mezzo soprano* (mezzo means "middle"), with the same overall range and quality of the lyric but with a little more power in the lower range.

Note

Mezzo sopranos are sometimes designated Soprano II or "second sopranos," and typically sing a harmony part a few notes below the main melody.

The soprano voice with the widest and most powerful range is the *dramatic soprano*, called *spinto* in Italian. Good dramatic sopranos are few and far between—especially in younger singers.

Alto

The lowest of the female voices is called the *contralto*, or *alto* for short. The range of a typical alto starts on the G below middle C and goes up two octaves to the first G above the treble clef staff.

In classical singing, the alto voice can be quite heavy and dark, sounding almost like a tenor. In popular singing (especially in jazz), this type of voice sounds warm and rich in its depth of tone.

Classifying the Adult Male Voice

Just as there are two main female voice classifications, there are also two primary classifications for the male voice—*tenor* and *bass*. There is also a third classification, halfway between the two, called the *baritone*.

Tenor

The highest and probably most popular of the male voices—especially in popular music—is the *tenor*. The tenor range extends from the C below middle C up to the A on the treble clef staff.

Most of the famous male popular singers—now and in the past—fall under the category of *lyric tenor*. Lyric tenors always get the "leading man" roles in musical theater or become the lead singer for dance bands and orchestras. Most popular contemporary male recording artists are tenors too—some more "lyric" than others! Think Paul McCartney or Jon Bon Jovi or Justin Timberlake or ... well, just about any male singer you can think of.

Note

While the tenor part is written on the treble clef, it actually sounds an octave lower than written. For example, when a tenor reads middle C, he actually sings the C below middle C.

The *dramatic tenor* has a similar range to the lyric tenor, but displays a heavier or perhaps more resonant quality. You often come across dramatic tenors in opera or classical music—guys like Placido Domingo or Luciano Pavarotti.

Baritone

Bridging the gap between the tenor and the bass is the *baritone*—sometimes referred to as Bass 1. (The traditional bass voice is then designated Bass 2.) It is a very popular and "listenable" voice, usually lyric in quality and lends itself well to a lot of popular repertoire.

The typical baritone range starts on the low G on the bass clef staff and goes up to the A above middle C—overlapping a large part of the female alto range.

Bass

The lowest and heaviest of the male voices is, of course, the *bass*. (That's pronounced like "first base," not like the fish.) The typical bass range can go as low as the first E below the bass clef staff, and as high as the E above middle C. These are the guys that provide the foundation to any harmony and amaze us with their power and their *looooooooow* notes.

Note

Most high school basses are actually baritones—and only become true basses as their voices deepen over time.

While there are subcategories of the bass voice, they're not often referred to. In most cases, a bass is a bass is a bass.

Determining Your Vocal Classification

Now that you know the different types of voices, how do you determine *your* vocal classification?

The best way to find where your voice fits is to compare your range to the set ranges for each voice classification. Whichever "official" range you best fit into then becomes your voice classification.

Caution

You will probably find that your voice doesn't fit neatly into a single classification—you might be able to go a few notes lower or higher, or not be able to reach the very highest or lowest notes in a range. You should pick the classification that *best fits* your individual range—even if it's not a perfect fit.

Table 4.1 presents the practical range, comfortable tessitura, and points of passaggio for each voice classification. For our purposes, think of the range as the ultimate, widest possible range of notes you can sing; tessitura as those notes that are most comfortable for you to sing; and passaggio as that note (or range of notes) where your voice "lifts" from your chest to your head.

Keep in mind that actual vocal ranges vary greatly from singer to singer. Tessitura and points of lift will vary and change as your voice develops with time and practice. It's best that you don't compare your relatively untrained voice to that of a professional singer; the pros develop greatly extended ranges and tessitura and pretty much eliminate the points of passaggio.

Note

I developed the chart in Table 4.1 with the nonprofessional in mind, while also taking into account the younger singer. While you might find other range charts that differ a little from these, I think these charts best represent the various ages of our readers and levels of singing expertise.

Finding Your Range—On the Audio CD

You can use Table 4.1, along with the accompanying audio CD, to find where you fall within these classifications. The way to do this is to advance to the section of the CD that contains the voice classifications. Each classification is sung by a professional singer; the singer sings a number corresponding to each note in a voice's range.

You should sing along with the singer, and mark those notes where you start to feel uncomfortable singing along. For example, let's say you start to sing along with the tenor. If you find yourself not being able to hit any notes above the number five or six, you're probably *not* a tenor. When you sing along with the bass, you should find that you can hit more of the notes within the range.

By this process of elimination, you should be able to determine which formal range best suits your voice.

Finding Your Range—On the Piano

If you have access to a piano or digital keyboard, you can use that instrument to help you find your vocal range. Table 4.2 shows where each voice falls on the keyboard; just play the notes and sing along to determine where your voice fits within the available ranges.

Table 4.1 Vocal Ranges

Voice	Range (Full)	Tessitura (Comfortable Range)	Passagio (Lift Range)
Soprano	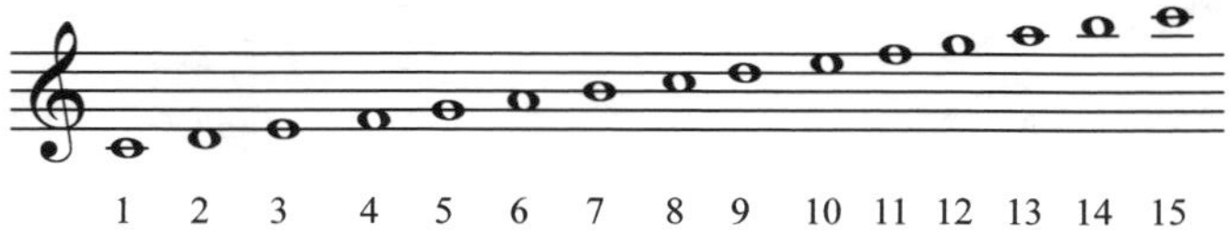 1 2 3 4 5 6 7 8 9 10 11 12 13 14 15	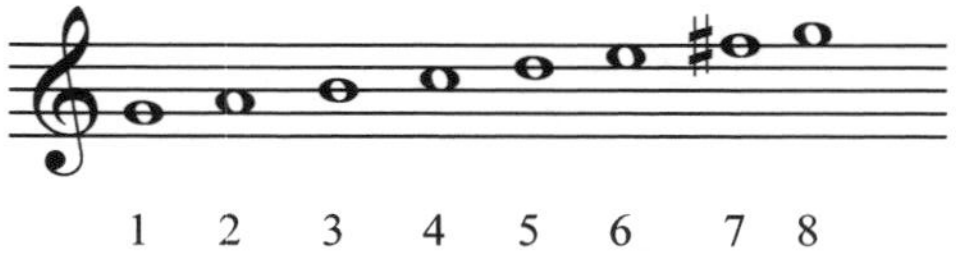 1 2 3 4 5 6 7 8	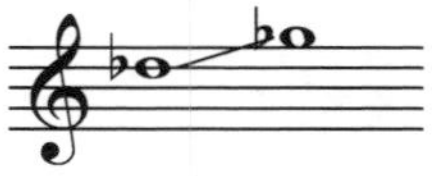
Alto	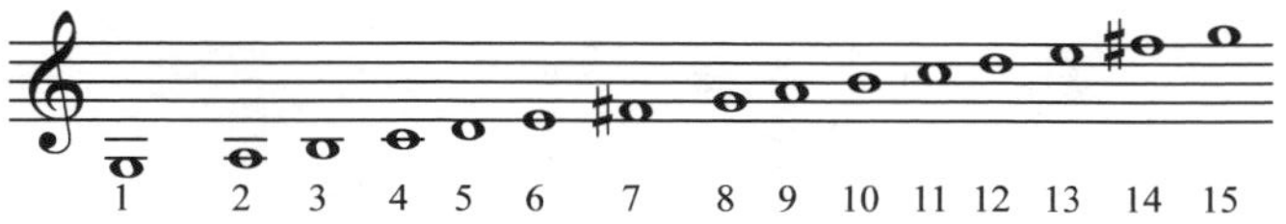 1 2 3 4 5 6 7 8 9 10 11 12 13 14 15	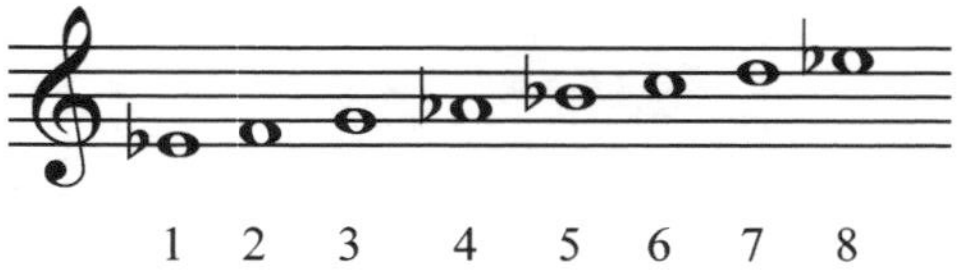 1 2 3 4 5 6 7 8	
Tenor	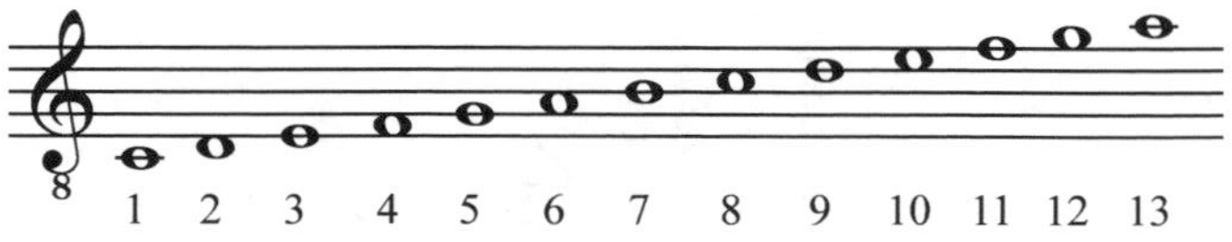 1 2 3 4 5 6 7 8 9 10 11 12 13	 1 2 3 4 5 6 7 8	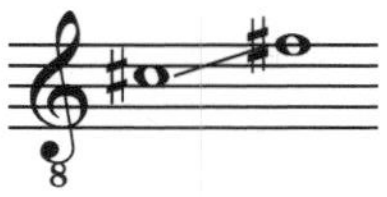
Baritone	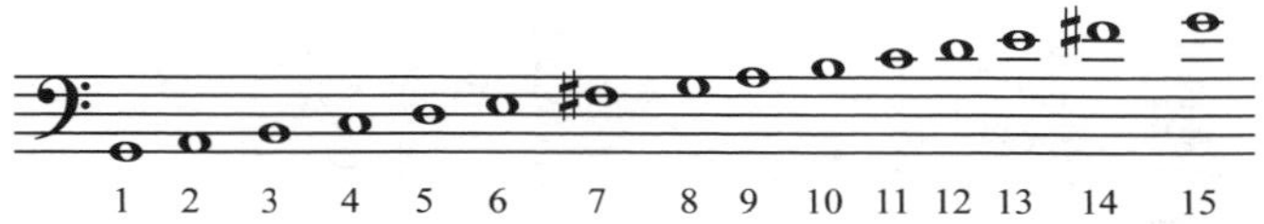 1 2 3 4 5 6 7 8 9 10 11 12 13 14 15	 1 2 3 4 5 6 7 8 9 10	
Bass	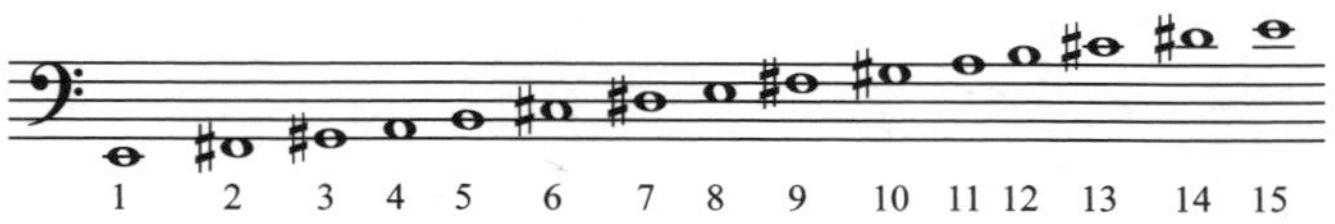 1 2 3 4 5 6 7 8 9 10 11 12 13 14 15	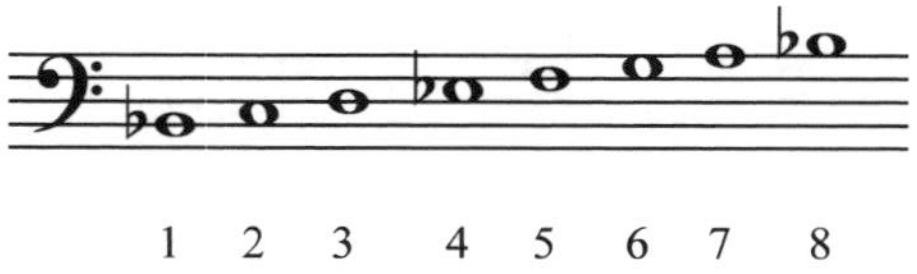 1 2 3 4 5 6 7 8	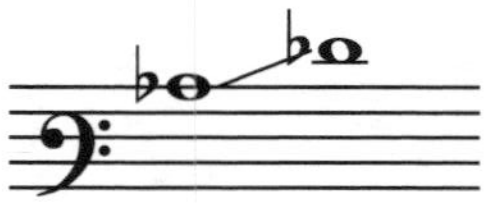

Table 4.2 Vocal Ranges—on the Piano Keyboard

Voice	Range
Soprano	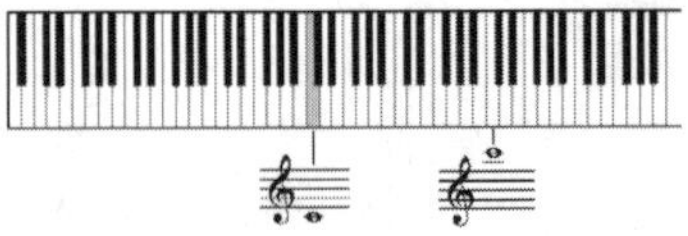
Alto	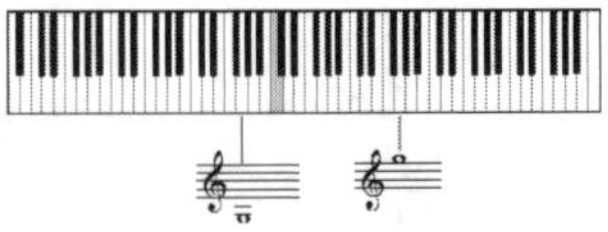
Tenor	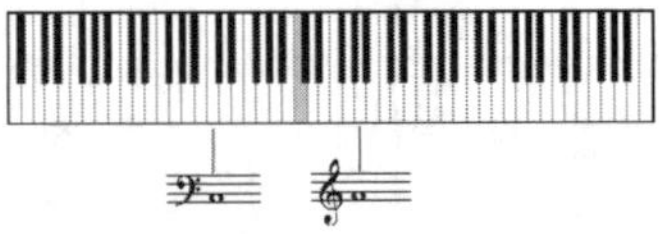
Baritone	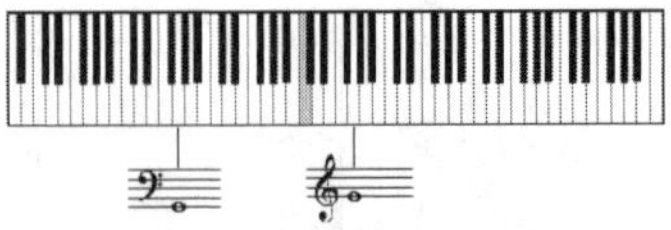
Bass	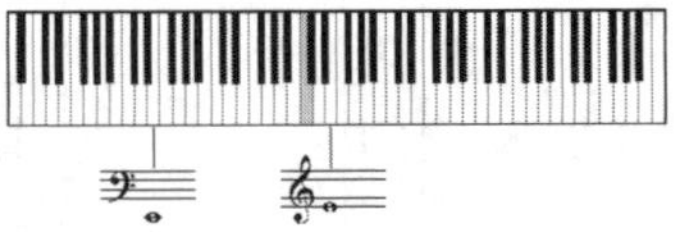

Age-Specific Considerations

If you are a young singer—between the ages of thirteen and eighteen, let's say—you need to be familiar with some specialized classifications that apply only to you.

Notice that when we talked about voice classifications earlier in this chapter, we called them "adult" categories? There's a good reason for this. You see, it takes many years for a voice to settle into a particular range and quality that can be labeled or classified. As you mature, not only your vocal range but also your tone quality—and thus your vocal classification—will change. That's why any voice classification should apply to mature voices only.

And this isn't something that applies only to junior high or high school singers. I've had college students come to me insisting that they were baritones, when they were actually tenors; their true tenor voice didn't develop until they studied privately. I've also had students who studied privately but still had some vocal maturing to do before their voices settled into the final, mature range and timbre.

So if you're a younger singer, read on to learn how to deal with any changes your voice might be going through.

The Maturing Voice

The boy's changing voice has been a subject of much scholarly research—and comedy. There is enough material on the topic to fill several whole books, so we don't need to write another one here. What I will do, for the benefit of our younger readers, is explain some of the changes that might be in store and how to navigate these waters of transformation.

It's no secret that dramatic physiological changes take place in both boys and girls in early puberty. Many of these transformations are quite obvious to the naked eye, but this physical growth happens on the inside, too—in our vocal mechanisms. During puberty, the vocal cords grow about 2 to 4 mm longer in girls, and about 1 centimeter longer and thicker in boys—thus the development of a more pronounced Adam's Apple in men.

The muscles in and around the larynx also grow, at varying rates, making it difficult to coordinate speech registers—not to mention the singing voice. The typical "cracking" voice has been a source of embarrassment for young men since time immemorial, but it doesn't have to be the case. If you understand what is going on and how to ease through the process, there is no reason why you can't continue to sing—and even make good vocal progress.

Girls' voices go through changes too, but they don't drop an octave while doing so. Young girls need to be reminded that immature vocal cords don't always operate in a fashion to produce a clear, focused tone. A certain amount of breathiness may remain in your tone, no matter what you do, until you are in your last years of high school. You should still work on focus and placement, but try to remain patient with your developing voice. The natural voice is always the best choice; you should never allow a teacher to try to force a false "mature" tone before it is ready.

A Survival Guide for Young Singers

Whether you're a boy or a girl, you need to know how to cope with the changes your voice is going through. With that in mind, here is my list of the most useful survival techniques for young singers:

- Always sing in a comfortable tessitura. It's singing outside your comfortable range for long periods of time that kills you, not the individual high or low notes themselves. In choir class, drop out for a phrase or two if your part stays too high or too low for too long.
- Be aware of signs of physical tension—stretched neck, forward thrust chin, clinched jaw, raised shoulders, and so on. When you feel that tension coming on, consciously relax yourself or drop out for a phrase or two.
- Boys should not be afraid to sing in their head tones, even though they might be able to sing in their "changed" voice. The head tones are how you *should* sing, carrying that feeling over into your newly found "changed" voice.
- Avoid singing only in the low voice register, using only low notes. Discuss your vocal needs and goals with your choir director and don't allow yourself to be placed in a particular section of the choir just to meet personnel shortages or to compensate for other weaknesses in the group.
- Avoid loud singing while your voice is changing; it forces the voice and can be really damaging. (This goes for yelling or cheering at ball games, too!)
- If your voice feels tired or hoarse, stop singing for a few days. See a doctor if the hoarseness continues when you resume singing.
- Drink a lot of water; it keeps the vocal cords moist and does a lot of other good things for you. Some singers benefit from a vaporizer in the winter months to keep their mucous membranes moist and less susceptible to colds.
- Avoid alcohol and smoking—good advice for singers of any age!
- As you mature, let your musical tastes mature with you. Listen to a lot of great singers representing all vocal styles. Don't limit your role models—branch out and get beyond the obvious, popular choices.
- If at all possible, take private or group voice lessons—especially important during this critical time in your physical and musical development.

Note

See Chapter 9 to learn more about head tones.

Note

No matter what your age, you can learn more about good vocal maintenance in Chapter 21.

Special Categories

While we're talking about younger voices, let's take a quick look at some special vocal subcategories for younger male singers:

- **The boy soprano:** This is the unchanged male voice that has particular strength and purity of tone. If you've ever listened to the Vienna Boy's Choir, you know the beauty of this highest unchanged male voice. It is considered a treasure among choir directors—and certainly should be among young men who possess it!
- **The male alto or countertenor:** As the boy's voice begins to change, the high notes get much more difficult to reach and the general range starts to diminish. These young men can no longer be classified as soprano and are often referred to as altos because they are most comfortable singing in the female alto range. More properly, these voices fall into a male alto or countertenor classification. (While these terms are often used interchangeably, I like to maintain a distinction between the two; younger singers in this range are called male altos, while more mature singers are called countertenors.)

> **Note**
>
> Some composers and choir directors refer to the changing young man's voice as the *cambiata* voice.

Countertenors are those adult men who have acquired the special ability to retain their high notes through the use of head voice. They have amazing range and power and are often hard to distinguish from an operatic alto. While this type of voice is not everyone's cup of tea, these singers do produce a haunting and truly unique sound.

> **Note**
>
> In the late 1960s I had the pleasure of being in a class taught by the great English countertenor Alfred Deller, a robust and charming bass-baritone who had perfected his head voice to an almost inhuman degree. A pioneer in popularizing authentic performances of early music, Deller is credited with starting a twentieth-century revival of music for countertenor. While his voice could soar to the heights of most sopranos, there wasn't a feminine thing about him!

The Least You Need to Know

- There are four main vocal classifications: the female soprano and alto voices, and the male tenor and bass voices.
- You can determine your individual vocal classification by singing along with a known soprano, alto, tenor, or bass, or by singing the notes within a given range as played on a piano.
- Range isn't the only criteria for vocal classification; you should also consider your tone quality, tessitura (comfortable range), and passagio (the point where your voice lifts from your chest to your head).
- Your voice range doesn't settle until your voice changes and you've had proper training and exercise.
- Young singers—particularly young male singers—have specific issues in terms of range. You should take it easy vocally while your voice is in the process of changing.
- Not every soprano can sing like Mariah Carey!

Chapter 5

Developing Your Technique with Vocal Exercises

In This Chapter

- Begin to develop your breath control
- Begin to focus your tone
- Start to develop resonance
- Begin to extend your range

Like any other muscle in your body, your voice has to be "warmed up" before it can really operate at maximum levels. Just as we wouldn't think of running a 10K run without stretching our feet, legs, and lower back muscles, we shouldn't sing without first loosening the parts of the singing mechanism.

The exercises you do to loosen your voice muscles are called *vocal warm-ups*. You probably did similar types of warm-ups at the beginning of choir rehearsals when you were in school. These exercises not only serve to relax, loosen, and prepare the voice for singing, but they can also be used to overcome specific hurdles when developing good singing technique. I compare them to the drills that basketball or football players repeat over and over in practice; the actual scrimmage or play (in your case, the singing of songs) comes only after you've completed the drills.

The 10 exercises in this chapter are designed to help you get a jump start on good technique and should be practiced faithfully as you begin that journey. You should never just go through the motions of singing exercises without taking the time to analyze and evaluate and even adjust the sensations you experience.

The exercises in this chapter are non-voice specific. That means they can be done by sopranos, altos, tenors, or basses—whatever your voice classification.

None of these exercises deals with the extremes of the vocal range. You are free to continue the sequences either upward or downward to better fit within your personal vocal range.

All notation is in treble clef (for simplicity), but changed male voices can sing them one octave lower than written. On the audio CD, some of the exercises are sung by women and some by men, so you can hear vocal models for both sexes. I hope it goes without saying that you shouldn't try to match pitches outside your gender!

Exercises for Breath Control

Since singing has to happen on the breath, let's begin there. These first three exercises will help you better control your singing breath and extend your breath capacity.

Exercise 5.1: Hiss Like a Snake

This first exercise is designed to help you control the release of air from your lungs. Follow these steps:

1. Stand with correct posture and inhale slowly.
2. Hold for a second or two then start to release your breath in a very controlled stream. Allow the air to "hiss" between your closed teeth on an "s" sound. Feel that you have emptied your lungs by the end.
3. Repeat steps 1 and 2, but rather than hissing the air out, this time use a high falsetto voice (for men) or a light high head voice (for women), count "one, two, three," and so on as you release the breath. You should count as far as you can before running out of air.

Keep a record of the final number you reach before you run out of breath, and track this number as you continue to practice. The better you get, the higher you'll be able to count!

Exercise 5.2: Hissy Doodle

A variation of Exercise 5.1 is to hiss an actual song. Follow these steps:

1. Stand with correct posture and inhale slowly.
2. Hold for a second or two, then start to release your breath in a very controlled stream. While you release your breath, hiss the rhythm (*not* the notes of the melody) to the song "Yankee Doodle."

When you perform this exercise, take special care not to breathe at points in the "tune" where you would normally breathe (if you were singing it). In other words, try to get all the way through it without a breath. And, as this gets easier with practice, try extending into a repeat of the song without a breath.

The next step is to apply a tone to this exercise. Instead of simply hissing the *rhythm* of "Yankee Doodle," try sustaining the lyrics on a high-pitched single tone. This shouldn't have a melody, but rather a head-voiced monotone. Remember, the focus here isn't on melody, it's on breath control.

> **Note**
>
> The key here is to focus on producing a rhythmic version of the song—no actual pitches. Your throat should feel relaxed and in an open, almost yawn-like position.

> **Caution**
>
> It will probably feel a little like you're holding your breath as you sing. This is okay, as long as you don't allow yourself to feel tension in the throat. You're just learning how to reserve your air supply!

Exercise 5.3: Sing the Alphabet—in a Single Breath

This exercise requires you to know your ABCs—in the form of the "alphabet song," to the tune of "Twinkle, Twinkle Little Star." Here's what you need to do:

1. Stand with correct posture and inhale slowly.
2. Using your elevated head voice, sing the "alphabet song" from start to finish, without taking a breath.

This isn't as easy as it sounds, and you might not be able to get all the way through at first. Don't worry; it'll come, with practice.

Exercises for Focusing the Tone and Developing Resonance

Good singers produce a focused tone, with plenty of resonance. The best way to practice this technique is with a kind of open-mouth hum, as you'll learn in the following exercises.

Exercise 5.4: Don't Get Hung Up!

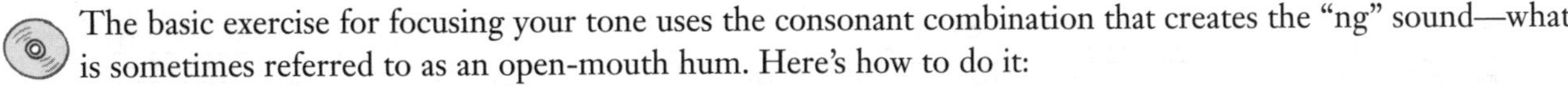

The basic exercise for focusing your tone uses the consonant combination that creates the "ng" sound—what is sometimes referred to as an open-mouth hum. Here's how to do it:

1. Say the word "hung" and immediately close to the "ng." Your lips should be apart and the tongue should be against the roof of the mouth. Your teeth should have space between them in back as if you were forming the "ah" sound.
2. Repeat at higher and higher pitches while always sustaining the "ng."

As you perform this exercise, you should start to feel a definite tingle or buzz in the area around your nose. (You may even feel the tingle just below your eyes in your cheekbones—if so, that's great!) You should repeat the exercise until you can consistently produce this very focused area of vibration around your nose while sustaining the "ng" sound.

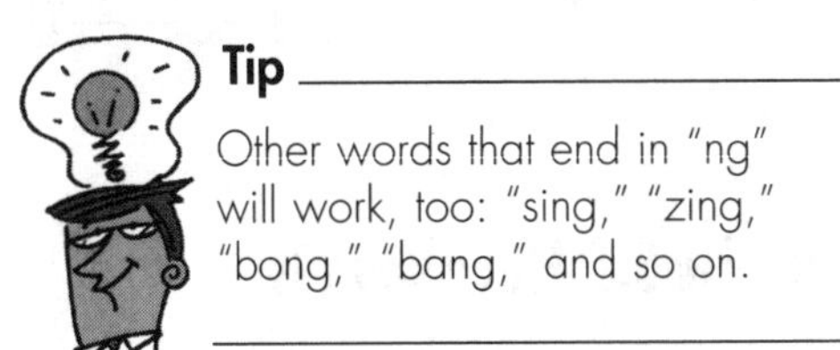

Tip

Other words that end in "ng" will work, too: "sing," "zing," "bong," "bang," and so on.

Exercise 5.5: Humming a Tone

This next exercise applies the same sense of focused vibrations to a specific tone. You should *sing* the word "hung" in the same manner that you did before, but this time starting on any pitch that's comfortable to you. You should feel increased vibrations when you sing the word.

Here's what to do:

1. Starting on G, sing the word "hung." Hold each whole note for as long as you can on one breath. As you sustain the "ng," try to gradually crescendo the tone and intensify the sense of vibrations around the nose and under the eyes.
2. Take a breath.
3. Repeat step 1 a half-step higher. Continue upward in half steps, as shown, until you reach C.

Exercise 5.6: Say Ah

You have produced a focused, resonant tone (using an open mouth hum) by performing the previous exercises. Now it's time to carry that focus and resonance into a tone that is *not* a hum.

"Ah" is one of the most open and often-used vowels in our vocal vocabulary, so we'll start with it. Follow these steps:

1. Sing the word "hung."
2. When you feel the "ng" really start to vibrate and focus, quickly drop your tongue and jaw to produce the tone "ah." This is a critical point and one you don't want to overlook—the "ah" should feel like it sits in the same place as the "ng" did. You should feel the vibrations around your nose and eyes just the same as you did on the "ng."
3. Once you feel that the sensations of the "ng" and the "ah" are similar, go ahead and descend to the other pitches as notated.
4. Continue upward in half steps, breathing slowly and deeply between each sequence, until the pitch C is reached.

Exercise 5.7: More Vowels

Once you've mastered the "ah" sound, you can move on to the other four basic vowel sounds. (You learned these back in Chapter 2—remember?) This exercise is a variation of Exercise 5.6, using a slightly different musical pattern, that gets the voice moving a little more and has you dropping open to different vowels as the pitch descends. You should concentrate on keeping the very same sensations on each of these vowels.

1. Sing "hung-ah," as you learned in Exercise 5.6. Remember to hold the "ng" until it starts to vibrate, and then drop your tongue and jaw to produce the vowel sound.
2. Once you feel that the sensations of the "ng" and the vowel are similar, go ahead and descend to the other pitches as notated.
3. Take a breath and repeat steps 1 and 2 for each of the other vowel sounds; you'll be singing "hung-eh," "hung-ee," "hung-oh," and "hung-oo."
4. Continue upward in half steps, breathing slowly and deeply between each sequence, until the pitch C is reached.

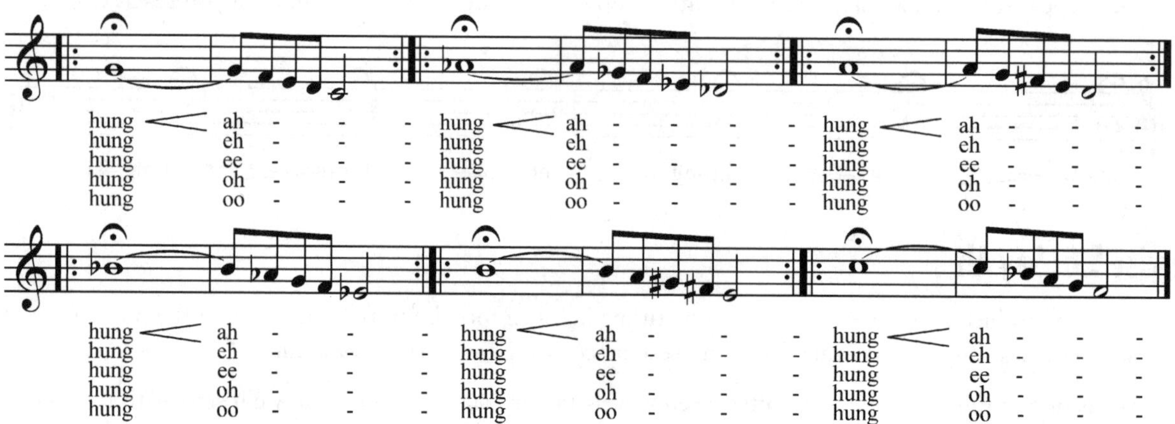

Exercise 5.8: Nee Neh Nah Noh Noo

This exercise helps you produce resonance without using the open mouth hum. In this instance we'll use the word "nee." Before you begin the exercise, practice saying "nee" in an elevated head voice. Sing it, then let it fall down (drop in pitch) as if it were falling off a cliff. Can you feel the vibrations in your face, much like the "ng"? If not, keep practicing until you can, then follow these steps:

1. Sing the series of five vowels as notated, striving to keep the facial tingle as you sing through the "n" to the vowel.
2. You may continue this upward or downward in pitch, noting the pure vowel sounds of the singer on the CD.

Exercises for Extending Your Range

Every singer wants to extend his or her vocal range. You'll always want to sing just a little bit higher (or lower) than you comfortably can. While it's physically impossible for a low bass to become a high tenor, you can "push the envelope" somewhat by using the next series of exercises.

Before you begin these exercises, however, you need to learn a particular practice technique that we'll call the Santa Claus laugh. This technique helps connect your tone with your breath.

Start by placing your hands on your stomach, just above your belt buckle. With your hands in place, make an exaggerated Santa Clause "ho-ho-ho." Make this a real belly laugh, so much so that the tone starts in your belly—without any mouth movement to form the words. Once you've mastered the basic belly laugh, gradually speed up the interval of your "ho-ho-hos."

In any case, do whatever works for you to begin to feel the involvement of the diaphragm in the production of the tone. If you do this right, the tone will feel really connected to the breath. It should also feel nice and low, around your beltline. Once you feel this diaphragm/beltline connection of the tone and the breath, you are ready to carry that sensation into a singing tone—which we'll do in the next exercises.

Tip

If you're having trouble connecting your belly with your breath, you might want to visualize panting like a dog on a very hot day. You'll feel silly, I guarantee, but it's an effective approach for a lot of singers.

Exercise 5.9: Ho-Ho!

This exercise helps to develop your range very quickly. Follow these steps:

1. Sing the words "ho-ho" or "he-he" on a low pitch.
2. Repeat the words an octave higher, as notated.
3. Repeat this pattern moving up through the notes of the scale.

It's important that you keep your mouth and throat in an open position at both the top and the bottom of the octave. Remember the panting or the "ho-ho-ho" sensation, and sing the octave jumps in a short and bouncy fashion.

Be sure not to allow your mouth or throat to change much at all on the high notes—which you might be inclined to do. If anything, open or drop the jaw *more* on the high notes. Strive to feel that they come from the same place as the panting did. You should continue the sequences upward in half steps until you feel that it simply gets too high for you. (You'll know when!)

Exercise 5.10: Ha-Ha!

This is a great exercise for pitch accuracy, flexibility, range extension, and connecting the tone to the breath. You'll also get some practice in outlining major chords, if you're into music theory!

Follow these steps:

1. Start slowly on the "ha" vowel sound, then sing the pattern notated.
2. Repeat this pattern a half-step higher, then work your way up through the notes of the scale.
3. Repeat the entire exercise using each of the basic vowels.

As you sing this exercise, your mouth and throat should remain open and stay quite still. Stay aware of the involvement of the beltline and always feel that the tones bounce up into the head from there. Remember to take a full, slow breath between sequences—and when you work through the basic vowels, make sure you keep them consistent on each pitch.

The Least You Need to Know

- A great way to practice breath control is to let out a breath in short, controlled hisses.
- To practice focusing your tone, create an open-mouth hum ("ng") until you feel a buzz around your nose.
- Use the Santa Claus laugh—or just pant like a dog—to practice connecting your breath.
- You should repeat most exercises using all five basic vowel sounds.

The Least You Need to Know

Part 2

Learning to Sing—Properly

Okay, so singing isn't as simple as just opening your mouth and letting loose. To be a good singer, you need to learn the right vocal technique—including how to stand, how to breathe, and how to properly place your voice for the best sound. This part shows you how.

Chapter 6

Let's Get Physical

In This Chapter

- Learn how to view your body as an instrument
- Discover how the vocal mechanism works
- Learn about the breathing system
- Understand the vocal tract
- Find out how to condition your body

If you're a tuba player, your musical instrument is that big conglomeration of brass tubing called a tuba. If you're a pianist, your instrument is the piano. And if you're a singer, your instrument is *you*—specifically, those parts of your body you use to create a vocal tone.

Just as tuba players or pianists must understand how their instruments work and how to take proper care of them, we vocalists must also understand how our "instruments" work and how to take care of ourselves to ensure our best performance. It pays to learn as much as you can about your body and how it relates to singing—so read on to learn how it all works!

Your Body Is Your Instrument

I've often thought how fortunate we are as singers to be able to carry our "instruments" with us at all times, conveniently ready to make music at the drop of a hat. This is especially true when I'm working with an orchestra and witness the sheer strength it takes to carry in and set up a tuba, stringed bass, or a harp. Compared to those musicians, we singers have it easy!

Compared to most instrumentalists, singers certainly have the advantage of portability. Then there's the issue of price; unlike those orchestral musicians, we didn't have to pay thousands of dollars to obtain our instruments.

However, just because you didn't buy your "instrument" at a music store doesn't mean you should take it for granted. In more ways than one, your "instrument" is truly priceless and should be treated as such.

The fact is, because your instrument—your vocal mechanism—is housed in your body, you have to deal with some issues and obstacles that are unique to singers—in particular, physical disorders and ailments.

Illness, allergies, stress, and even weather conditions can wreak havoc on the voice and directly affect your vocal performance. If you're a piano player with a bad cold, you can still play the piano; yeah, your performance might suffer because you don't feel well, but the tone quality of the piano will remain unchanged. That isn't the case when you sing. Any condition that affects your body affects the quality of your voice and thus your performance. That's an issue tuba players simply don't have.

So as you continue on your singing career, view your voice as your treasured instrument—just as the violinist treasures his Stradivarius. After all, your voice is priceless, and it's the only one you'll ever have.

We'll examine the maintenance of your "instrument" in more depth in Chapter 21. For now, let's look at the parts of your vocal instrument, and how they work together to make singing possible.

Understanding the Vocal Mechanism

The vocal mechanism—the instrument you use to sing—is made up of assorted body parts, from your derrière up through your nose and throat. I'll be the first to admit that memorizing the scientific names for muscles, ligaments, and bones isn't going to help you sing any better, so I'm not going to load you up with a lot of medical terminology. You should, however, have a basic understanding of vocal anatomy in order to become more aware and sensitive to what your body is doing when you sing—in other words, to better control how your instrument actually works. With awareness comes control.

Unfortunately, your instrument isn't as easy to observe as a tuba or piano; most of the parts are hidden under a layer of skin. That means that it's not possible to actually watch your instrument function in the same way that a tuba player or pianist can. Instead, you have to *visualize* what's happening internally.

Remember the important role of imagery in singing (back in Chapter 3)? All singing begins in your imagination. To supplement your imagination, you can refer to the illustrations and analogies throughout this chapter to help you better understand your body as your instrument.

Let's start with the basics.

The human voice is a wind instrument, like a clarinet or a tuba. You "play" your voice by a controlled stream, or flow, of air.

The wind instrument that is your voice has the same basic characteristics as all of the man-made wind instruments:

- A source of air
- A vibrating mechanism
- A pitch selection mechanism
- A chamber that amplifies the sound

In the case of the human body, this process breaks down like this:

1. Your *lungs* provide the source of air.
2. The air causes your *vocal cords* to vibrate.
3. Your vocal cords' rate of vibration determines the pitch of the tone.
4. The *resonators* in your head—including your throat, mouth, and nose—amplify the basic sound.

As you can see in Figure 6.1, all these parts work together as a single instrument, and enable you to sing.

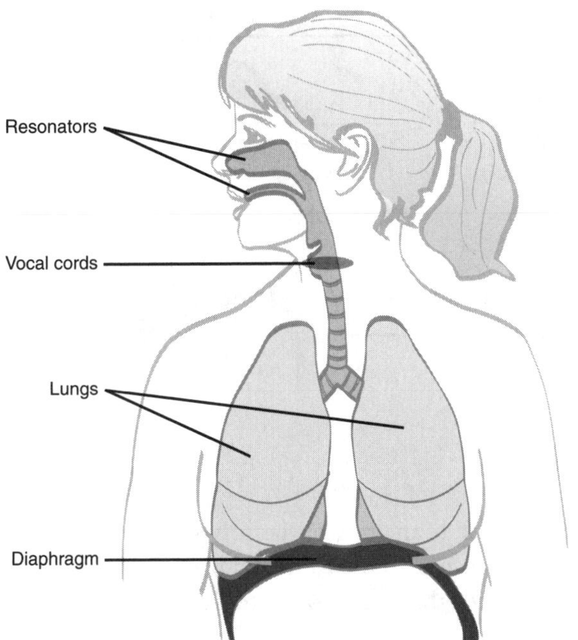

Figure 6.1

How the human vocal mechanism produces a tone.

Let's compare the human instrument to another wind instrument—the clarinet. With the clarinet, the player provides the source of air, the reed vibrates against the mouthpiece, the pads and keys alter the pitches, and the body and bell act as the amplification chamber.

Interestingly, even though the human voice is a wind instrument, it also has a lot in common with a particular string instrument—the violin. The violin strings and the human vocal cords both vibrate to produce a tone. These vibrations are set into motion by drawing the bow across the strings (in the case of the violin), and by the breath passing over the vocal cords (in the case of the voice). The quality of tone then depends on the sensitivity of the resonating chambers; in the violin, it's the body of the instrument, and in the human voice, it's (primarily) the head.

The balance of this chapter takes a closer look at the human vocal mechanism. For our discussion, we're going to break the mechanism into two distinct parts—the *breathing system* (consisting of the lungs, trachea, and breath support muscles) and the *vocal tract* (consisting of the vocal cords, resonators, and articulators like the tongue and lips).

The Breathing System

It's impossible to separate the breathing system from the vocal apparatus because without the breath, there would be no voice. As you can see in Figure 6.2, the human breathing system consists of four distinct parts:

- Diaphragm
- Lungs
- Trachea (wind pipe)
- Supporting muscles of the back and the abdominal area

While not all vocal teachers agree on the best way to achieve breath control, all agree that it is essential to good singing technique. So let's examine the complete breathing system—starting at the bottom (so to speak) and working our way up.

Figure 6.2

The parts of the human breathing system.

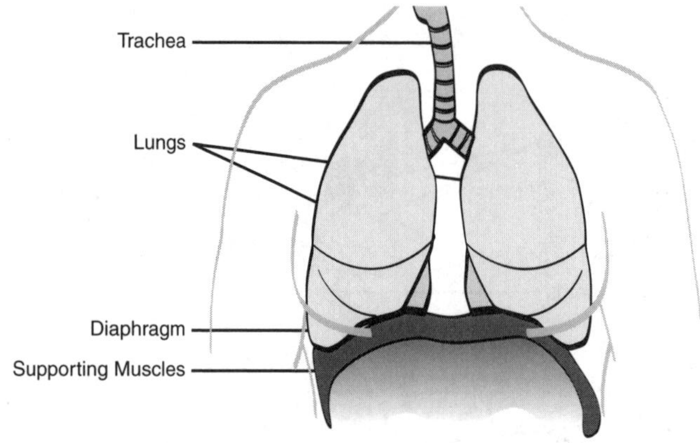

The Support Muscles

The *gluteal muscles* (buttocks) attach to the rear of the pelvis and aid in supporting it and the lower back. The *pelvic* and *lower back muscles* are attached to the front and back of the diaphragm, respectively. These muscles are as important to proper deep breathing as they are to lifting heavy objects.

The Diaphragm

The *diaphragm* is like a strong, muscular drumhead that separates the lungs and chest cavity from the abdomen. It is the most important muscle of the inhalation process. The flexing or lowering and flattening of the diaphragm allows you to take air into your lungs—in other words, to inhale. When you subsequently exhale, the diaphragm resumes its relaxed, arched position.

> **Note**
>
> You can feel the diaphragm's spasmodic power when you have the hiccups.

The Lungs

We all know that the lungs inflate and deflate automatically, without our conscious thought. Most of us also realize that we only use a small portion of their capacity in our everyday activities. However, many inexperienced singers have a number of misconceptions about the role of the lungs in the process of singing, primary of which is that filling your lungs up with air is the key to singing long phrases and having vocal "power."

As far as the singing process is concerned, the lungs are a wonderful set of bellows that are controlled by neurological impulses and the muscle groups surrounding them. If you think too much about your lungs and your breathing, it's likely that your breathing will be shallow and insufficient for really fine singing. Better to let your lungs do what they do naturally—and put your breathing on autopilot.

It is far more productive to concentrate on the parts of the body that are more obviously under our control—in particular, the muscular support system and the diaphragm. As you'll learn in Chapter 8, the best thing you can do to improve your breathing during the singing process is to lift your rib cage, allow your diaphragm to lower, and expand your back muscles during inhalation. Do this, and your lungs will thank you!

The Trachea

The trachea, also called the *windpipe*, functions much like the hose on a vacuum cleaner as a conduit for air flow. Anything you do to keep it open and clear is helpful to tone production.

> **Note**
>
> Unlike the hose on a vacuum cleaner, the trachea tends to expand during exhalation.

The Vocal Tract

Once the breathing apparatus does its job and produces a controlled flow of air, it's time for the rest of the vocal mechanism to kick in—and turn that air flow into a distinct, focused tone. The part of the vocal mechanism responsible for producing the tone is called the *vocal tract*, and it consists of the vocal cords, larynx, pharynx, mouth, and mask.

The Vocal Cords

The miraculous little set of muscles and ligaments we call the *vocal cords* are one of the most misunderstood parts of the vocal anatomy. This is in part because we can't see them, and also because they're extremely complex. The actual workings of such a complex little body part are only overshadowed by the neurological miracles that innervate it!

The vocal cords (shown in Figure 6.3) function like a fluttering valve, controlling the flow of air to and from the lungs. They also control pitch and influence vocal timbre. Quite a Herculean task for a structure that's barely over a half-inch in length!

Note

The vocal cords are sometimes referred to as the *vocal bands* or the *vocal folds*. These are particularly descriptive terms, as the vocal cords are more like small folds of tissue rather than individual cords or strings. The space for air flow between the two vocal cords is known as the *glottis*.

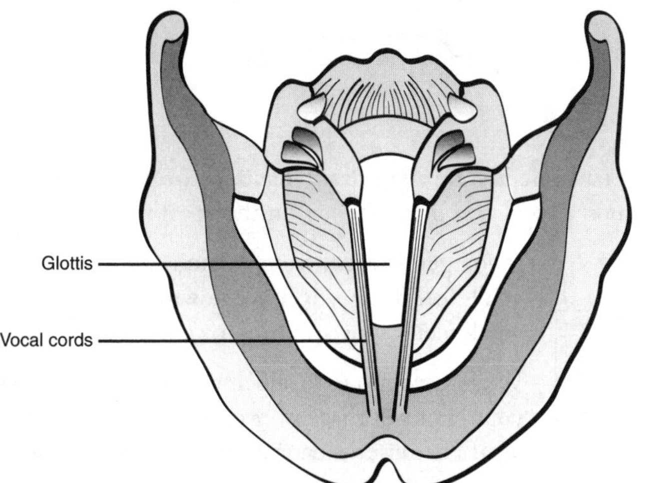

Figure 6.3

A birds-eye view of the vocal cords.

Remember when you were a kid and made rude noises by pinching the neck of an inflated balloon? The escaping air through the fluttering neck of the balloon can produce some pretty funny sounds. The tighter you pull the neck, the higher the pitch of the sound.

This is basically how the vocal cords work. The fluttering edges open and close rapidly, or vibrate, at a rate of hundreds or even thousands of times per second. The vibration is caused by the alternating increase and decrease of air pressure below and above the vocal cords—just like when you're letting the air out of a balloon. Thus sound is created.

The quality and intensity of the sound, as well as the pitch, are determined by the size, shape, and texture of the vocal cords. The more the vocal band is stretched, the thinner it becomes and the higher the pitch produced.

In addition, longer vocal cords produce lower pitches than shorter vocal cords, much like a larger balloon produces lower sounds. Thus men's voices are deeper than women's voices because men have longer and thicker vocal cords.

The Larynx

The *larynx* (or *voice box*) is located at the top of the trachea, as shown in Figure 6.4, and encases and protects the vocal cords. It's composed of cartilage and measures about one and a half inches from top to bottom.

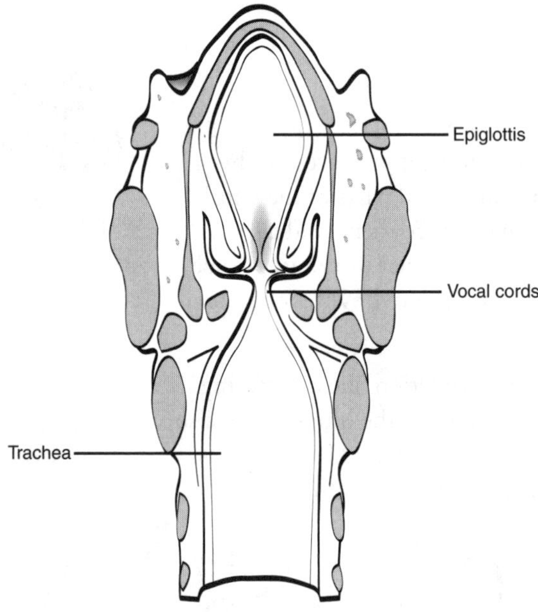

Figure 6.4

The larynx and the vocal cords.

The larynx plays an important role in tone amplification and, according to respected voice specialist William Vennard, it may be "the most prized area of resonance" in the vocal mechanism.

> **Note**
>
> Some people call the larynx the *Adam's Apple*. It sits in the front of the throat and can be felt moving up and down when you swallow.

If you gently touch your Adam's Apple and start to yawn, or simply inhale, you'll feel the larynx move downward as your throat opens. If you swallow, you'll feel it move upward, or constrict.

When it comes to producing a beautiful singing tone, you want to keep your larynx in that lower position that results from taking a deep breath. That's because when the larynx is lower, your throat is more open and free, thus creating more resonating space and minimizing muscle tension.

The Pharynx

While it's generally understood that our throats are involved in the process of singing, few people understand the real role of the pharynx in vocal production. The area called the *pharynx* extends from the top of the larynx to the area behind the nose. It is much more than what we commonly call the throat, and its impact on our singing tone is dramatic.

As you can see in Figure 6.5, the pharynx is divided into three parts that must work together to produce a free and resonant tone:

- The *laryngo-pharynx*, the bottom of the throat that surrounds the larynx
- The *oro-pharynx*, or the back of the mouth; includes the soft palate
- The *naso-pharynx*, or the area behind the nose; includes the hard palate

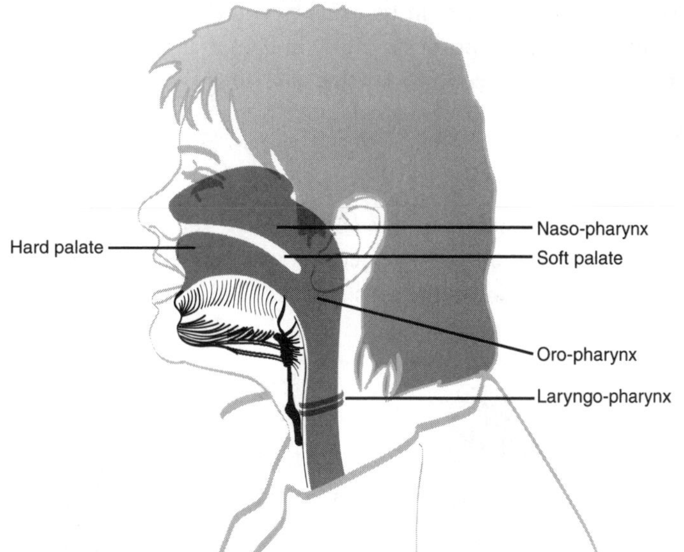

Figure 6.5

The parts of the pharynx.

All the areas of the pharynx are important in the production of your singing tone, and even the smallest adjustments can make big differences in the resulting sound. However, the area I want to concentrate on is the *soft palate*, or the *velum*, which is located in the oro-pharynx.

If I had to choose one single key to singing success—or obstacle to it—it is the position of the soft palate. If you want to be a good singer, you have to learn to raise your soft palate.

I've worked with a large number of young singers who have grown up trying to imitate their favorite pop/rock idols, and more often than not, the model was really nasal and pinched sounding—not a good thing. This nasal sound is the unfortunate result of a lowered soft palate that cuts off the air—and thus the vibrations—going into the head.

Learning how to raise your soft palate is relatively easy. Go to the mirror and look inside your mouth. You see the little punching bag hanging down from the top, in back? (It's called the *uvula*.) Watch yourself in the mirror as you raise the uvula a few times. Now close your eyes and internalize the sensation as you repeat the same action.

Another good exercise for raising the soft palate is simply to yawn gently or to sigh. Focus on the feeling at the back of your throat as you do so.

> **Caution**
>
> Some teachers stress the concept of *forcing* the larynx into a low position to produce a big vocal sound. Unfortunately, this can lead to some unnatural and tense manipulations that will only get in the way of good vocal development.

> **Caution**
>
> It's easy for any of us to unthinkingly lower our soft palate when singing. That's because American English (talking, not singing) tends to be produced with a lazy, lowered soft palate. Thus lowering the soft palate when singing sometimes feels "natural" to untrained singers.

The Mouth

Just as the vocal cords, larynx, and pharynx play important roles in your tone production, your mouth contributes greatly to your own unique sound. It is perhaps the most obvious and easily adjusted part of the resonating system.

In addition, your lips, teeth, hard and soft palate, and tongue all act as *articulators* in forming words when we sing. They also play a role in adjustment of tone quality—particularly the tongue.

While the role of the mouth is important, I want to stress to you that it is not the primary source of your singing voice. This is a common misconception (or faulty image) that many inexperienced singers have. The mouth is best thought of as an adjustable conduit for the tone—*not* the originator of the tone.

The Mask

Just above your mouth, in the area around your eyes and nose is a very important resonator we call the *mask*. (Think of the black mask of Zorro or the Lone Ranger.) As you can see in Figure 6.6, the mask consists of the bones and sinus cavities of the face and is the area we'll concentrate on in Chapter 9. The mask is responsible for adding the qualities of brilliance, focus, and "buzz" (or "ping") to your singing tone.

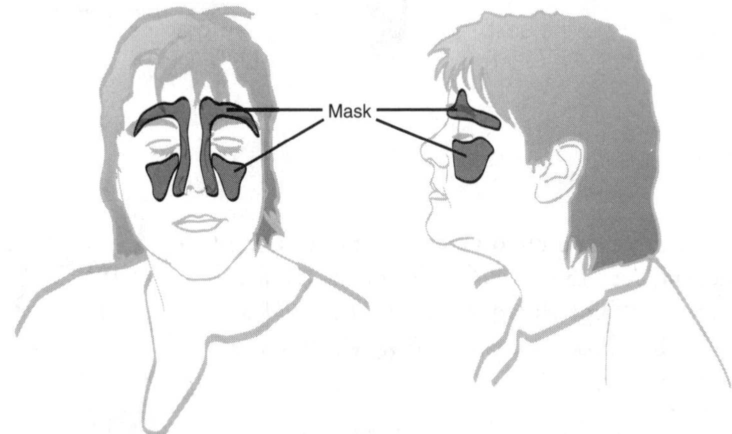

Figure 6.6

The mouth and mask.

The mask and other resonators (sometimes called *resonating chambers*) are very important in the production of vocal tone. Just think what your voice would sound like without these resonators.

Consider, for a moment, the solid-body electric guitar. If you've ever played an electric guitar "unplugged," you know that there's not much sound produced by simply strumming the strings. That's because the guitar body is a solid structure that doesn't provide a resonating chamber for the vibrations from the strings to bounce around in. (The big sound you get from an electric guitar comes from the electrical contacts and the amplifier—not from the guitar itself.)

Compare this with the hollow-body acoustic guitar. Here the vibrations from the strings are "amplified" by the resonating chamber that is the inside of the guitar body. The bigger and more "well tuned" the body, the bigger and better the sound of the guitar.

If you don't make maximum use of your natural resonating system when you sing, the result will be much like that unplugged electric guitar—weak and thin. Use your natural resonators, and you'll sing out like the finest acoustic guitar—rich and loud!

Conditioning Your Instrument

If you view your voice as your instrument, then you must also view your body as your instrument's "case." It's easy to see that a fit and healthy body correlates to a very protective instrument case. No serious instrumentalist would carry his valuable instrument around in a paper bag, and no serious singer can ignore the physical condition of his body—his instrument's case.

When considering proper fitness, the first point to consider is your weight. You probably grew up with the image of the opera Diva as a rather large, physically imposing person—which is where the old saying, "it's not over 'til the fat lady sings" comes from. But the notion that great big bodies produce great big voices is only true to a point.

Excess body fat never helped anyone do anything—in fact, carrying all that weight around is a lot of work and a big hindrance in any physical activity. Unless you're considering a career in Sumo wrestling, you should try to keep your weight at a healthy level for your body type. Today we know much more about the negative effects of excess body fat on our entire physical condition, particularly on our respiratory system—which is so critical to the singing process. While there are always exceptions to any rule, look at the vast majority of successful singers today, from opera to rock, and you won't find many out of shape bodies among them.

Tip

The practice of Yoga can improve both posture and breathing; the mind/body coordination with emphasis on breathing can also help you focus as you mentally prepare for a performance. What's great about Yoga is that it's easily accessible and can be practiced at any age and by nearly every body type; see Chapter 7 to learn more.

Any vigorous physical activity—jogging, biking, even brisk walking—will strengthen and develop your respiratory as well as your cardiovascular system. Of course, you should always check with your doctor before starting any exercise program, but most anyone can safely start with regular, brisk walking and work their way up to more vigorous activity. Make conditioning part of your daily routine, and you'll be able to feel the difference in your singing.

Note

I have a dear friend who sings professionally in New York City. Here's how he describes his three to five workouts per week at the gym: "It's just part of my job."

The Least You Need to Know

- You should view your body as your instrument—and care for it just as you would the most expensive musical instrument.
- An intimate knowledge of your vocal anatomy will make it easier to use imagery as you develop your voice.
- You should relate breathing to the muscle groups around your diaphragm and beltline—more than to your lungs.
- A good physical fitness program will assist your vocal progress.

Chapter 7

Straight and Tall: Why Posture Makes a Difference

In This Chapter

- Learn how all your body parts work together for proper singing posture
- Find out how to plant your feet for different types of music
- Discover why loose and flexible is better than stiff and locked
- Determine the best singing posture for you—both standing and sitting

If you've ever watched a gymnast pause and straighten her body before beginning floor exercises, or observed a diver start his preliminary steps before springing off the board, you've witnessed excellent singing posture. Maybe you didn't actually analyze the lifted sternum, the relaxed shoulders, or the slight tuck of the pelvis. But you surely knew that by their posture, their stance, their attitude, if you will, that they were ready to put their entire body into "action."

This is the very same physical approach that the singer must use before a tone is ever produced. After all, singing is truly an athletic endeavor, involving the entire body—something that many average singers fail to realize. Never forget that the singer's instrument *is* his body and, just like a clarinet or trombone, can only be "played" when it's put together correctly.

Try to think of correct singing posture as putting your instrument together. You remember those old days back in high school band? With the clarinet players inserting and adjusting their reeds and the trombone players fitting their slides and mouthpieces? It's the same thing for a singer—you have to put it all together before you can start.

Tip

At this point, I could probably skip all the details of correct singing posture and suggest that you purchase *The Yoga Manual: A Step-by-Step Guide to Gentle Stretching and Total Relaxation* by Rosemary Lesser (Todtri Publications, 1998). That's because singers who practice Yoga not only feel better, physically, but they sing better, too! If you want to learn Yoga, *The Yoga Manual* provides step-by-step lessons for movements, stretches, and breathing techniques. The lessons are easy to follow, thanks to more than 200 illustrations that present "real folks" doing Yoga—not the typical svelte physical specimens you might find in other books.

Proper Posture—From the Bottom Up

Proper posture involves all the different parts of your body. It's not just about standing straight and tall, it's about making all the parts of your body work together to produce the correct vocal tone.

Fortunately, the proper posture for singing is relatively easy to achieve. Good singing posture is nothing more than good whole body posture—aligning all the parts of your body in their normal balance.

That said, let's examine the proper singing posture—from the ground up.

The Feet

Start with your feet about shoulder width apart. They should be firmly planted on the floor, with the sense that your weight is on the balls of your feet, as shown in Figure 7.1.

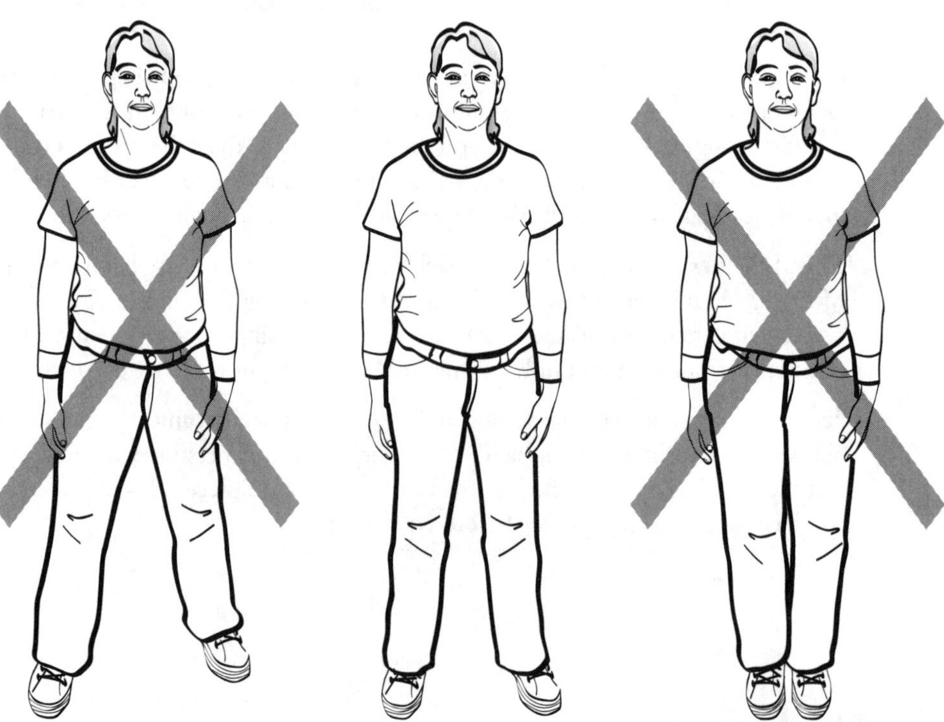

Figure 7.1

Plant your feet shoulder-width apart.

This stance can and should vary a little, depending on the "mood" of the repertoire being sung. For example, if the song is forceful or powerful or has a quick tempo, the feet should probably be spread a little wider, definitely no less than shoulder width. If the song is contemplative, slower in tempo, or of a more subdued nature, then you should place the feet a little closer together.

Remember that a wide stance implies power and stamina, while a narrower stance is more appropriate for a less "commanding" presentation. Regardless of the mood of the repertoire, however, *never* stand with you feet nearly touching! That's just not a sturdy enough base to work from. You need to feel planted firmly to the earth, as sturdy as a rock, ready to sing to the mountains. You don't want to be so unstable that a good fortissimo will send you toppling to the ground!

The Knees

In the proper singing posture, your knees should be slightly bent and fairly flexible. In fact, you should be able to bounce up and down easily when singing. (Not that you'll be doing a lot of bouncing—it's just that you should be able to do so, if you wanted to!) Think of the way tennis players flex their knees when waiting for a serve; it's the same thing here.

If your knees are locked, you're like a stiff board standing against the wind—one good puff and you're on the ground! It's true; a fixed or rigid knee has sent many a young chorister to the floor, flat on their face. In addition, blood flow is restricted if the knees are locked, so keep them feeling fluid or "soft."

The Pelvis

Yes, Elvis did have something here. Like the knees, your pelvis should also feel free and relaxed, but with a slight tuck.

The tuck is important, because when many students are told to stand straight, they tend to make their back concave—sway-backed, if you will. Thus I always tell students that the pelvis should feel slightly tucked, with the main objective of keeping the spine as vertical and straight as is comfortable.

The Sternum

The sternum is your breast bone, and it should be in a lifted position.

I tell my younger students to pretend that there is a vertical handle between their breasts, and then have them "lift" the handle up and out. The sensation when this is done is that there is a greater or taller space between the breasts and the belt line. Now, since nobody stands like this normally, don't feel too strange when you lift that imaginary handle!

Note

You can keep the sternum in this lifted position throughout inhalation and exhalation. (It takes practice!) Turn to Chapter 8 to learn more.

Since all your body parts are interconnected, it's not unusual for your work on one part to affect another related part. Case in point: When you lift the sternum into proper position, you can inadvertently screw up the positioning of your shoulders. Read on to learn more.

The Shoulders

Many people, when lifting the sternum, also lift the shoulders. Don't do this! They really are independent body parts and should be treated as independently as possible.

What you need to do is keep your shoulders down and loose. If you have to, roll your shoulders back and down to keep them as relaxed as possible.

Tip

If anything feels rigid or tense in this posture check, chill a bit. Singing is a freeing event, and much damage can be done by rigid body tension.

This is also a good time to gently roll your neck from side to side—but not too far! If you can touch your ears to your shoulders, your shoulders are too high. This indicates that you're tense, and if you're tense, the vocal mechanism will never work correctly.

Instead, feel the space between your ears and shoulders without exaggerating anything. Scrunching your shoulders up to your ears and then dropping them is a good exercise to discover the different sensation of tension and release.

Tip

When you line up your body like this, you should feel a sense of lift, or elongation in the spine, as if you are growing taller.

The Spine

Your spine has three natural curves: the cervical curve (neck), the thoracic curve (middle back), and the lumbar curve (lower back). To line up your three spinal curves in their correct position, imagine a plumb line running beside your body with your ears, shoulders, pelvis, knees, and ankles all lined up. Figure 7.2 shows how these body parts should be aligned.

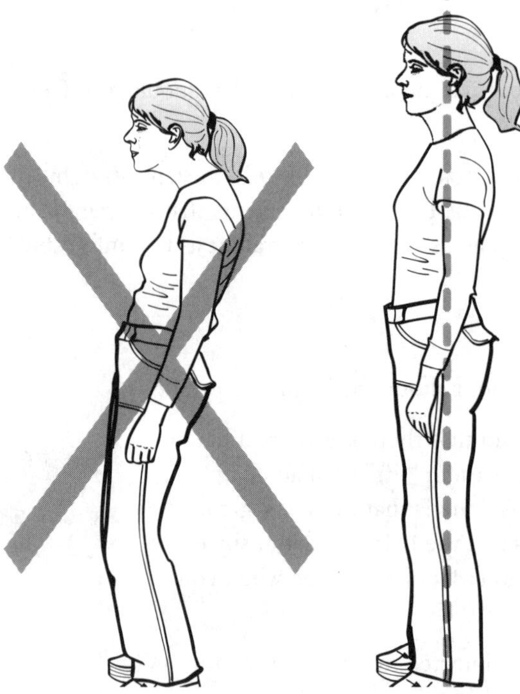

Figure 7.2

Align the parts of your body for proper spinal posture.

The Neck/Chin

Caution

Physical therapists say that many people develop neck and shoulder pain by allowing their chins to jut forward, thus compressing the vertebrae in the neck. This usually results in a slumped shoulder posture, which can contribute to all kinds of body pain.

Suffice to say that the neck is a critical area for singers. It not only encases the spinal cord, nerves, blood vessels and our vocal mechanism, but this narrow little body part has the added job of supporting our heads—which, on average, weigh twenty pounds! Proper alignment of the neck will produce proper chin position, which in turn affects not only posture but also actual tone production. (Figure 7.3 shows proper neck and chin alignment.)

In your effort to stand straight, make sure that you don't jut your jaw forward. You also don't want to tuck it in too much; this isn't the time for a tucked chin military inspection! What you want is just a slight chin tuck, with the emphasis on an open and free throat.

Figure 7.3

Align your neck and chin naturally.

Here's one way to look at proper chin alignment. Try feeling like you are singing a little "over your glasses," so that the back of your neck feels longer than the front. This really helps keep the chin in proper alignment—which is critical for good tone production.

The Arms

Okay, we've checked our posture from the ground up—but what in the world do we do with those two dangling things on either side of our bodies? What do the arms do when we sing?

The answer is simple: nothing much! Unless you want people to think you are a singing traffic cop, you should simply allow your arms to hang loosely at your sides, with your fingertips lightly touching your upper thighs. You should hold your arms loosely in place, not flopping back and forth, not dragged down like a pair of weights. Loose and natural is the key here.

Your arms (and hands) should be as inconspicuous as possible. You certainly don't want to hold one hand in the other; that went out about the time the steam engine was invented. When it comes to your arms, less is always more. Unless you are acting or singing on stage—as a character in a role—just forget about those limbs!

Note

There are certain arm and hand aspects that are unique to good microphone technique. Turn to Chapter 23 to learn more.

Seated Posture

Since we don't always stand when we sing (although it would be best if we could!), it's important to know how to sit properly. As with good standing posture, good sitting posture allows your back to do its job of supporting you.

Note

Fortunately, very few choral directors insist on standing for the entire length of a rehearsal—they would probably lose half their choir members if they did!

There is some argument as to what is the best posture for singing while in a seated position. Some choir directors teach that the feet should be firmly planted on the floor and the back should not touch the back of the chair at all. (See Figure 7.4.) Others permit the singer's back to stay in contact with the back of the chair, but insist that it be in touch from the small of the back to the shoulders, as shown in Figure 7.5. (This is to avoid the natural tendency to slump while sitting.)

I believe that both these postures are fine, as long as the chair is one designed for the choral rehearsal. Even better, I suggest switching from one posture to the other every 10 to 15 minutes. This shifting of postures keeps the back from becoming fatigued.

Tip

You can stretch your back by pushing it (the lumbar curve) firmly into the back of a straight chair, holding that position for a few seconds, and then releasing. Try this in a comfortable straight chair and you'll not only feel it in your back muscles, but also in your abdominals.

Figure 7.4

Sitting posture #1: Your back doesn't touch the chair.

Figure 7.5

Sitting posture #2: Your entire back touches the chair.

Most of the time, a singer will need to hold a choral score while rehearsing. Never allow it to rest in your lap. Instead, hold it out in front of you, as if it were on a music stand. This keeps the back straight, the chest elevated, and your neck in a better position to sing. (You can also see the conductor a lot better—so you won't be the only one singing after a cutoff!)

Practice Your Posture: Some Fun Posture Exercises

As mentioned previously, Yoga is one of the best forms of physical conditioning for singers. The term Yoga literally means "union," and it focuses on the integration and harmony of mind, body, emotions, and spirit.

The physical practice of Yoga is *Hatha Yoga* ("the union of the opposites"). The *asanas* (physical poses) practiced in Hatha Yoga will improve your posture and focus attention on the breath and how it brings the mind into harmony with the body. There is great benefit in this for singers.

Exercise 7.1: The Mountain Pose

Let's look at one of the most basic asanas, the Mountain Pose (*Tadasana*), which teaches correct posture. You don't need any special props, but I suggest you do this pose barefoot and in front of a mirror, if possible. You'll soon see how similar this asana is to the posture instruction you learned earlier in this chapter.

Here's how to do it:

1. Stand with your feet slightly touching and your weight evenly distributed between the heels and the balls of each foot.
2. Spread your toes so as to feel firmly "planted" on the ground.
3. Use your thigh muscles to lift your kneecaps and focus on a feeling of stability and strength. You should feel as if you're balancing your pelvis on your legs. This may require a small sense of tucking the tailbone under or a tightening of the abdominals. This is due to the fact that most of us have grown accustomed to lazy posture and have allowed the lower back muscles to weaken, producing a kind of "sway backed" stance. As you align your pelvis over your legs, you'll feel the involvement and support of the abdomen.
4. From the ground up, slowly stretch your inner legs and continue the feeling of lengthening upward along your entire spine.
5. Lift and open the chest as you inhale slowly. Feel as though the breath goes to your toes.
6. Drop your shoulders and feel the back of your neck become elongated. Don't allow any tension in the neck, only a gentle sense of stretch.
7. Hold this pose for about a minute while breathing deeply and slowly. Become aware of the firmly supported "stretch" of your body from your toes upward through the crown of your head.
8. Release the pose.

> **Note**
>
> For singing purposes, you may want to stand with your feet hip-width apart instead of touching.

Did you notice some "opposite" pulls while performing this exercise? The straight spine and the lifted chest seem to be in opposition, don't they? The lowered shoulders and the elongated neck also seem to oppose each other. This is because we have practiced such poor posture habits all our lives!

> **Note**
>
> There is one big difference between proper singing posture and the Mountain Pose exercise. When singing, you should never feel that the knees are tense or locked, which can result from lifting the kneecaps in the Mountain Pose.

Exercise 7.2: Interlocking Fingers

Another way to achieve the lifted chest and elongated spine is a bit of a stretch—literally.

1. Stand with your feet apart and interlock your fingers in front of you.
2. Turn your interlocked hands out and away from your body.
3. Raise your interlocked hands above your head with your palms toward the ceiling. Your arms should be aligned with your ears.
4. Stretch and hold for ten seconds as you breathe normally.
5. Inhale somewhat deeply and hold your breath, then unlock your hands and allow the arms to float down to your sides—keeping your chest elevated as it was while stretching. As the arms lower, make sure that the shoulders lower too. Everything *but* the chest should slowly lower.

6. Exhale slowly, keeping the chest in this lifted position.
7. Repeat this exercise three or four times.

Exercise 7.3: Tighten That Butt!

Here's another exercise that isn't too physically demanding, but works to strengthen both your abdominal and lower back muscles.

1. Stand straight, feet comfortably apart. (You can also do this one seated.)
2. Exhale and tighten the buttocks and abdominal muscles for a count of four seconds, then release.
3. Repeat step 2, this time holding the "tightened" position for much longer and adding deep, slow breathing. (This helps you feel the relationship of the lower body to breath support.)

Repeat this exercise several times and you'll start to understand how a properly aligned and balanced pelvis supports a straight spine. You will also find out just how much you've allowed your abdominal and lower back muscles to waste away!

Exercise 7.4: Chin Tucking

Remember how, with proper posture, you're supposed feel an elongation in the back of the neck? Here's an exercise to help your neck posture, one you can perform while standing or seated—or even when you're at your computer or in the car driving!

1. Tuck your chin down or slide it backward, creating a big double chin. (This is easier for some of us than others!)
2. Hold for four counts, then release.

Notice what the "normal" position of the head and neck is upon release. Most of us tend to allow our chins to jut forward, causing contracted tension in our shoulders. Pain and poor tonal quality can result from tension or compression in the neck.

Note

You can find more exercises like this in the book *Yoga Journal's Yoga Practice for Beginners* by Patricia Walden (Healing Arts Publishing Inc., 1990). Just about any Yoga exercise is also good for improving your singing posture.

The Least You Need to Know

- Proper singing posture is more than just standing straight and tall; it's about aligning all your body parts, from your feet to your head.
- Your feet should be firmly planted on the ground, about shoulder's width apart.
- Your knees should be flexible, not locked.
- Your pelvis should feel free and relaxed, but with a slight tuck.
- Your sternum should be in a lifted position—but without making your shoulders lift.
- Your shoulders should be loose and low.
- Your neck and chin should line up naturally, neither too far forward nor too far back.

Chapter 8

Waiting to Exhale: Learning Breath Control

In This Chapter

- Discover how breathing impacts your singing
- Learn proper inhalation techniques
- Find out how to control your exhalation
- Use breathing exercises to develop better breath control

Most vocal teachers agree that control of the breath is the foundation on which all other vocal technique rests. Put more simply, good breathing is fundamental for good singing.

Many vocal students realize the importance of good breath control, even though their reasoning for this is sometimes a little out of whack. When I ask students why they should work on their breath control, I often get the answer, "So I can sing through the whole phrase," or "So I can hold long notes when I need to."

While these are both good reasons for working on breath control, neither is the primary reason. The most important reason to work on breath control is that *singing tone is affected by the way you breathe*.

That's right—the better your breath control, the better the singing tone you'll achieve. Sure, developing lung capacity, learning to inhale fully and deeply, and controlling the breath's release will enable you to sing those long phrases and notes. But more important, developing good breath control will allow your voice to sound full and clear, instead of weak and breathy.

So let's get to work!

Breathing In: Inhalation

As you're aware, breathing is a two-step process. Step one, you breathe in. (This is called inhalation.) Step two, you breathe out. (This is called exhalation.)

We'll work on your inhalation first, by performing some simple exercises.

Expand Your Diaphragm

You probably remember (from Chapter 7) the important role that posture plays in preparing the breath. Posture is also important in keeping your sternum steady as you expand your diaphragm when you inhale.

> **Note**
>
> Now would be a good time to review the breathing-related content of Chapters 2, 6, and 7, and get ready to put your newfound knowledge of vocal anatomy to work with the exercises in this chapter.

Let's examine exactly which body parts do what when you inhale. Start by standing in a good singer's posture, then place both hands on your chest, on either side of your sternum, just above your breasts. Practice raising and lowering your sternum a few times as you breathe in and out, respectively. The movement of your hands on your chest will help you see the up and down "heaving" motion as you breathe.

Unfortunately, this is what a lot of people do when they inhale (and exhale)—and it's *wrong*. What you're currently experiencing is a shallow and insufficient kind of breathing for singing. You should avoid it at all costs.

What you should do, instead, is work to expand your diaphragm as you inhale. So let's repeat this little exercise, but this time do it the *right* way:

1. Stand in good singer's posture and place your right hand on your chest and your left on the area just above your beltline (your diaphragm), as shown in Figure 8.1.
2. Lift your sternum *before* you inhale.
3. Take a slow deep breath.

Figure 8.1

Learning to expand your diaphragm.

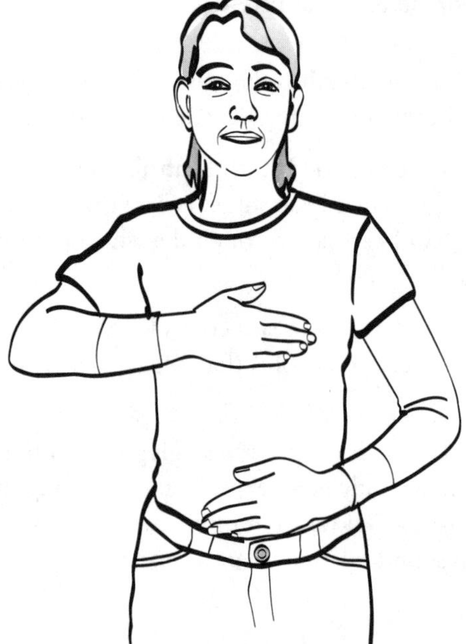

The only movement you should feel (or see, if you're working in front of a mirror) is the expansion around the diaphragm.

I recommend you practice taking long, deep breaths while focusing on the image of filling a water balloon. Why? Because the water fills a balloon from the bottom up, and that's how you should imagine filling your lungs—from the bottom up, as shown in Figure 8.2. Too many students have the reverse image, which often leads to shallow breathing.

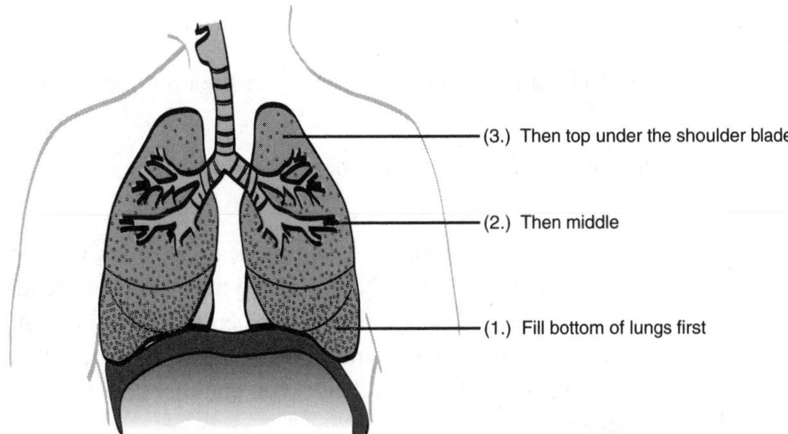

Figure 8.2

Fill your lungs with air from the bottom up.

Breathe with Your Back

When we're discussing inhalation, we shouldn't forget the role of the back—even though it's often overlooked, especially by inexperienced singers.

In Chapter 6 you learned how the abdominals, intercostals, and back muscles work together with the diaphragm to provide support to the whole vocal mechanism. You can feel this happen by placing your hands on your sides at the bottom of your rib cage, just above your belt. (Make sure your thumbs are wrapped around to your back, as shown in Figure 8.3.) As you inhale, you should feel your thumbs being pushed apart as your back muscles expand.

Caution

When practicing your inhalation, try to avoid the common mistake of sucking in your stomach when you inhale. You can learn a lot by watching a sleeping baby breathe—slow and steady, with no unnatural contraction of the stomach muscles.

Figure 8.3

Feel your back muscles expand when you inhale.

Practice taking deep breaths until you can produce a noticeable spread. This may take some work, since most people don't consciously involve the back in their breathing to any noticeable degree.

Mouth vs. Nose Breathing

When students ask me whether it's better to breathe through the mouth or the nose, I answer with all certainty: "It depends."

As with many aspects of life, the question of mouth vs. nose breathing depends on the situation. Both have their pros and cons.

Tip

If you have trouble feeling and controlling this all-around expansion, try tightening a belt (unbuckled) around the area of your diaphragm. When a proper breath is taken, you should be able to feel the belt actually stretch open. (The next step is to attempt to keep the belt in place while singing an exercise—try it!)

You can see this when you take a deep breath through your mouth, then another through your nose. Notice how your soft palate tends to lower when you inhale through your nose? When singing, you want to keep your soft palate high, so you might think that breathing through your nose is a bad thing—which it would be if you couldn't also adjust the position of your palate.

Let's demonstrate this with another little exercise. Take another deep breath through your nose, but this time *imagine* that you're yawning through your nose. Did you feel the velum rise? (If so—and you should have—you've just seen another example of vocal imagery at work.)

Still, even though you can consciously affect the position of the soft palate when breathing through your nose, mouth breathing tends to better prepare the vocal mechanism. You'll also get more air more quickly into your lungs by breathing through your mouth. However, the downside of mouth breathing is that it tends to dry out the throat—which is not desirable.

So my best advice is to let the music and the situation dictate which technique—nose breathing or mouth breathing—to use for inhalation. When making the choice, remember these two points:

- When mouth breathing, the nasal passage should remain open and involved.
- Whichever method you choose, your inhalation should be silent—no audible "gasping," please!

To that last point, it's actually possible to take in *too much* air. If you hyperinflate your lungs, you create a lot of pressure on your vocal cords—and that's something you definitely don't want.

Breathing Out: Exhalation

Contrary to popular myth, good breathing technique has much more to do with exhalation than inhalation. There are numerous reasons why exhalation is so important, including the fact that less breath is needed to sing than you might think, and that sound (phonation) doesn't occur until the breath leaves the lungs and passes over the vocal cords.

A person's natural tendency is to just let the breath escape "at will" as he talks or sings. You can confirm this by reciting a familiar passage (something you don't have to read or concentrate on) and, while you're reciting, think about what's happening to your breath. You'll discover that your exhaled breath sort of rushes out, so that there is a considerable amount of breath in your speaking voice.

Note

I know you can't produce a sound when you're really holding your breath—remember how the vocal cords work?—but, for the sake of this exercise, try to approximate that feeling.

What you want to work toward is a more controlled exhalation. You want your breath to seep out in a more measured manner, rather than in uncontrolled bursts.

One way to develop a controlled exhalation is to recite that same passage while imagining that you're holding your breath. This is a very different feeling, isn't it? You should feel more involvement of your midsection muscle group, and you may even feel a more open throat and hear a clearer speaking tone.

Now, I'm not suggesting that you should hold your breath when you sing, since we have to sing "on the breath" and without the tension that holding it produces. However, when you practice controlled exhalation, it should *feel* more like you're holding your breath than it does allowing it to escape at will.

Exercises for Better Breath Control

The following exercises will help you develop an increased awareness of your breath capacity and flow, and thus develop the controlled release of your breath. These exercises can be done just about anyplace and don't require you to have this book's CD nearby. So don't complain that you don't have time for these exercises—you can do them while driving in your car or even lying in bed!

Exercise 8.1: Inhale and Hold

This exercise helps develop your lung capacity. You should record your progress as you repeat this exercise over time.

1. Inhale and hold your breath.
2. Mentally count to the highest number possible before release.

When you perform this exercise, remember to keep a "silent yawn" position in your throat. You should gradually be able to make it to higher numbers before releasing your breath.

Exercise 8.2: Exhale Like a Snake

This exercise helps you develop controlled exhalation. You should record your progress as you repeat this exercise over time.

1. Deeply inhale.
2. Exhale slowly, sustaining a slow "*sss*" while mentally counting as the air escapes.

You should make sure that your sternum stays elevated while the air escapes—and resist the urge to slump down as you exhale. As in the previous exercise, you should be able to increase the length of your exhalation over time.

Exercise 8.3: Hiss a Song

We've done this one before (in Chapter 5), but it's worth repeating here as it's great for developing controlled exhalation.

1. Hiss the rhythm (not the tune) of the song "Yankee Doodle" and strive to get through it without a breath.
2. Repeat, and try to get through the song two—or maybe even three—times without a breath.

Exercise 8.4: Sing a Song

This exercise is similar to the last one, except you're singing the song instead of hissing it.

1. Sing the song "Yankee Doodle" and strive to get through it without a breath.
2. Repeat, and try to get through the song two or more times without a breath.

Compare how long you were able to sustain a tone while "hissing" verses singing. Some surprising differences?

Exercise 8.5: Sing a Scale

This exercise has you singing the first half of a major scale, over and over.

1. Sing up and down the first five notes of a major scale, singing numbers on each note. (Instead of singing "Do-Re-Mi-Fa-So-Fa-Mi-Re-Do," you'll sing "1-2-3-4-5-6-7-8-9—where the "9" is a repeat of the starting "Do.")
2. Keep singing the same five notes, up and down, while continuing to count upward, as many times as possible before you run out of breath.

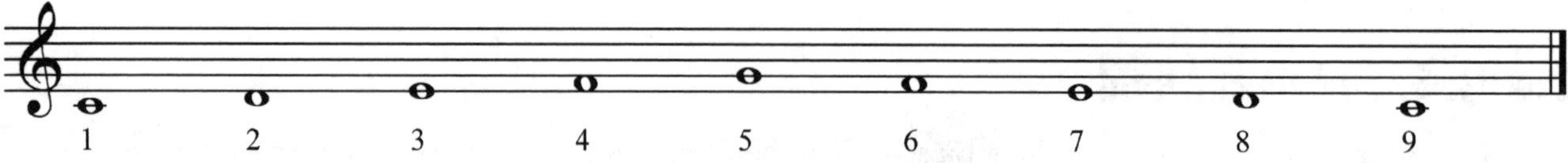

The goal, obviously, is to count as high as possible on a single breath. (We use numbers here instead of the "Do-Re-Me" Solfeggio to provide a benchmark for your progress.)

Exercise 8.6: Keep Your Chest High

Earlier in this chapter, when we discussed inhalation, I had you place one hand on your chest and the other on your diaphragm area while inhaling. We're going to take that same practice technique and apply it to exhalation, with the goal of keeping your chest high as you exhale.

1. Place one hand on your chest and the other on your diaphragm area.
2. Take a deep breath.
3. Exhale steadily, while keeping the space between your hands constant.

The key here is to pay close attention to the space between your hands. Don't allow your hands to drift together as you empty your lungs. If they do, you're allowing the chest to fall as you exhale—which is a bad, but common breathing fault. The only movement you should feel is your beltline "deflating" as your diaphragm returns to its resting position.

The Least You Need to Know

- The way that you breathe affects your singing tone—as well as your ability to sing long notes and phrases.
- When you inhale, you should avoid raising and lowering your sternum as your diaphragm expands.
- When you take a deep breath, your back muscles should expand.
- Exhalation is even more important than inhalation.
- You should work toward a controlled exhalation, instead of letting your breath escape at will.

Chapter 9

Finding Your Focus: Vocal Placement and the Even Voice

In This Chapter

- Choosing the right path
- Discovering the open throat
- Understanding vibrato
- Learning about the even voice and vocal registers
- Using exercises to develop the even voice

In Chapter 2 I had you speak the word "we" and then repeat it as if you were a child going down a slide—"whee!" When you called out "whee," you used that powerful tool we call vocal imagery—and it helped to elongate and raise the pitch of your voice.

That exercise, even though you didn't know it at the time, was all about finding your *vocal focus*—or what some educators call *placement*.

When you imagine the feeling of that gleeful childhood "whee," your voice seems to get out of your throat and travel upward into your head. It automatically finds the correct pathway to the area for maximum resonance and carrying power—the mask, which you learned about in Chapter 6. Placing your voice in the mask is crucial for producing the best, most focused vocal tone.

This concept of placement is a bit tricky, since it can be argued that we don't have the ability to actually make our voices "go someplace." Yet it's a fact that your voice takes on a ringing quality when it is directed or "placed" in the front of your face, in that area we call the mask. The mask works like the lens of a camera as it pulls fuzzy images into sharp and clear focus. The "ping" or "buzz" produced in the mask is also what gives your voice its volume and carrying power, as well as its clarity of tone.

The Path to the Mask

Getting the voice elevated and in the right pathway toward the mask can be accomplished in several ways. I'm a dedicated fan of vocal imagery when teaching focus and placement because I've seen it work so well with both young and inexperienced older singers.

Remember, if you can imagine it, you can produce it. Your ability to achieve proper placement or focus depends on your ability to imagine the tone quality and your willingness to experiment with your vocal sounds.

Imagining the Path

Figure 9.1 shows the correct path you should choose to place your voice in the mask area. As you can see, the vibrating airflow should be aimed at the *top* and *rear* portion of your head.

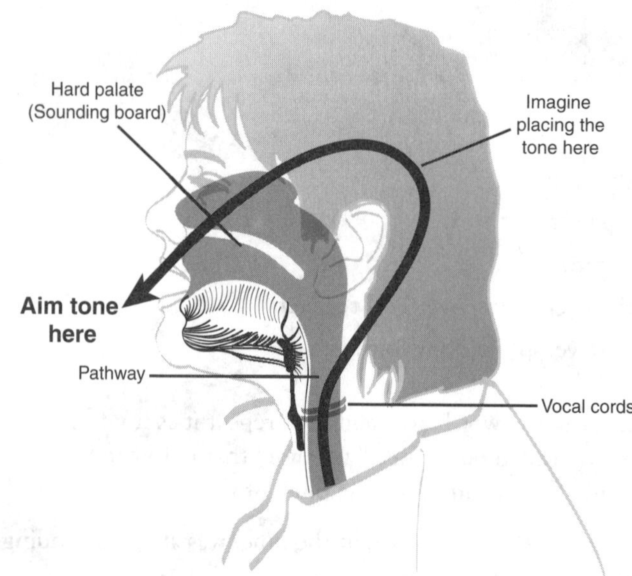

Figure 9.1

The path to proper vocal placement.

Palates and the Path

There are several obstacles to moving your voice through or along this pathway—the first of which is the soft palate, which you also probably remember from Chapter 6. If the soft palate is lowered, it blocks the pathway—and prevents vocal focus.

You need to make sure that the soft palate is lifted or raised, just like you are starting to yawn. In fact, you tend to naturally find this pathway when you sigh while yawning. Experiment with that feeling for a while and you'll realize that you knew the right path all along—you just didn't realize it applied to singing!

> **Caution**
>
> Many inexperienced singers wrongly imagine the voice to be in the throat. You should always imagine it to be in your head.

A better target to shoot for when trying to focus your tone is the *hard palate*, shown in Figure 9.1. If you have trouble focusing on the hard palate, try using the image of singing "over your glasses" or "out your eyes," or even "into the upper row of teeth." Use whatever image works for you to get your voice up and out of your throat and into your head—you'll feel and hear a less breathy and more focused tone.

Good—and Bad Vibrations

When your voice is focused, you will feel and hear it differently—on the inside. A focused tone sometimes creates a "buzzing" feeling in the ears or behind the nose or eyes. This is a good vibration.

If you're feeling lots of vibrations in your throat, you may be keeping your throat too tight, or even closed. Sometimes this tension is increased when you raise your tongue in the back of your mouth.

Tip

Always be aware of the physical sensations that occur as you experiment with new sounds—and be open to change.

You need to imagine your throat as nothing more than an open passageway for the stream of air to reach the sounding board of your mask. Keeping the throat open and free is critical to good tone production—and the only way to ever develop the ability to sing high notes.

Now let's examine the vibrations you should be feeling in the front of your face, in your mask. Turn back to Chapter 2 and repeat Exercises 2.1 and 2.2—the speaking versus singing voice exercises. When you switch to your singing voice, note the vibrations you feel in the area of the mask.

By now, you should be able to apply this feeling of elevation and focus to actual sustained singing tones. As you repeat these exercises, make sure you keep a sense of vertical space in your mouth (the "egg" imagery) so you don't sound tight or strained as you concentrate on centering your tone in the mask.

Your mouth, chest, and throat should also be filled with vibrations, since they all act as resonators. These parts of the vocal mechanism provide a certain richness or fullness of tone that the mask alone does not.

Understanding Vibrato

Vibrato is that slight fluctuation in pitch and intensity that gives warmth and vibrancy to the singing tone. (Actually, I prefer to think of vibrato as a "spinning tone," since the image of spinning tends to be more focused and controlled than the image of wavy vibrations.) In any case, vibrato is a good thing; any freely produced and properly placed voice will generate some degree of vibrato.

Vibrato is an indicator that we are doing things right. A forced or tight voice won't have it. It is a quality that is a natural attribute, and it will begin to show itself as you develop focus and balanced breath support.

Developing Vibrato

If you are a young singer, don't get discouraged if you don't seem to have vibrato in your tone. That's because vibrato is a characteristic of the more mature voice. Younger voices tend to be more "pure" or straight, with vibrato developing as they mature. Good technique will be fertile ground for its development.

Vibrato is something you can't artificially reproduce. I've encountered some vocal students who tried to introduce a kind of shake or tremor into their voices, attempting to produce a vibrato that otherwise didn't exist. That's not a real vibrato, and it doesn't sound all that good. Remember, vibrato will happen and happen naturally when your vocal placement is correct and properly supported.

Controlling Vibrato

You can control the degree of your vibrato (to some extent) by applying specific breath control techniques. In particular, when you balance the breath pressure from below and above the vocal cords, you can decrease—or even eliminate—vibrato from your voice.

If vibrato is a naturally occurring component of the mature voice, why would we want to eliminate it? Well, some types of music (mostly older classical forms) demand the pure tone of a younger, vibrato-less voice. In addition, some (but certainly not all) choir directors like to reduce individual vibrato in an attempt to create a more uniform choral sound.

The point is, if you practice good breath control, you can also control the degree of your vibrato.

Dealing with Unwanted Vibrato

Another reason you might need to control your vibrato is that vibrato—like many things in life—is good only in moderation. Think of vibrato as a rare and very expensive spice; a little goes a long way. Too much vibrato draws unwanted attention to itself—and away from what you're singing. Moderation, again, is the key.

I'm sure you've heard older voices that have an uncontrolled wobble, or oscillation, when singing. The saying "You could drive a truck through that vibrato" (meaning the vocal wobble was extremely wide) is laughingly applied to such cases. Sadly, aging can cause a loss of elasticity in the vocal cords and diminish a singer's breath support, resulting in an uncontrolled vibrato. (This condition, unfortunately, tends to show up more dramatically in older women.)

Note

We'll look further into both vibrato and straight tone when we examine different vocal genres in Part 5 of this book.

While an unwanted wobble or tremolo in the voice is often caused by inadequate breath support, the lack of vibrato is typically caused by *too much* pressure and tension during exhalation—what we could call *improper* breath support. You'll hear that kind of singing tone called "straight tone" or "white tone"—and you probably don't want to listen to it very long. (It's the aural equivalent of watching a single stationary laser beam—straight and boring!)

Vocal Registers and the Even Voice

We all know that our voices can produce a range of vocal qualities, or "colors." We use the term *timbre* to describe this type of tone color, and the different timbres of the human voice are called *vocal registers*.

When you hear singers referring to "chest voice" or "head voice," they're talking about different vocal registers. Let's take a look at these registers and how to either get rid of them or make them work for you—not against you!

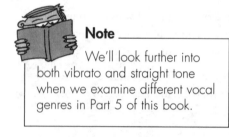

Note

You can interchange the term *resonance* with voice—as in "head voice" and "head resonance."

Caution

A common fault of many inexperienced singers is using the chest voice for their entire range—even the high notes. We call this "belting," not singing.

Chest Voice and Head Voice

A vocal register is described by the sensation of the source of the vocal tone. For all practical purposes, there are two main registers, based on the two most common resonating areas—the head and the chest. One of the objects of good vocal technique is to develop the ability to blend these two timbres so that your high notes have a certain depth and warmth, and your lower notes retain focus and resonance.

We just looked at producing focused, brilliant tones in the area of the head we call the mask. This focused tone is called the *head voice*, since the source of the resonance is in the head.

Of course, there are other resonators in the vocal mechanism, such as the throat and the chest. When it feels like your voice is produced more in the throat or the sternum, this register is called the *chest voice*.

Figure 9.2 shows the resonating areas we've identified as head and chest. As you look at it, note that there should always be a "two-way street" on which the vibrations travel between the sounding boards in the head and around the sternum.

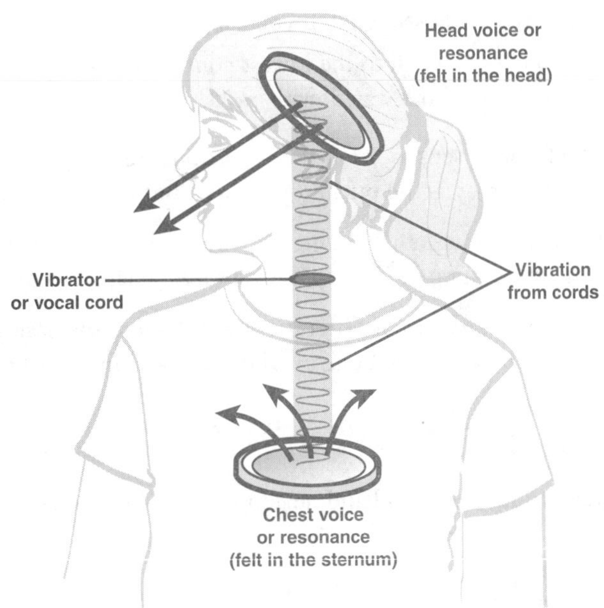

Figure 9.2

Blending the voice between the two registers.

Balancing the tone between these two resonating areas is called *blending* the voice, and the ability to do so is called the *even voice*. When you sing low notes, you should still retain the sensation of head voice—keeping the velum high and the space in the mouth big—or your notes will sound raucous and harsh. Conversely, when you sing high notes, you should retain the image and sensation of the vibrating sternum to keep the voice from sounding too bright or shrill.

Make It—Don't Break It

Now that you know what registers are and how they impact vocal color, you need to negotiate a great big stumbling block called the *break*. The break is the area between your chest and head voice where you must make some physical adjustments in order to avoid a "flip" or "crack" in your tone quality.

Singers hate the break because it requires a lot of work to eliminate. In fact, some singers never do eliminate the break—and wind up sounding like two or three different people in the course of one song! Of course, the most blatant example of the break is found in a young man's changing voice, but *all* singers have to contend with it—which is where the following exercises come in.

Exercises to Develop the Even Voice

The following exercises will help you smooth out the passages between registers and develop the even voice. Work through them carefully; they're certainly not as easy as you might think.

Remember, keeping a seamless tone between registers is a very advanced technique—sometimes taking *years* to develop.

Exercise 9.1: Stay in the Mask

This is a great exercise for all beginning or otherwise untrained singers. The focus is on keeping your voice in the mask area throughout your entire vocal range.

1. Sing a free "naw" at the highest possible pitch you can reach.
2. Allow your voice to gradually descend to the lowest comfortable note you can sing—while imagining your voice staying in the mask all the way down.

Concentrate on keeping the forward sensations in the mask consistent as the pitch drops slowly. Your voice will want to drop back into the throat as the pitches get lower, but don't allow that to happen.

It may be helpful *not* to think of this as actually "singing," but rather just making a sound. Most likely, the untrained singer will feel the voice jump, flip, or at the very least change in tone quality as it slides downward.

You may have to experiment with loudness or different vowels to find the easiest combination for your success. This one really takes concentration and control, and you shouldn't expect success on your first few tries.

Exercise 9.2: Feel the Vibrations

Here's another good exercise to help you find and develop blended registers.

1. Place one hand on your sternum and one on your forehead.
2. Start with a high pitched "hum," lips closed and teeth clenched.
3. Slide down to a very low pitch and then slide back up, paying attention to the vibrations you feel.

You should feel the vibrations seem to move from your head to your chest and back up again. You'll also exaggerate the break in the registers with your teeth clenched.

Now try the same exercise with an "open hum"—lips together, but with that feeling of the egg between your teeth. This open hum should help you better negotiate the break between registers—or at least make it a little less blatant!

Exercise 9.3: Falsetto to Full

Male singers have some unique vocal abilities that women don't. While both men and women have a type of higher "half voice," men have two distinct voices, dramatically distinct in both timbre and pitch. This voice is called the *falsetto* voice, and if you've ever heard Frankie Valli sing with the Four Seasons, you know what it sounds like.

So this next exercise is just for the guys. Since you have all those high notes, why not learn to incorporate them into your singing range—seamlessly?

1. Repeat Exercise 9.1, starting high in your falsetto voice.
2. As you descend in pitch, attempt to "sneak" into your full voice, without allowing any blatant tone color changes or octave drops.

The Least You Need to Know

- Correct vocal placement aims the tone to the mask—that area of the head just behind your eyes.
- There are two main registers to the singing voice—the head voice and the chest voice.
- Making the break between these registers seamless results in what we call the even voice.
- Properly trained voices not only strive for an even voice, they also blend the warmth of the chest voice with the brilliance of the head voice.

Part 3 Sight Singing and Vocal Theory

The best singers know how to read any piece of music put in front of them. Use the chapters in this part to learn basic vocal theory, Solfeggio techniques, and sight singing—both notes and rhythms.

Chapter 10

Basic Vocal Theory

In This Chapter

- Learn how to read different pitches on a sheet of music
- Discover how to sing intervals
- Learn about major and minor scales
- Figure out different key signatures
- Learn how to read note values and rhythms
- Figure out different time signatures
- Discover different tempo markings—and how to navigate a complete piece of music

This chapter is a little different from the others so far in this book. Instead of focusing on the "how" of singing, it focuses on the "what"—the notes and rhythms that are written on paper that you have to read in order to sing.

That's right—this chapter is all about reading music.

But it's more than that, really; it's about learning how to read, yes, but it's also about the building blocks of the music itself—the scales and keys and rhythms that are used to create the songs you sing. Or, to use a better phrase, this chapter is about *vocal theory*, that aspect of general music theory that applies specifically to singing.

So if you already know how to read music and can tell a major scale from a minor, feel free to skim or skip this chapter completely. But if you want to know what all those black dots are on the music you're handed to sing, then read on—and pay close attention. Learning how to read music is just like learning how to read a foreign language; once you figure out some key concepts, it's pretty easy.

Singing Pitches

Sing an "ah"—any "ah."

You are now singing a *pitch*. Pitch describes how high or low a note is—and you can sing lots of different pitches, from the very top of your range to the very bottom. Different voices

Note

Want to learn more about music theory? Then check out *The Complete Idiot's Guide to Music Theory* (Alpha, 2002), written by Michael Miller—the co-author of the book you're currently reading!

(and different instruments) produce different ranges of pitch. For example, women tend to have higher-pitched voices than men, which means they can sing higher notes. Men have lower-pitched voices, so they can sing lower notes. (There are exceptions to this rule, of course; a high tenor might be able to sing a higher range of pitches than a low alto.)

Time for another quick exercise: Sing the lowest pitch you can sing, then gradually raise the pitch until you're singing the highest pitch you can sing.

You just sang a whole lot of different pitches—dozens of them, in fact. But how do we indicate just one of those pitches, and do so in a way you know which specific pitch you're supposed to sing?

Pitches by Number

One way to designate pitches is to number each individual pitch. All melodies are constructed from a series of notes (called a *scale*) that starts on a specific pitch, and ends on a higher version of that same pitch. We can then number each of the pitches in the scale, starting on the number "1" and *ending* on the number "1." (Remember, a scale starts and ends on different versions of the same pitch.)

In the Western world, we divide our scales into seven main notes—eight if you count the first note, which is repeated at the end of the scale. Because there are seven notes, it's easy to number them—one through seven. Let's use this numbering system to describe the melody of "Frere Jacques." We'll call the first pitch you sing "1" and go from there.

1 2 3 1

1 2 3 1

3 4 5

3 4 5

"Frere Jacques" by the numbers

Pitches by Solfeggio

Another way to describe a pitch is to assign a simple syllable to each pitch in the scale. Remember the song from *The Sound of Music* that goes "Do, a deer, a female deer"? That's what we're talking about here.

In this particular method, called *Solfeggio* (or Solfège), each of the seven notes of a scale has its own name. Table 10.1 shows the words to use.

Table 10.1 The Solfeggio Method

Tone	Solfeggio name	Pronunciation
1	Do	Doh
2	Re	Ray
3	Mi	Mee
4	Fa	Fah
5	So (or Sol)	So (or Soul)
6	La	Lah
7	Ti	Tee
8	Do	Doh

Here's what the first half of "Frere Jacques" looks like using the Solfeggio method:

```
Do Re Mi Do
Do Re Mi Do
Mi Fa So
Mi Fa So
```

"Frere Jacques" in Solfeggio

Solfeggio is a great way to develop your sight singing skills. We'll work more with Solfeggio in Chapter 11.

Pitches by Name

It's important to know that both the numbering and the Solfeggio methods are *relative* ways of naming musical pitches. That is, the first note in a scale is always number one and is always called Do. The second note is always number two and is always called Re. It doesn't matter what actual pitch you start with—these names always apply.

The problem with using relative naming is that it doesn't tell you what *precise* pitch to start with. You might start your Do Re Me on a low pitch, and your neighbor might start hers on a higher pitch, and your duet will end up sounding like two water buffaloes in heat—and that's not good. (Unless you're a water buffalo, of course.)

No, what we need is a way to designate the *specific* pitches that you're supposed to sing.

The way we do this is to assign letters of the alphabet to specific pitches, using the first seven letters of the alphabet—A, B, C, D, E, F, and G. While the numbering and Solfeggio methods are relative (the number 1 can be assigned to any pitch), the letter method is absolute. This means that A always refers to a specific pitch. When someone tells you to sing an A, you'll always know which specific pitch to sing.

Try this exercise: Sing A B C D E F G A (think "Do Re Mi Fa So La Ti Do"). The first A and the second A should be the same pitch, with the second A an *octave* higher than the first A. (You'll learn about octaves a little later in this chapter—suffice to say it's a way of presenting a lower or higher version of the same note.)

Pitches on a Piano Keyboard

A good way to visualize the seven basic notes (A through G) is to look at a piano keyboard. Each white key on the keyboard corresponds to one of these seven main notes, as shown in the following figure. (And ignore the black keys, for the time being.)

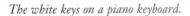

The white keys on a piano keyboard.

As you can see, the black and white keys on a piano form a certain pattern. If you start in the right place, you'll see that the black keys are arranged in groups of twos and threes. The first white key to the left of a group of *two* black notes is always assigned to the tone of C. The first white key to the left of a group of *three* black notes is always assigned to F. Once you know where C and F are, you can figure out the location of the other notes.

To figure out which A (or F or C) to play, know that the C located in the middle of the piano keyboard—directly underneath the manufacturer's logo or pull-down door handle—is called *middle C*. (It's the C in the middle of the keyboard—easy to remember.) All other notes can be described relative to middle C—as in "the F above middle C" or "the D below middle C."

Pitches on a Musical Staff

Now that you know the seven basic notes and where they lie on a piano keyboard, how does a composer or arranger go about communicating those notes to you? The composer could just spell out a song; if he used this method, the first half of "Frere Jacques" would look like this:

C D E C
C D E C
E F G
E F G

The notes of "Frere Jacques"

Now, that's more specific than using numbers or Solfeggio, but it's really difficult to read. A better way to notate pitches is to do so *visually*, using a graphic that in some ways resembles a basic piano keyboard. This graphic is called a *staff*.

The basic music staff is composed of lines and spaces, like this:

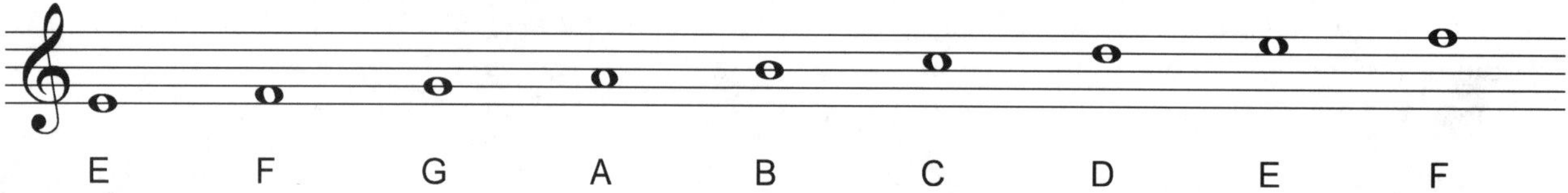

The notes of the treble clef staff.

As you can see, the staff has precisely five lines and four spaces. Each line or space represents a specific pitch. The pitches are determined by the *clef* at the beginning of the staff; the staff we're looking at here uses what is called the *treble clef*. (There are several different types of clefs, which we'll discuss later in just a minute.)

This treble clef staff pictures the notes in the exact middle of a piano keyboard—just above middle C. (The bottom line of the staff represents the E above middle C.) The following figure shows how the notes of the staff relate to specific piano keys.

Where treble clef notes fall on the piano keyboard.

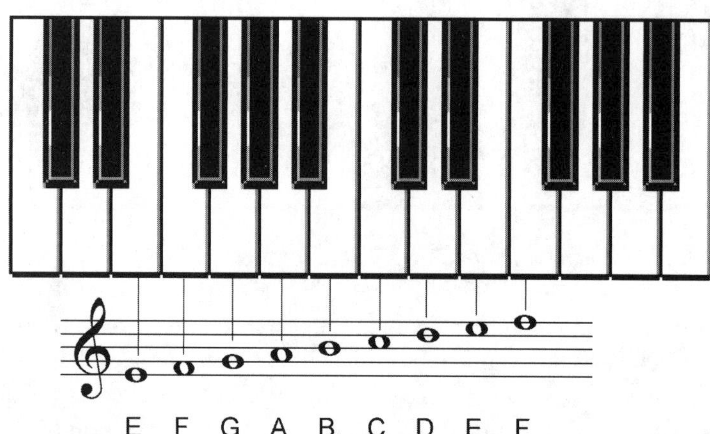

Back to "Frere Jacques"—here's what the first part of that song looks like on a music staff:

"Frere Jacques" in standard musical notation.

Tip

Notes higher than the F at the top of the staff are written in the lines and spaces *above* the staff. (For example, the first space above the staff is the first note after F: G.) Notes lower than E are written in the lines and spaces *below* the staff. (For example, the first space below the staff is the first note before E: D.

Different Clefs

Up till now, we've been looking at a staff that represents the notes just above middle C on the piano keyboard. The notes of this staff are determined by the type of *clef* that appears at the beginning of the staff—and there are two primary types of clefs used in vocal music.

The Treble Clef

The clef we've been working with so far is called the *treble clef.* As you've already learned, in real-world terms, the treble clef is positioned just above middle C. The bottom line of the treble clef staff is an E; the top line is an F.

Tip

Here's an easy way to remember the lines and spaces of the treble clef staff. The lines are assigned, bottom to top, to the notes E, G, B, D, and F; just remember the first letters in the phrase, "Every Good Boy Does Fine." The spaces of a staff are assigned, bottom to top, to the notes F, A, C, and E; remember the word "FACE."

All female voices read music using the treble clef. Tenor parts are also written using the treble clef, although tenors actually sing each note an octave below what is written.

The Bass Clef

Basses and baritones are used to reading music written with a different clef, called the *bass* clef. The bass clef is positioned just *below* middle C.

Here's what the bass clef looks like, with the notes of a bass clef staff:

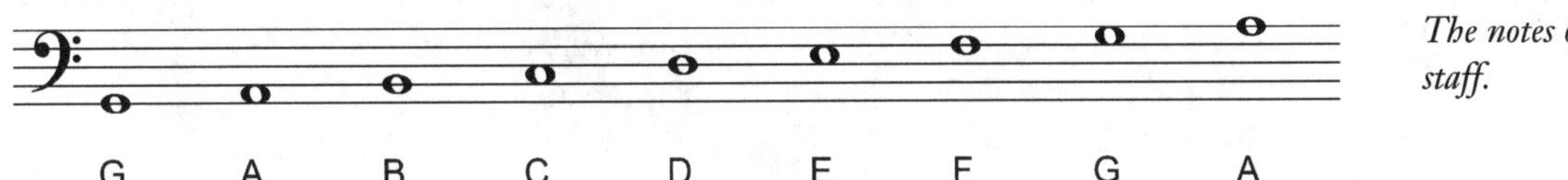

The notes of the bass clef staff.

Sharps and Flats

The lines and spaces on a music staff correspond exactly to the white keys on a piano. But what about those black keys? Where are they on the staff?

When I told you that there are seven main pitches in a Western musical scale (A through G), I was simplifying things a little. There actually are 12 possible notes in an octave, with some of them falling between the seven main pitches.

> **Tip**
>
> An easy way to remember the lines of the bass clef is with the phrase, "Good Boys Do Fine Always." (The first letter of each word describes each line of the staff, from bottom to top.) To remember the spaces of the bass clef, remember the first letters in the phrase, "All Cows Eat Grass."

Just count the keys between middle C and the next C on the piano—including the black keys, but without counting the second C. If you counted correctly, you counted 12 keys, which represent 12 pitches; each pitch/key is the same interval away from the previous pitch/key.

These black keys are called *sharps* and *flats*. A sharp raises the natural note; a flat lowers the note.

Take the black key above the middle C key, for example. You can refer to this key as *C-sharp*, because it raises the pitch of C. It also can be called *D-flat*, because it lowers the next white key up, D. (C-sharp and D-flat are just two different ways of describing the same pitch; any black key on the piano can be described as either a raised or lowered note.)

On a music staff, sharps and flats are designated by special characters placed *before* the affected note. These characters, called *accidentals*, look like this:

♯ ♭ ♮

Three accidentals: a sharp, a flat, and a natural.

That third character is called a *natural*. When you see a natural sign on a piece of music, it means to return the specific note to its natural state, without any sharps or flats.

Singing Intervals

When you sing two pitches in a row, the space between the two pitches is called an *interval*. The smallest interval in Western music is the *half step*. On the piano keyboard, half steps appear between the white keys B and C and between E and F, and between any adjacent white and black key. (For example, D to D-sharp and F-sharp to G are both half-step intervals.)

> **Note**
>
> Now that you know about steps, it's a little easier to understand how sharps and flats work. When you sharpen a note, you move the pitch up a half step. When you flatten a note, you move the pitch down a half step.

Two half steps equal one *whole step*. The interval between F and G is a whole step; the interval between B and C-sharp also is a whole step.

You can use the step method to describe the intervals between two notes—although once you get more than a few steps away, the counting becomes a tad difficult. When you're trying to figure out which note is seven half steps above middle C (it's G, in case you're counting), it's time to utilize another method to describe your intervals.

Intervals by the Numbers

Another way of describing intervals is to use the numbers of the scale to denote the basic intervals between notes. The first note of a scale is numbered one, the second note is numbered two, and so on. Instead of counting half steps and whole steps, you can simply describe an interval by using these relative numbers.

For example, let's say you want to describe the interval between C and D. If you count C as number one (the first degree), D is number two and the interval between them is called a *second.* The interval between C and E (the first and third degrees) is a *third;* the interval between C and F (the first and fourth degrees) is a *fourth* … and so on.

There are two special terms used to describe notes that have the same number/name/pitch. When two notes of the same pitch are sung by two different voices, they're sung in unison. Two identical notes with the same name, played eight degrees apart, form an octave, which comes from the Latin letter octo, for eight. For example, if you go from middle C to the next C up the keyboard, that's an octave; F to F is another octave … and so on.

Note

The lowest note of an interval, chord, or scale is called the *root.*

The following figure shows the basic intervals, starting with a unison and ending with an octave, with C as the *root.*

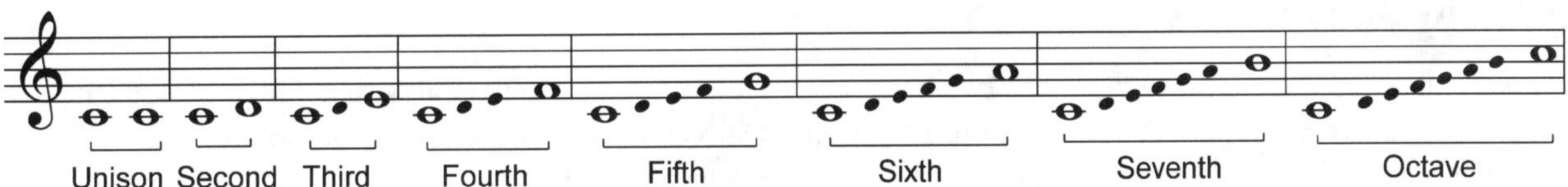

Basic intervals in the C Major scale.

Intervals and Half Steps

The only problem with describing intervals by degree is that most intervals can exist in two different forms—major or minor. A minor interval is a half step less than a major interval—for example, the interval from F to A is a major third, while the interval from F to A-flat is a minor third.

In addition, some intervals exist naturally in only one form. These intervals—fourths, fifths, and octaves—are called *perfect* intervals.

And there's more. When you flatten a minor or perfect interval you create what is called a *diminished* interval. When you sharpen a major or perfect interval, you created an *augmented* interval. Diminished and augmented intervals are particularly difficult to sing, as your "internal ear" will undoubtedly hear the more traditional perfect interval within a given scale. You really have to force yourself to raise or lower that second note to force the somewhat unnatural diminished or augmented interval.

If all these major and minor and diminished intervals confuse you, you're not alone; there are a lot of variations to keep track of. It might be easier for you to think of all these intervals in terms of half steps. To that end, Table 10.2 shows how many half steps are between these major and minor intervals.

Table 10.2 Half Steps Between Intervals

Interval	Number of Half Steps
Perfect unison	0
Minor second	1
Major second	2
Minor third	3
Major third	4
Perfect fourth	5

continues

Table 10.2 Half Steps Between Intervals (continued)

Interval	Number of Half Steps
Augmented fourth	6
Diminished fifth	6
Perfect fifth	7
Minor sixth	8
Major sixth	9
Minor seventh	10
Major seventh	11
Octave	12

Singing Scales

Now that you know how to deal with two notes in a row (an interval), let's deal with a bunch of notes in a row—what we call a *scale*. A scale is, quite simply, eight successive pitches within a one-octave range. All scales start on one note and end on that same note one octave higher.

For example, every C scale starts on C and ends on C; an F scale starts on F and ends on F; and they all have six more notes in-between.

The first note of a scale is called the first degree of the scale. (Or, sometimes, the *tonic*.) Not surprisingly, the second note is called the second degree, the third note is called the third degree, and so on—until you get to the eighth note, which is the tonic again.

There are many types of scales, but the two most common are the *major* and *minor* scales. Both of these scales can start on any note—from A-flat to G-sharp.

Major Scales

The most common type of scale is called the *major* scale. Major scales are happy scales; they have pleasant and expected intervals at every turn. (Just sing "Do Re Mi Fa So La Ti Do" and you'll hear this pleasant quality.)

What makes a major scale major are the specific intervals between the notes of the scale. Every major scale uses the same intervals, as shown in Table 10.3.

Table 10.3 The Intervals of the Major Scale

Note	Steps to Next Note
Tonic	Whole
Second	Whole
Third	Half
Fourth	Whole
Fifth	Whole
Sixth	Whole
Seventh	Half

Here's what a typical major scale looks like; this is the C Major scale, which is composed of all the white keys on the piano.

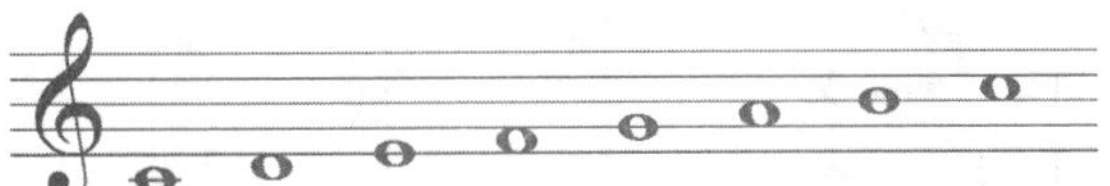

The C Major scale.

You'll be singing a lot of major scales as you practice your vocal techniques. Any time you're asked to sing the Solfeggio "Do Re Mi Fa So La Ti Do," you're singing a major scale. The specific major scale you sing determines which pitch you sing for "Do."

Minor Scales

Minor scales are sadder sounding than major scales. This is partly because the third note of the minor scale is a minor interval, whereas the third note of the major scale is a major interval. That little half step between a minor third and a major third makes all the difference in the world!

Table 10.4 shows the intervals between notes in what we call the *natural minor* scale.

Table 10.4 The Intervals of the Natural Minor Scale

Note	Steps to Next Note
Tonic	Whole
Second	Half
Third	Whole
Fourth	Whole
Fifth	Half
Sixth	Whole
Seventh	Whole

The natural minor scale is easy to sing because it's directly related to a corresponding major scale. All you have to do is think of a major scale, but start (and end) singing on the sixth note of the scale, rather than the tonic. The minor scale that starts on the sixth of the corresponding major scale is called the *relative minor* of that major scale.

Here's an example: Sing a C Major scale (C D E F G A B C). Now move up to the sixth note—or just move down two notes. (It's the same thing—up six or down two—both put you on the A.) Now sing an eight-note scale, but using the notes in C Major. What you get—A B C D E F G A—is the A minor scale. The relationship between C Major and A minor is shown next:

Note

Sometimes the seventh note in a minor scale is raised. (Using the A minor scale as an example, the G would become a G sharp.) This type of scale is called a harmonic minor scale.

The A minor scale and its relative major scale, C Major.

Singing in Keys

When a piece of music is based on a particular musical scale, we say that music is in the "key" of that scale. For example, a song based around the C Major scale is in the key of C Major. A song based around the B-flat Major scale is in the key of B-flat Major.

When you see that a piece of music is written in a specific key, you can assume that most of the notes will stay within the corresponding scale. So if a piece is written in A Major, most of the notes in the melody should be within the A Major scale. (There are exceptions to this, of course, which is where accidentals come in.)

Using Key Signatures

Key signatures are combinations of sharps or flats that designate a specific scale. By specifying which notes are flatted or sharpened up front like that, the composer doesn't have to insert individual flats and sharps throughout the piece of music.

For example, if you see a B-flat in the key signature, like the one below, every B you see in the piece should be sung as a B-flat. (And which major scale contains a single B-flat? If you said F Major, you win a gold star!)

The key signature of F Major.

Major Keys

Every major scale has its corresponding key signature, as shown in the following tables. Table 10.5 presents those key signatures with flats; Table 10.6 presents those key signatures with sharps.

Table 10.5 Major Keys with Flats

Key	Key Signature
C Major	

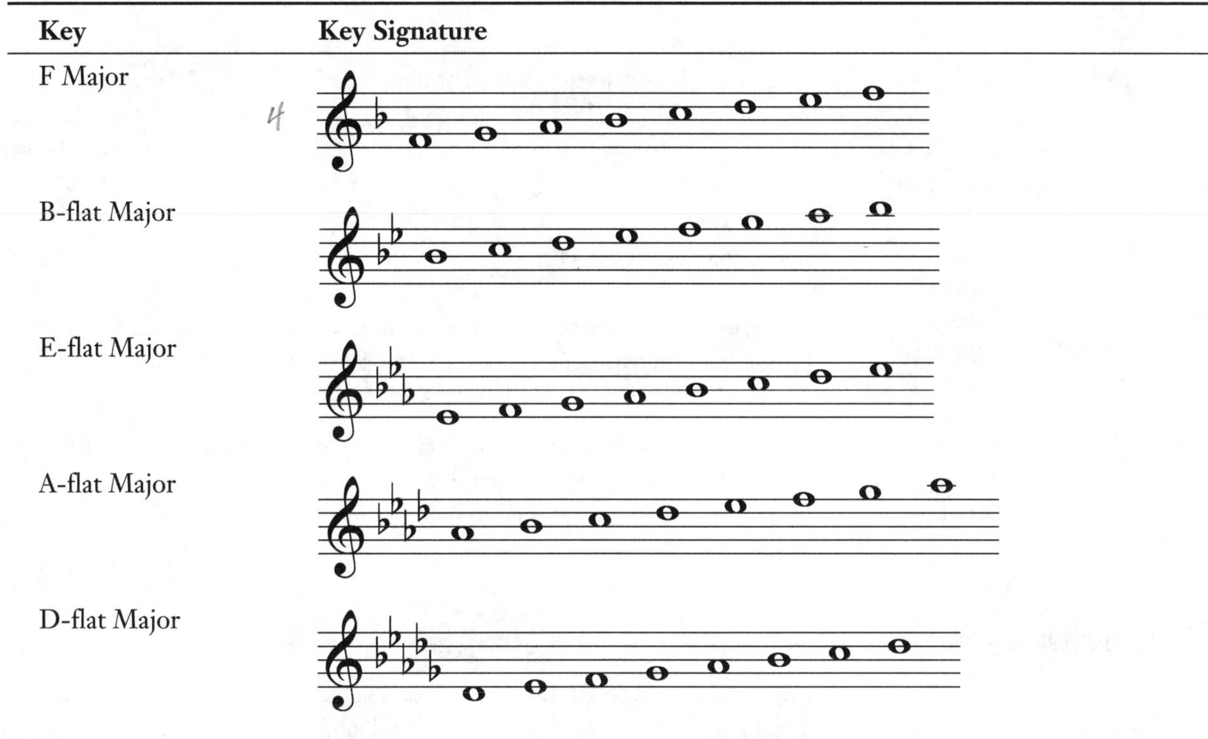

Key	Key Signature
F Major	
B-flat Major	
E-flat Major	
A-flat Major	
D-flat Major	

Table 10.6 Major Keys with Sharps

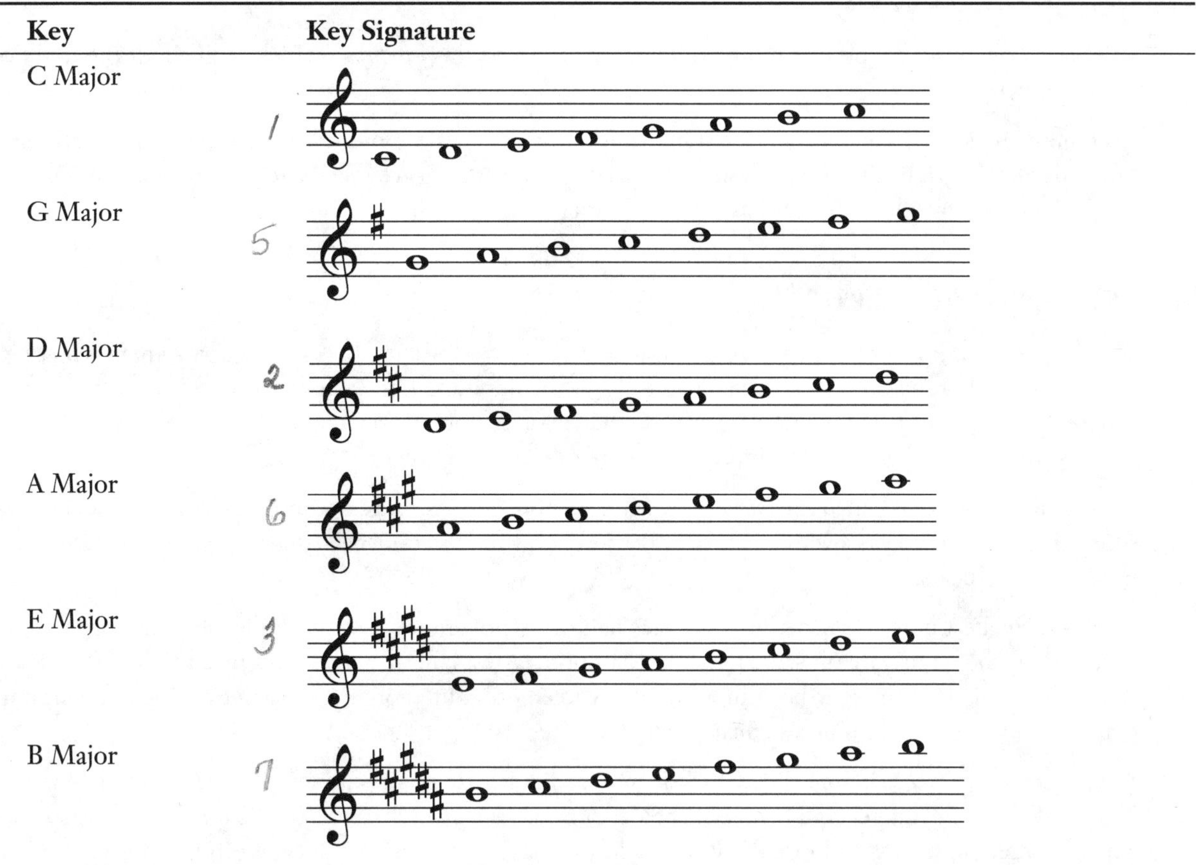

Key	Key Signature
C Major	
G Major	
D Major	
A Major	
E Major	
B Major	

Minor Keys

The key signatures used to indicate major keys also can represent natural minor keys. As you remember from earlier in this chapter, a natural minor scale is based on the same notes as a major scale, but starts on the sixth note of the scale. This same method applies to keys, so that (for example) the key of A minor uses the same notes—and the same key signature—as C Major.

Note

When a note is changed with an accidental, that accidental applies until the end of the current measure. At the start of the next measure, it's assumed that all notes revert to what they should be, given the current key.

Accidents Will Happen

When a song is written in a particular key, you can assume that all the following notes will correspond to that particular key. But how does a composer indicate notes for you to sing that are *outside* the given key?

When a song includes a note that isn't within the current key, this is indicated by a sharp, flat, or natural sign. When you see the inserted sharp, flat, or natural, you know to play the note as written, rather than as indicated by the music's key signature.

Changing Keys

Some songs don't always stay in the same key throughout. When you encounter a key change in the middle of a song, that song is said to *modulate* to another key. Songs can modulate from any one key to any other key. Key changes are indicated by the insertion of a new key signature.

Singing in Rhythm

When you sing a song, you sing more than pitches. You also sing *rhythm*—which is all about the duration of the notes you sing.

Each note you sing has a certain value. There are different types of note values, with each note value signifying a specific length of time—as measured by parts of a measure. (We'll get into measures in a minute; for the time being, consider a measure as a container that holds four beats.)

Understanding Note Values

To better explain how note values work, we have to get into a little math. (Don't worry—there won't be any story problems!) You see, each note value lasts a specific duration, and each duration reflects a ratio to duration. As you can see from the following figure, each shorter note is precisely half the duration of the previous note. So, if you can divide and multiply by two, this should be fairly easy to grasp.

The most basic note is called the *whole note*. A whole note gets its name because, in 4/4 time (we'll get to this soon—I promise!), it lasts a whole measure. Because 4/4 time has four beats in a measure, this means a whole note lasts four beats.

The next smallest note is called a *half note*. (It's half of a whole note—pretty simple, eh?) Because a whole note lasts a whole measure (in 4/4, anyway), a half note lasts a half measure. This means a half note lasts *two beats*, which is half of the four-beat duration of a whole note. Put another way, you can sing two half notes in a measure because two half notes equal one whole note.

Let's keep going. If a half note is half a whole note, what is half a half note? Well, do your math, and when you divide ½ by 2, you get ¼. This means half a half note is a *quarter note*. Because a half note lasts two beats, a quarter note—which is half that duration—lasts one beat. Put another way, you can fit four quarter notes in a measure—one to a beat.

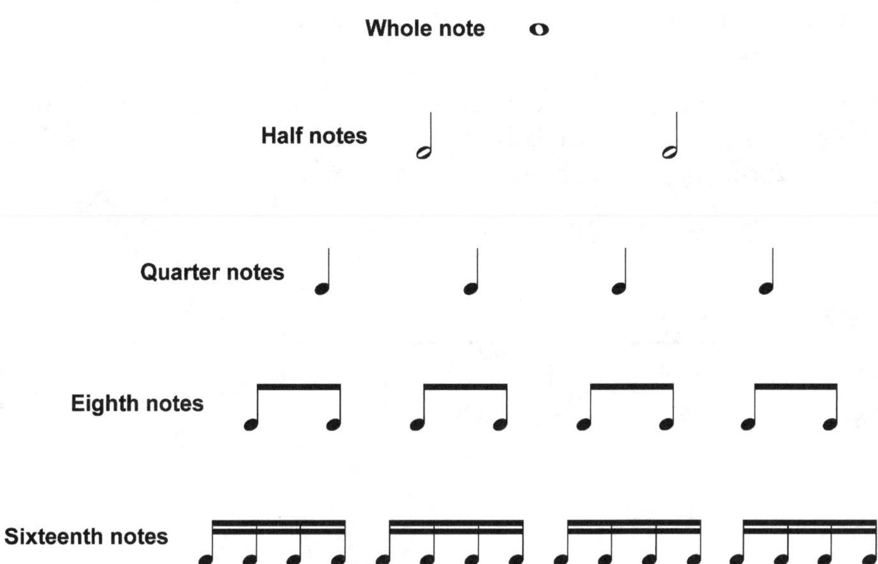

The most common note values—each smaller note is exactly half the previous note.

Now let's take a quarter note and divide it in half. Doing the math, $1/4$ divided by 2 equals $1/8$—so the next-smallest note is the *eighth note.* Just as there are four quarter notes in a measure of 4/4 time ($4 \times 1/4 = 1$), each measure holds eight eighth notes ($8 \times 1/8 = 1$). Put another way, there are two eighth notes for every quarter note ($2 \times 1/8 = 1/4$)—or two eighth notes for every beat.

Tip

When you tap your foot to the beat of most popular songs, your foot is tapping quarter notes. One, two, three, four—each of those counts is a quarter note.

Okay, you know where this is going. Half an eighth note is (do the math!) a *sixteenth note* ($1/8 \div 2 = 1/16$). There are 16 sixteenth notes in a measure ($16 \times 1/16 = 1$), or 4 sixteenth notes per one quarter-note beat ($4 \times 1/16 = 1/4$).

There are even smaller notes out there (thirty-second notes and sixty-fourth notes and so on), but for all practical purposes, the sixteenth note is the smallest note you're likely to encounter in vocal music.

Taking Count

When your choir director or producer is trying to talk you through a piece of music, how does he communicate note values verbally?

It starts fairly simply, in that each beat in a measure is counted as either one, two, three, or four. So if you're counting off four quarter notes, you count them as one, two, three, four.

If the beat is always one, two, three, or four, what about the eighth notes that lay between the beats? It's simple: Count them as "and," as in "one-and, two-and, three-and, four-and," all very even.

For sixteenth notes, you use the nonsense syllables "e" and "ah" to represent the sixteenth notes between eighth notes. So if you're counting a group of straight sixteenth notes, you'd count "one-e-and-ah, two-e-and-ah, three-e-and-ah, four-e-and-ah," all nice and even.

Taking a Rest

If a note represents the duration of a pitch you sing, what do you call it when you're *not* singing? In music, when you're not singing, you're resting—so any note you don't play is called a *rest.*

When you see four quarter notes, you sing four tones—one per beat. When you see four quarter note rests, you don't sing four tones; you rest over four beats.

Each type of note—whole note, half note, and so on—has a corresponding rest of the same duration. So you have a whole rest that lasts a whole measure, a half rest that lasts a half measure, and so on. Rests are used to indicate the spaces in between the notes and are just as important as the notes you sing.

Table 10.7 shows all the notes you've just learned and their corresponding rests.

Table 10.7 Notes and Rests

Duration	Note	Rest
Whole note	𝅝	𝄻
Half note	𝅗𝅥	𝄼
Quarter note	𝅘𝅥	𝄽
Eighth note	𝅘𝅥𝅮	𝄾
Sixteenth note	𝅘𝅥𝅯	𝄿

Taking a Note—and Dotting It

Sooner or later you'll run into something a little different: a note or a rest with a dot after it. When you run into one of these *dotted notes*, that note should have a longer duration than the normal version of that note—one and a half times longer, to be precise.

Sing a dotted note 50 percent longer than normal.

When you see a dotted note, hold that note 50 percent longer than you would do normally. So a dotted half note is equal to a half note and a quarter note (or three quarter notes). A dotted quarter note is equal to a quarter note and an eighth note (or three eighth notes). A dotted eighth note is equal to an eighth note and a sixteen note (or three sixteenth notes).

You can also have dotted rests, which work the same as dotted notes. When you see a dot after a rest, that rest should last one and half times the value of the main rest.

Taking Two Notes—and Tying Them Together

Another way to make a note longer is to tie it to another note. A tie is a little rounded connector placed between two notes; it essentially tells you to add the second note to the first note.

Sing two tied notes as a single long note.

When you see two or more notes tied together, you sing them as if they're a single note; for example, two quarter notes tied together equal one half note.

What do you do if the tied notes are on different pitches, like the next example? Well, this may *look* like a tie, but it isn't really a tie—it's a *slur*. A slur is a way of indicating that two (or more) notes are to be sung in a smoothly connected fashion, rather than as distinctly separate notes.

A slur ties together two different pitches.

Taking the Beat and Dividing by Three

There's another little oddity in rhythmic notation—and this one is very important. Everything we've done up to now has divided notes and beats by two. What happens, then, if you divide by something other than two?

The most common division other than two is dividing by three; this is called a *triplet*. When you see the number three over a group of three notes (or three rests—or any combination of three equal notes and rests), you know that those three notes have to fit into a space that would normally hold just two notes. Triplets have more of a rolling feel than straight notes and are counted as "trip-ah-let."

The three notes of a triplet fit in the space of two regular notes.

Singing in Time

> **Tip**
>
> Just as songs can change key anywhere in the middle, they can also change time signatures. A change in time is indicated by the insertion of a new time signature. From that point on, the song should be counted using the new time signature.

Written music uses something called a *time signature* to signify how many beats are in a measure and what kind of note is used for the basic beat. A time signature looks kind of like a fraction, with one number sitting on top of another number. The top number indicates how many beats are in a measure; the bottom number indicates the note value of the basic beat.

Let's take the four-quarter-notes-to-a-measure form we've been using throughout this chapter. Because we have four beats in a measure, the top number in the time signature is a four. Because the basic beat is a quarter note, the bottom number is a four (as in the 4 in 1/4). So the standard form we've been using is called "four four" time (because of the 4 on top of the 4) and looks like this:

The time signature for 4/4 time.

Other time signatures follow this same form. For example, if our measures have three beats instead of four and still use a quarter note for the beat, we have a 3/4 time signature. If you have three beats per measure but the basic beat is an eighth note instead of a quarter note, that time signature is "three eight," or 3/8.

Singing in Tempo

Now that you know how to figure out how many beats there are in a measure, how do you determine how *fast* those beats should be played?

The speed of a piece of music—how fast the beat goes by—is called the *tempo*. A faster tempo means a faster beat; a slower tempo makes for a slower song.

You can indicate tempo in one of two ways: by indicating the precise number of beats per minute or by using traditional Italian terms. We'll discuss both methods next.

Beats per Minute

The most accurate way to indicate tempo is by specifying a certain number of *beats per minute*, or *bpm*. This gives you a precise speed for your performance, especially when you use a *metronome*. You set your metronome to a specific bpm number, and it tick-tocks back and forth at the proper speed. When you sing along to the metronome, you're singing the song at exactly the right tempo.

Italian Tempo Markings

The second way to indicate tempo, typically found in classical music, is through the use of traditional Italian musical terms. These terms correspond to general tempo ranges. For example, *Grave*, *Largo*, *Lento*, and *Adagio* are used to indicate slow tempos; *Adante* and *Moderato* are used to indicate moderate tempos; and *Allegro*, *Vivace*, and *Presto* are used to indicate fast tempos.

Speeding Up—and Slowing Down

Some pieces of music retain the same tempo throughout the entire song (think most popular music here). Other pieces of music speed up and slow down at times, often for dramatic effect.

If a tempo change is immediate—that is, you go directly from one tempo to another, with no gradual transition—the change is indicated by the insertion of a new tempo marking.

If the tempo change is meant to be gradual, you're likely to see one of two new Italian markings. *Ritardando* (often abbreviated *Rit.*) means to gradually slow down the tempo, while *accelerando* means to gradually speed up the tempo.

Hold That Note!

Sometimes the music is meant to actually stop—right in the middle of the thing! When you see what is called a *fermata* (looks like a little bird's eye) placed on top of a note or a rest, that means to hold that note (or rest) until the director tells you to stop. Then you can take a break and start up with the next note after the fermata, at normal tempo.

When you see a fermata, hold the note.

Singing from Start to Finish

Reading a long piece of music is a little like reading a roadmap. You'll see various indications in a score that provide direction, to repeat a section or to jump to another section within the song.

Repeating Sections

There are various shorthand methods used to tell you to repeat a section of a song. The most common method is the use of *repeat marks*, which are used in pairs. One repeat mark indicates the start of the section to be repeated; the other one indicates the end of that section. Unless noted otherwise, you repeat a section only once (that is, you sing it twice), and then you move on to the next section.

Repeat marks tell you to sing a range of measures twice.

Sometimes you'll need to repeat a section but sing a slightly different ending the second time through. When you see this in the music—called a *first ending* and a *second ending*—you sing the first ending the first time through, and then when you repeat the section, you skip the first ending and sing the second ending.

First and second endings tell you to end a repeated section two different ways.

Following the Signs

You also can repeat a section of a song by returning to a section designated with a sign, called a *Segno*. (Segno means "sign" in Italian.) For example, when you see the notation "D.S. al Fine," you jump back to the sign and sing through to the end of the song.

Another navigation technique indicates a separate ending section of music called the *Coda*. When you insert a *Coda sign* in your music, it indicates that you should jump to the section marked Coda. A common navigation technique is notated "D.C. al Coda" or "D.C. al Fine," where you jump to the beginning of the song and then follow through to the Coda or the end (Fine).

Table 10.8 details these and other common navigation markings.

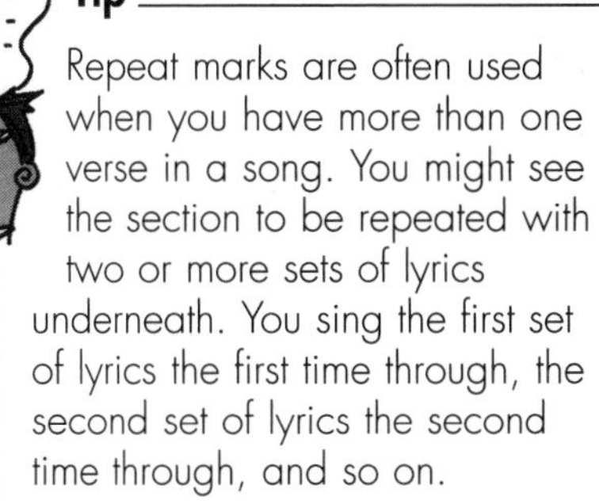

Tip

Repeat marks are often used when you have more than one verse in a song. You might see the section to be repeated with two or more sets of lyrics underneath. You sing the first set of lyrics the first time through, the second set of lyrics the second time through, and so on.

Use the Segno and Coda signs to navigate a piece of music.

Table 10.8 Common Navigation Markings

Marking	Means …
D.C. al Fine	Go back to the beginning and play through to the end.
D.C. al Coda	Go back to the beginning and play to the Coda sign; then skip to the Coda section.
D.S. al Fine	Go back to the Segno sign and play through to the end.
D.S. al Coda	Go back to the Segno sign and play to the Coda sign; then skip to the Coda section.

The Least You Need to Know

- There are seven basic pitches in a musical scale.
- Scales can be either major (happy) or minor (sad).
- The key signature tells you what key a song is in—and which scale you'll be singing.
- The distance between any two pitches is called an interval.
- The basic rhythmic note values are whole notes, half notes, quarter notes, eighth notes, and sixteenth notes—each note half as long as the previous.
- The time signature tells you how many beats in a measure and the duration of each beat.

Chapter 11

Do, a Deer: Using Solfeggio Techniques

In This Chapter

- Learning how to read notes with the Solfeggio method
- Discovering how to find Do in different keys
- Learning how to read and sing different intervals
- Working with accidentals and minor keys

Back in Chapter 10, I mentioned that wonderful song from *The Sound of Music* that had Julie Andrews and the kids dancing through the streets of Salzburg singing "Do, a deer, a female deer." The charm and appeal of that song does much more than simply entertain—it serves as one of the most effective learning tools ever used in a classroom. Everyone loves to sing this engaging tune and lyrics—lyrics that actually teach a very old method of singing called Solfeggio.

Solfeggio is a particular method of sight singing that has been around for hundreds of years and is still being taught today in fine music programs around the world. In fact, you probably learned it when you were in school. The 1990s saw a real revival of the use of Solfeggio as a reading tool in music education—which is significant, as many state school music contests require sight singing skills as a part of a choir's adjudication.

In this chapter we'll use the Solfeggio method to provide some practical application of the vocal theory you learned in the last chapter. So get ready to brush up on your "Do Re Mi"—and start sight singing!

How Solfeggio Works

I'm embarrassed to admit this, but singers are notorious for their "illiteracy" when it comes to reading music. Sure, you don't have to be able to read music to sing well, but if you never develop your basic reading skills, you're limiting your potential as a musician. If you want the respect of other musicians—or ever hope to get a job in a recording studio—you'd better learn how to read music. You'll also need music reading skills if you choose to sing in a choir, or onstage in a musical. It's an essential skill.

Let's face it—if you can't pick out a written melody on a piano, how are you going to learn a piece of music that's brand-new to you? I suppose you *could* search for a recording of that particular song, but that might take days—and will always represent someone else's interpretation of the music. You could even go running to the nearest "literate" musician to play it for you, if you're lucky enough to have someone like this at your beck and call. (Most of us don't, however.)

Or you can learn to read the music yourself.

One of the easiest ways to learn to read music is with the Solfeggio method of sight singing. The Solfeggio method assigns a particular syllable (Do, Re, Mi, Fa, So, La, Ti, and Do again) to each of the eight degrees of a major scale. This assists your memory of a particular pitch as it relates to a *tonal center*.

Note

The **tonal center** is the key in which the music is written.

The Solfeggio method also helps you identify relationships between notes of a scale—without having to know the actual pitch names. We call this *relative pitch*, and it's something that all singers need to develop.

There are two different methods of Solfeggio in use today. One is called Fixed Do; in this method, the note C is always Do, regardless of the key. The other method, which we'll learn here, is called Movable Do; in this method, the note that Do represents changes as the key changes.

The Movable Do

As you remember from Chapter 10, one way to represent pitch is to assign numbers to each step of the scale. Another way is with the Solfeggio syllables. As you learned in Table 10.1, Do equals 1 (the first pitch in a scale), Re equals 2, Mi equals 3, and so on. When you want to indicate the first pitch in a scale—any scale—you use the Solfeggio Do. When you want to indicate the second pitch in the scale, you use Re. And so on, all the way up the scale.

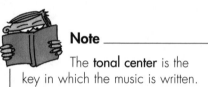

Note

In addition to the syllables used in the major scale, the Solfeggio method also includes syllables for sharped or flatted notes of the scale. (We call these *chromatic* notes.) That's a little too complicated for this book, however, so we'll stick to the seven main Solfeggio syllables here.

It doesn't matter which key you're in—the first note of the scale is always Do. If you're singing in the key of G, Do is G. If you're singing in the key of B-flat, Do is B-flat.

That's your movable Do.

Let's look at how this movable Solfeggio works on a real piece of music—using "Twinkle, Twinkle Little Star" as an example. If you want to represent the melody of "Twinkle, Twinkle Little Star" by the numbers (with each number representing a degree of the scale), it looks like this:

```
1  1  5  5  6  6  5
4  4  3  3  2  2  1
```

"Twinkle, Twinkle Little Star," by the numbers.

Since you know which Solfeggio syllables represent which numbers, you can then notate "Twinkle, Twinkle Little Star" in Solfeggio, like this:

```
Do  Do  So  So  La  La  So
Fa  Fa  Mi  Mi  Re  Re  Do
```

"Twinkle, Twinkle Little Star" in Solfeggio.

And finally, here is what "Twinkle, Twinkle Little Star" looks like in traditional music notation:

"Twinkle, Twinkle Little Star" in traditional music notation.

In our little example, you see that Do is written on the second line of the treble clef, on the pitch G. That's because "Twinkle, Twinkle Little Star" is written here in the key of G, and when you're in the key of G, the first note of the scale (Do) is G.

To refresh your memory, here's where the Solfeggio syllables fall on the staff when you're in the key of G:

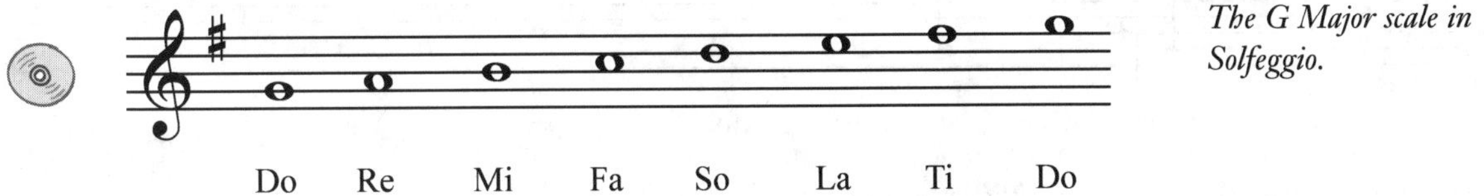

The G Major scale in Solfeggio.

Since there are many other keys in music, you have to be able to assign the Solfeggio syllables to these different keys. It's easy, really, since all you do is shift Do to the beginning note of the key (or major scale) being used.

For example, you can shift "Twinkle, Twinkle Little Star" to the key of C, as shown below. Do is now the pitch C—in this example, the third space on the treble clef staff.

"Twinkle, Twinkle Little Star" in the key of C.

Finding Do—In Different Keys

Now that you see how this works—and recognize that a song can be written in any number of keys—the next step is to learn how to identify different keys. Remember, in the Moveable Do method, the absolute pitch of Do changes when the key changes. (That's where we get the term "moveable Do.")

The first step in identifying a particular key is figuring out where your "home base" is—which you do by reading the song's *key signature*, which we'll discuss shortly. It's kind of like the game of baseball, where one base is designated as home—the place you start from and (hope to) return to. Just imagine the chaos of a baseball game without a home base! The same is true of sight singing, where you have to be able to find "home base" before you do anything else.

Once you find "home" (which is Do), you have a point of reference for all the other notes in a melody. This is important, as learning how to sight sing is all about *relative* pitch relationships—how the other notes of the scale relate to Do, whichever absolute pitch it is.

Note

You can get lots of hands-on experience with sight singing in Chapter 12.

Understanding Key Signatures

If you remember back to Chapter 10, the key of a song is indicated by its key signature. This is the group of flats or sharps found at the beginning of a staff, right after the bass or treble clef, as shown here:

America the Beautiful *in a handful of different key signatures—Db, D, and Eb.*

Key signatures are important to singers because they tell us where Do is. That is, the key signature designates the scale to be used; once we know that, we know what note is Do, since Do is always the first step of that scale.

> **Note**
>
> The fact that Do moves around from key to key is relatively insignificant with the Solfeggio method. What's important are the relative pitch relationships to Do, the home tone. All you have to do is figure out the underlying key, and you know where Do is—and how all the other notes of the scale lay out.

For example, when you're singing in the key of E, the underlying scale is the E Major scale, and Do is E—the first note of that scale. When you're singing in the key of E-flat, the underlying scale is the E-flat Major scale, and Do is E-flat. Just like that.

Some key signatures are composed of a group of sharps, while others are composed of a group of flats. It's the number of sharps and flats in the key signature that determine the key of the song. (There's even one key signature—the key of C—that doesn't have any sharps or flats.)

There are many different ways to figure out the "home base" of a given key signature. One way is to refer back to Tables 10.5 and 10.6 in Chapter 10. Another way is to follow a handful of easy rules—which I'll tell you about now.

> **Note**
>
> The following rules (The Key Signature with No Flats or Sharps, Key Signatures with Flats, and Key Signatures with Sharps) apply to reading key signatures for major keys; we'll discuss key signatures for minor keys later in this chapter.

The Key Signature with No Flats or Sharps

This isn't really a rule—it's just something you have to memorize. When you see a key signature without any sharps or flats, as shown here, you're in the key of C. That means that the underlying scale is C Major, and that Do is the note C.

The key signature for the key of C—no flats or sharps.

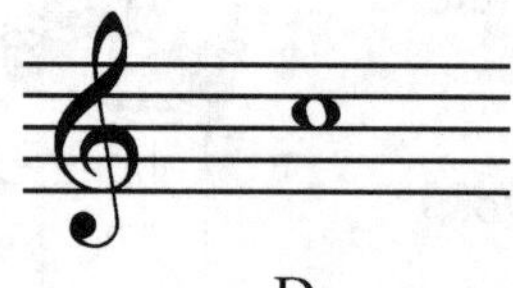

Key Signatures with Flats

Now let's look at those key signatures that include flats. The key (no pun intended) is to look at the next-to-last flat—the one that's next to the farthest one on the right. This note is your home base.

For example, take a key signature with six flats, like the first one in the following figure. The next-to-last flat is on the G line of the staff, indicating the note G-flat, so the key signature is G-flat—and Do is G-flat. In a key signature with five flats (the second one in the figure), the next-to-last flat is D-flat, so the key signature is D-flat, and Do is D-flat. And so on.

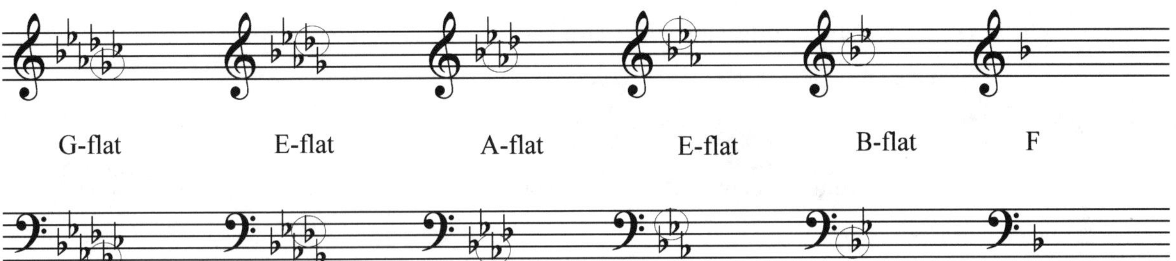

The next-to-last flat determines the key signature.

So here's your rule:

When you see flats in the key signature, the next-to-last flat is Do.

What about that last key signature, the one with only one flat? There's no next-to-last flat to circle? This is another one you'll probably have to memorize; the key signature with one flat is the key of F.

For a quick exercise, return to the preceding figure and draw a whole note on the line or space where Do would be. (And don't forget about the key of F!)

> **Note**
>
> For this and several other examples, we're presenting the examples in both treble and bass clef—so that all the voices will be familiar with what they're seeing.

Key Signatures with Sharps

There is a different rule to use for identifying key signatures with sharps. It comes from the fact that the last sharp in a key signature always represents the seventh note ("Ti") in a scale. If you know the last sharp is Ti, then the next note up must be Do.

So here's your rule:

When you see sharps in the key signature, Do is one space or line up from the last sharp.

For example, the first key signature in the following figure has a single sharp, F-sharp—which means that Do is G (one line up), and you're in the key of G. The last sharp in the second key signature is C-sharp; the next line up from this is D, which means that Do is D, and you're in the key of D. And so on.

> **Note**
>
> If you remember your theory from Chapter 10, you know that the interval between the seventh step of a scale (Ti) and the tonic (Do) is always a half step. So when you're going up to the next line or space above a sharp, you're going up a half step.

Go to the next line or space up from the last sharp to determine the key signature.

Another quick exercise—find Do for each of the sharp key signatures in the preceding figure.

The Next Steps

Once you've found Do, it's time to identify the other steps of the scale—which is really easy.

All you have to do is follow the scale.

For example, if you've determined that a song is in the key of F (that's the one with only one flat, remember?), you know that Do is the note F—the first note of the scale. You can then figure out the other notes in the scale. The second note—Re—is G. The third note—Mi—is A. The fourth note—Fa—is B-flat. The fifth note—So—is C. The sixth note—La—is D. And the seventh note—Ti—is E.

I told you it was easy!

Try to figure the next one for yourself. Let's say that you see a key signature with no sharps or flats. (Hint: It's the key of C.) Where do the Solfeggio syllables fall? (The answer follows.)

The key of C in Solfeggio.

Once you figure out the key and the Solfeggio, you can use the Solfeggio method to sing any melody you run into. For example, here's the first part of "Mary Had a Little Lamb," notated in the key of D. (Remember the rule? The next line above the C-sharp in the key signature is D, so Do is D).

"Mary Had a Little Lamb" in the key of D.

Look closely and you'll see that this tune doesn't start on Do, but on Mi—three notes above D. This illustrates an important point: Not all songs start on Do. (This means you can't just look at the first note of a song and assume that's the key you're in.)

Tip

More songs *end* on Do than start on Do—it's musically satisfying to end a melody on the home note!

Exercises for Finding Do

Now it's time for some exercises. Look at the following examples, then:

- Find Do (by reading the key signature)
- Label the Solfeggio syllable for each note (as we did with "Mary Had a Little Lamb," earlier)

Exercise 11.1

Exercise 11.2

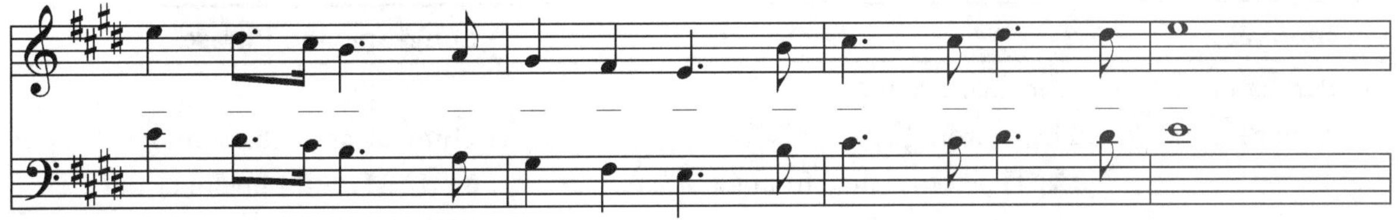

Exercise 11.3

Sight-Singing Intervals

Since melodies don't always follow a scale-like pattern, moving only in steps, you'll often have to be able to sing pitches that are several notes apart. As you learned in Chapter 10, this distance between two pitches is called an *interval.*

Since intervals are relative, you use the numbers of the scale to denote the basic interval between any two notes. We identify basic intervals by counting the lines and spaces between two pitches. Remember to always count the first note as "one" before continuing your counting. So if you're counting the distance between the first and second notes of the scale, you count "one, two"—and the interval is called a *second.*

Using Solfeggio examples, the interval between Do and Re is a second, since Do is the first note of the scale and Re is the second. The interval between Do and Mi is a *third*, and the interval between Do and Fa is a *fourth*. And so on up the scale, as shown next:

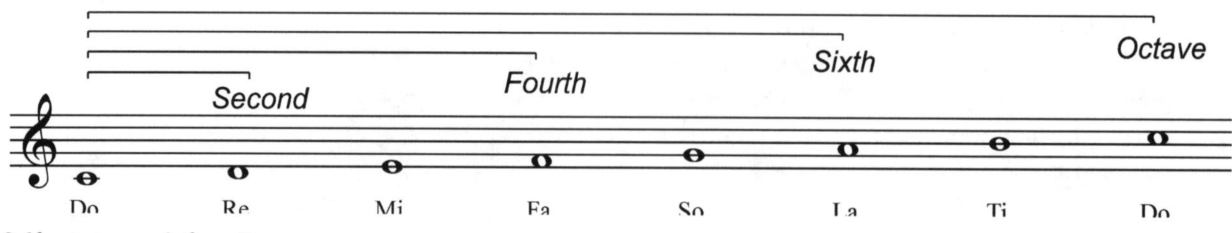

Solfeggio intervals from Do.

But what do you call the interval between Re and Mi—the second and third notes of the scale? This interval is just like the interval between Do and Re—a second. You get there by counting Re as one and Mi as two, which gives you the interval of a second. And the interval between Fa and La—counting Fa (one), So (two), La (three)—is a third.

Note

If you remember when we discussed intervals in Chapter 10, some intervals can be major and some can be minor, depending on the number of half-steps between the notes. There's not enough space here to repeat that whole concept; just know that you can have minor seconds and major seconds, minor thirds and major thirds, and so on, and that the difference between a minor interval and a major one is a half step.

Some intervals sound quite natural and are very easy to sing. Other intervals are less common and harder to sing. In any case, it helps if you know how an interval sounds before you try to hit that second note. And the easiest way to do this is by listening to the intervals used in some popular melodies.

We'll start with some examples of *ascending* intervals—intervals where the second pitch is above the first pitch. Table 11.1 provides some melodic shortcuts you can use to sing specific ascending intervals.

Table 11.1 Ascending Intervals

Interval		Song-Specific Phrase
Perfect unison	Exact Same note	
Minor second	Theme from *Jaws*	**Dum-dum …** (bass line)
	"As Time Goes By" (from *Casablanca*)	**YOU MUST** remember this …
Major second	"Frere Jacques"	**FRE-RE** Jacques …
	"Happy Birthday"	Hap-**PY BIRTH**-day to you …
Minor third	"To Dream the Impossible Dream"	**TO DREAM** the impossible dream …
	Brahm's Lullaby	**LULLA-BY** and goodnight …
Major third	"Have Yourself a Merry Little Christmas"	**HAVE YOUR**-self a merry little Christmas …
	"Oh When the Saints Come Marching In"	**OH WHEN** the saints …
Perfect fourth	"Here Comes the Bride"	**HERE COMES** the bride …
	"We Wish You a Merry Christmas"	**WE WISH** you a merry Christmas …
Tri-tone	"Maria" (from *West Side Story*)	**MA-RI**-a … (also called an augmented fourth or diminished fifth)
Perfect fifth	"My Favorite Things"	**RAIN-DROPS** on roses …
	"Twinkle, Twinkle Little Star"	**TWINKLE, TWINKLE** little star …
Minor sixth	"Sunrise, Sunset" (from *Fiddler on the Roof*)	**IS** this **THE** little girl …

Interval		Song-Specific Phrase
Major sixth	"NBC" chime	**N-B**-C (first two notes)
	"Jingle Bells"	**DASH-ING** through the snow ...
Minor seventh	"There's a Place for Us"	**THERE'S A** place for us ...
	Theme from *Star Trek*	**Doo-doooo** ... (first two notes)
Major seventh	"Somewhere Over the Rainbow"	**SOME**-where **O**-ver the rainbow ...
Octave	"Somewhere Over the Rainbow"	**SOME-WHERE** over the rainbow ...
	"A Christmas Song"	**CHEST-NUTS** roasting on an open fire ...

While intervals are the same going up or down, it's sometimes harder to sing descending intervals. The following table presents some song snippets you can use to "hear" descending intervals.

Table 11.2 Descending Intervals

Interval		Song-Specific Phrase
Minor second	"Joy to the World" (Christmas carol)	**JOY TO** the world, the Lord is come ...
	"Spinning Wheel"	**RIDE A** painted pony ...
Major second	"Three Blind Mice"	**THREE BLIND** mice ...
	"Yesterday"	**YES-TERDAY**, all my troubles seemed so far away ...
Minor third	"Jesus Loves Me"	**JE-SUS** loves me this I know ...
	"Hey Jude"	**HEY JUDE** ...
Major third	"Swing Low, Sweet Chariot"	**SWING LOW**, sweet chariot ...
	"Summertime"	**SUM-MER**-time, and the livin' is easy ...
Perfect fourth	"Born Free"	**BORN FREE** ...
	"My Girl" (The Temptations)	**MY GIRL**, talkin' 'bout my girl ...
Tri-tone	European police siren	
Perfect fifth	Theme from *The Flintstones*	**FLINT-STONES,** meet the Flintstones ...
Minor sixth	Theme from *Love Story*	**WHERE DO** I begin ...
Major sixth	"Over There"	**O-VER** there ...
	"Nobody Knows the Trouble I've Seen"	**NO-BOD**-y knows ...
Minor seventh	"Watermelon Man"	Water-**MEL**-on **MAN**
Major seventh	"Have Yourself a Merry Little Christmas"	So **HAVE YOUR**-self a merry little Christmas now ...
Octave	"Salt Peanuts"	Salt **PEA-NUTS**, salt peanuts ...

Tip

If you want to practice your ear training and sight singing skills in real-time, check out the lessons at the Musictheory.net website (www.musictheory.net). This site is great; it's the Internet equivalent of the listening labs we had when I was a student!

Singing Notes Outside the Scale—and Keys That Aren't Major

So far in this chapter we've only addressed major keys and scales—and within them, simple melodies that move in a fairly step-wise manner. If you can master these basic concepts—and use them in your day-to-day music study—you're a step ahead of a lot of other singers.

Dealing with the eight notes of the major scale, however, only touches the proverbial tip of the iceberg when it comes to reading music. Melodies don't always stay within the scale and key signatures don't always indicate major keys.

Music is sometimes more complex than this.

You need to read a whole book about music theory to understand all the different ways that nonscale notes and nonmajor keys can be used in different pieces of music. We don't have space for all that here; instead, I'll present a brief explanation of the concepts involved and present some tips you can use when you see a flat or a sharp in the middle of a melodic line.

Dealing with Accidentals

As you learned back in Chapter 10, composers and arrangers use flats and sharps to change the basic notes in a scale. When you see a flat in front of a note, you know to sing that note a half-step lower; when you see a sharp, you sing the note a half-step higher.

For example, if you're in the key of C (no sharps or flats, remember) and you see a sharp in front of a D, you know that something is up. Instead of singing Re as usual, you have to sing Re raised a half step (D-sharp, in this example), as shown below:

A raised Re and a lowered Ti, in the key of C.

Tip

The natural sign can be used to raise a flat, lower a sharp, or return an altered note to its original state.

Conversely, if you see a flat in front of a B, you have to sing a Ti lowered a half step (B-flat, in this example).

This is where knowing your intervals pays off. It's relatively easy to sing the standard "Do Re Mi" notes of the major scale, even if they're not in order; it's when you're presented with altered notes that you can use your memorized interval examples to help you hit the right note.

Dealing with Minor Key Signatures

When you see a lot of accidentals in a piece of music, there's a good chance that the composer or arranger is changing scales on you—in particular, changing a major scale to a minor one.

As you remember from Chapter 10, every major scale has a related minor scale. These two scales share a lot of the same notes and—most importantly for singers—they also share the same key signatures.

A relative minor key starts on the sixth note of its "cousin" major scale. This puts the Do of the minor scale on the same note as the La of the relative major scale.

How do you know that you're singing in a minor key? Here are some ways you can tell:

- Look through the piece of music to see if there are any accidentals within the piece. If there are—and they tend to appear on the same notes—that's your first clue that the piece is written in the relative minor key.

- Look to see what pitch the piece ends on. Since the relative minor scale is built on the sixth step of the major scale (La), if a piece ends on what would be La in the major key, that's your second clue.
- Assuming that Do has moved to the relative minor, look to see if the seventh scale step (Ti) is raised with either a sharp or a natural sign. (The seventh degree of the minor scale is often raised in this fashion.)
- If you can hear the tune played or sung, you should be able to hear that it's in a minor key. Minor tonalities have a melancholy or ancient flavor about them.

If two or more of these points prove true, chances are the song is in the relative minor key—which means that the new Do is found on the sixth step of the relative major scale.

For example, if the key signature says C (no sharps or flats) but the piece is minor, the actual key is A minor, and Do is A. If the key signature says F (one flat) but the piece is minor, the key is D minor and Do is D. If the key signature says B-flat (two flats) but the piece is minor, the actual key is G minor, and Do is G.

You can practice figuring out relative minor scales with the following exercises:

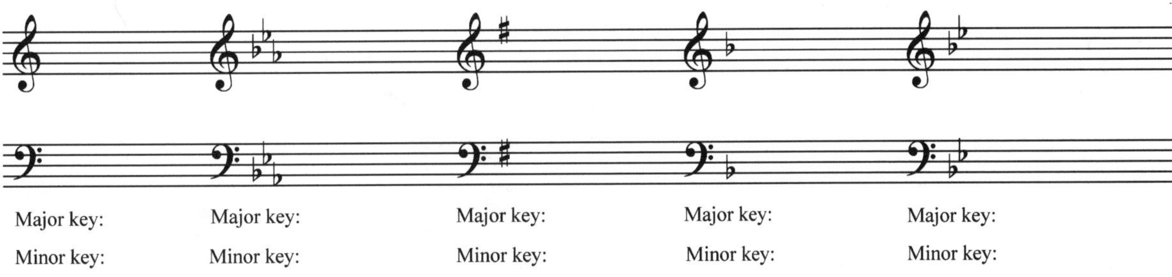

Enter the major and relative minor keys for these key signatures.

The Least You Need to Know

- Reading music is important for all singers, especially if you're singing in a choir, a musical, or a recording studio.
- The eight degrees of the major scale in Solfeggio are Do, Re, Mi, Fa, So, La, Ti, and Do (again).
- The Solfeggio method helps you understand the notes in any key, since Do is always relative—and movable.
- To determine the correct pitch for Do, you have to read the song's key signature; Do is always the first note of the key.
- Notes in a melody often jump from pitch to pitch, not always in a step-wise motion; the difference between two pitches is called an interval.
- Notes outside the designated key are indicated by the use of accidentals—sharps, flats, and natural signs.
- A scale that starts on the sixth degree (La) of the major key—and shares the same key signature—indicates a relative minor key.

Chapter 12

Practicing Your Sight Singing

In This Chapter

- Practicing singing intervals
- Using familiar tunes to practice your sight singing
- Learning how to sight sing rhythms
- Discovering how to put notes and rhythms together

Chapter 10 described the fundamentals behind reading music. Chapter 11 provided a method for reading music and for sight singing. Now it's time to put those fundamentals and methods to use.

Which means that it's time to practice!

Now, I know some of you are saying something along the lines of "practice—we don't need no stinking practice!" Practice sounds like work, and who wants to work? You just want to sing!

The thing is, if you want to become a *good* singer, you *do* have to work. And the biggest part of that work is *practicing*. That doesn't mean that practicing has to be hard or boring. In fact, there are lots of ways to make practice fun—which is where this chapter comes in.

So brush up on your theory and get ready to put your Do, Re, Mi's to good use. It's time to practice your sight singing!

Understanding Sight Singing

When musicians use the phrase *sight singing*, they're referring to the ability to read—and sing—a piece of music without first hearing it played on another instrument. That is, you see a group of notes in a melody, and you sing that melody, without the assistance of other instruments or singers. It's just you and the notes.

You see the notes on paper, and you sing them. It takes practice (which is what this chapter is all about), as well as a firm grounding of the theory behind the notes (which is what the previous two chapters were about). You need to figure out what key you're in (that's your key signature), what note is the home note of the scale (that's your Do), and how to move from one note to the next (that's your intervals). Put it all together, and you're singing complete melodic lines.

Some people are just naturally talented at sight singing. For the rest of us, it takes a little work—in the form of constant practice. But practice really does make perfect, and we'll begin by practicing how to sight sing specific intervals.

Sight Singing Intervals

These first exercises will help you develop your ear for intervals. Here's how to practice singing them:

1. Start by attempting to "hear" each interval in your head.
2. Now try singing the interval. (If you have a piano—or any other instrument—handy, you can give yourself the first pitch as notated and then try to sing the indicated interval.)
3. Check your results by playing the interval on your instrument.

> **Note**
>
> For these exercises, the absolute pitch you start with isn't important; what's important are the relative pitch relationships. So use any starting pitch you like.

Apply this approach to the following exercises, which let you practice both major and minor intervals—with a few augmented fourths/diminished fifths thrown in for good measure. I've included both ascending and descending intervals, and don't be shy about referring back to Tables 11.1 and 11.2 if you have trouble "hearing" any of them.

Exercise 12.1: Prime (Unison) Intervals

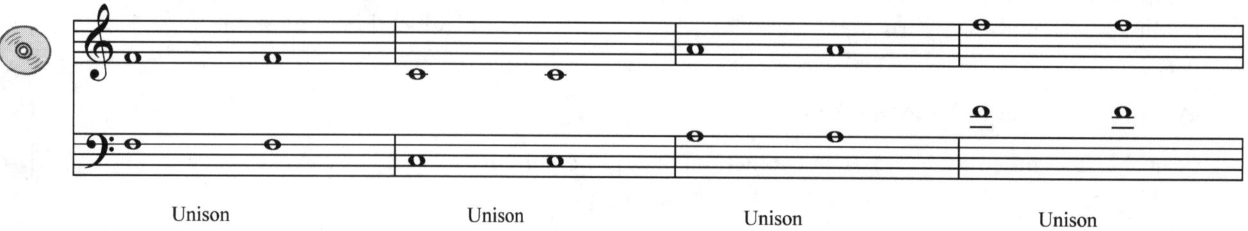

Unison Unison Unison Unison

Exercise 12.2: Major and Minor Seconds

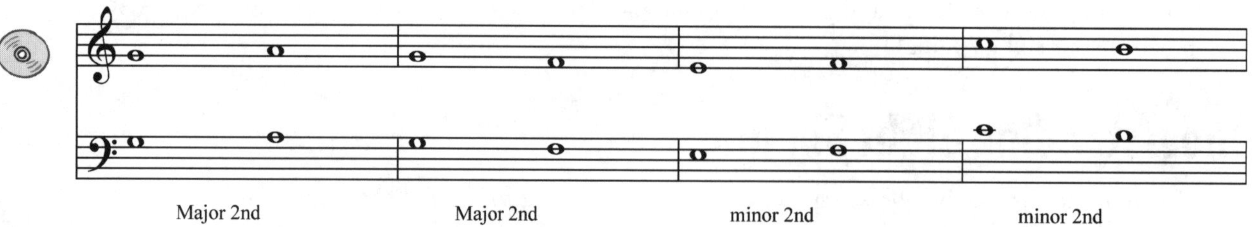

Major 2nd Major 2nd minor 2nd minor 2nd

Exercise 12.3: Major and Minor Thirds

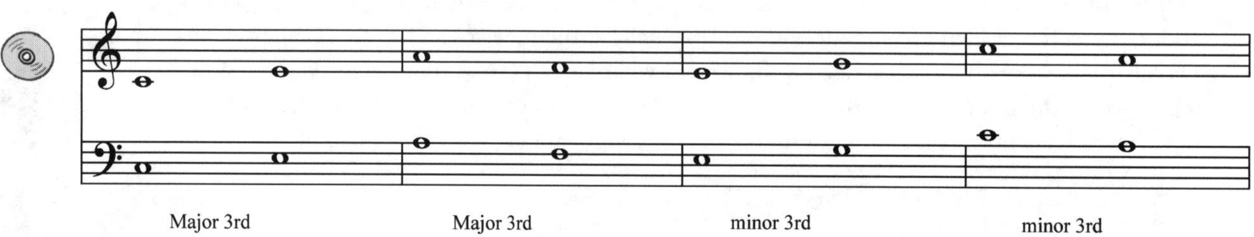

Major 3rd Major 3rd minor 3rd minor 3rd

Exercise 12.4: Perfect and Augmented Fourths

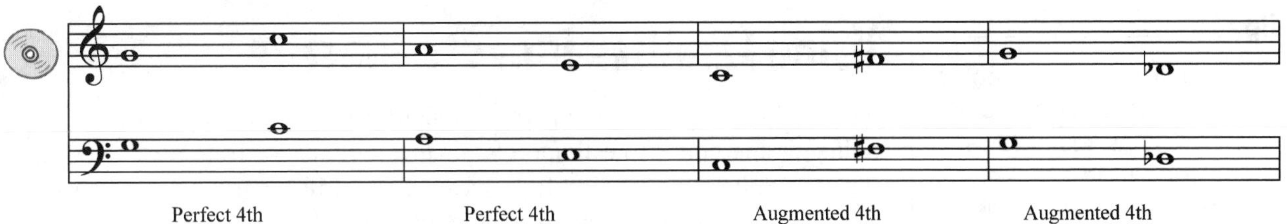

Exercise 12.5: Perfect and Diminished Fifths

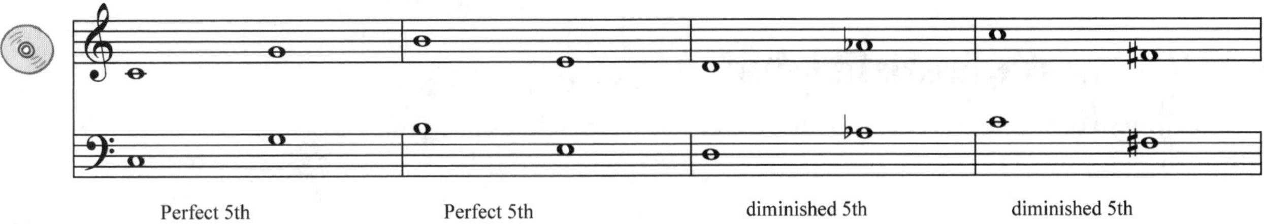

Exercise 12.6: Major and Minor Sixths

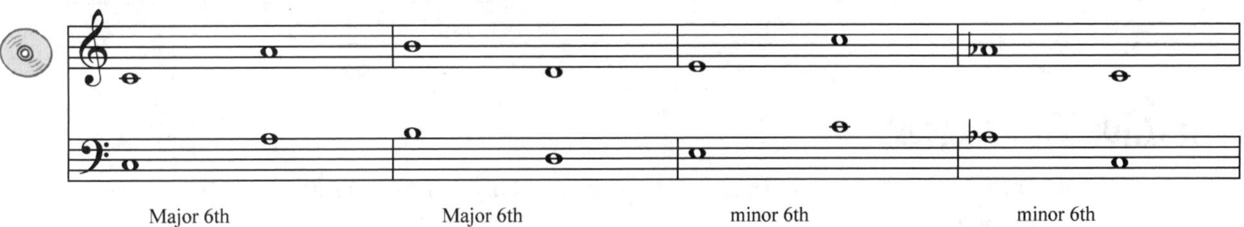

Exercise 12.7: Major and Minor Sevenths

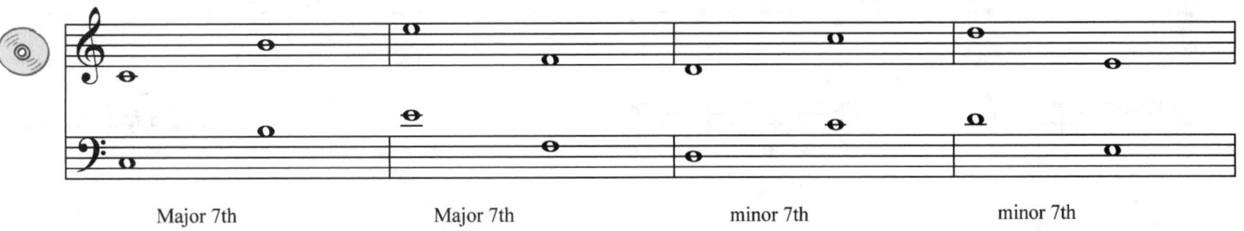

Exercise 12.8: Octaves

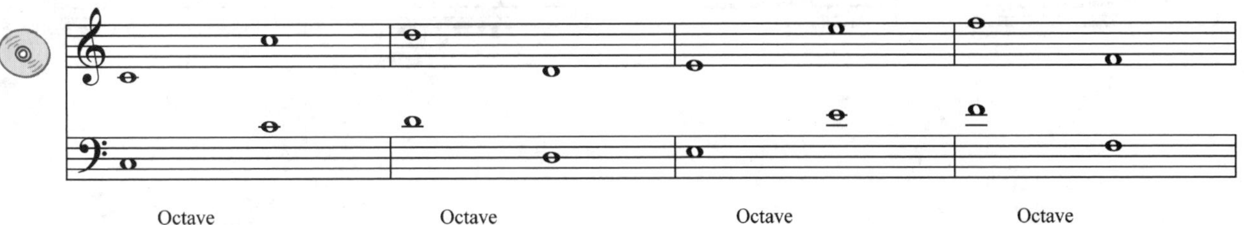

All of the exercises in this chapter are presented in both treble and bass clef. (They're the same, either way.) If you're a soprano, alto, or tenor, read the treble clef; if you're a bass or baritone, read the bass clef.

> **Tip**
> It's important to always keep a sense of tonal center (or Do) in your memory as you practice. At any point in an exercise or piece of music you should be able to instantly sing "Do"—no matter what note you're currently on.

Using Familiar Tunes to Practice

The best way I know to improve your sight singing and practice the Solfeggio method is to call upon familiar tunes, but to "translate" and sing them on Solfeggio syllables. It's a great way to utilize your tonal memory and apply it to a new, more advanced skill that will carry over when you start sight singing less familiar or unknown songs.

You can practice this Solfeggio sight singing with any simple song or hymn that you know, but the following exercises give you a place to start.

Exercise 12.9: "Twinkle, Twinkle Little Star"

Before you start singing this one, note that the key signature tells us that this song is in the key of G—thus the note G is your Do.

Exercise 12.10: "Frere Jacques"

The melody of "Frere Jacques" moves in steps, starting on Do. This should be pretty easy for you to sight sing with the Solfeggio syllables.

This exercise is actually in two parts. For the first part, you sing "Frere Jacques" in the key of G:

For the second part of this exercise, you sing the tune in the key of D. This is designed to help you get the hang of the "Movable Do" concept we discussed in Chapter 11.

Exercise 12.11: "Amazing Grace"

For this exercise, let's try a song that doesn't start on Do. As always, start by looking at the key signature and finding Do. (Hint: It's on the next line above the last sharp—a G#—which means Do should be A.)

Note

Notice that "Amazing Grace" starts on a note that is lower than Do, which some call "low So" and mark as "LS." The song is also in 3/4 time, which means there are three beats in a measure, instead of the normal four.

Exercise 12.12: "Go Tell Aunt Rhody"

"Aunt Rhody" is a tune that starts on Mi and moves pretty much in stepwise motion up and down the scale. Here's your chance to label the syllables yourself, rather than have me do it for you, so get out a pencil and fill in the blanks under each note with the proper Solfeggio syllables.

Sight Singing Simple Rhythms

As if it weren't enough to read the pitches of a song, we singers are called upon to make some sense out of the rhythms, too! But fear not, dear singer; practice also helps you improve your rhythmic sight reading.

For some of us, rhythmic notation is easier to read than melodic notation. That's because our natural speech patterns follow common rhythmic patterns. For example, say the word "Alabama," placing the emphasis (called an *accent*) on the first syllable rather than the third. Surprise—you've just "spoken" a group of sixteenth notes! And they look like this:

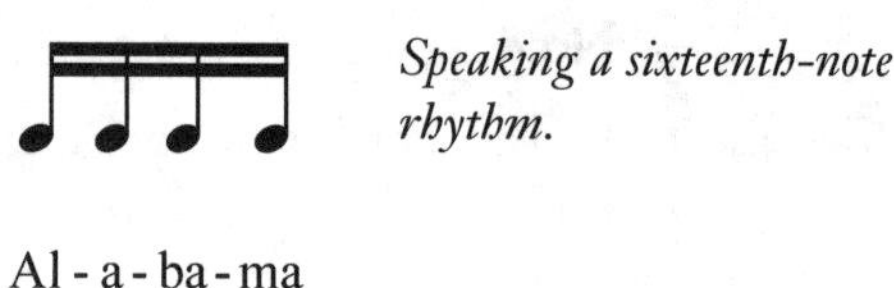

Speaking a sixteenth-note rhythm.

Just like the "Alabama" example, you can use your natural speech patterns to learn rhythmic notation. This approach is similar to the Suzuki method, which has been used in early childhood music education for years; what works for small children works equally well for adults.

Adapting Speech Patterns to Music Notation

The first thing you need to do is establish a basic beat. You do this by tapping your hand against your knee, in a slow and deliberate tempo—"one, two, three, four." This will serve as the pulse, or the unit of the beat, as you "say" the following rhythms. You can then use these units of rhythms as you practice your sight singing.

Note

The examples and exercises in this section are for basic groupings of notes written in the most common time—4/4, where a quarter note gets one beat in a measure with four total beats. This is a good place to start (as the majority of pop songs are written in 4/4 time), and these examples will show you how you can quickly learn to read rhythms.

Let's start with a whole note. If you recall from Chapter 10, a whole note lasts for four beats. So to practice singing/playing a whole note, get your knee-slapping beat going, then say "whole, two, three, four." Each word you say should fall on a knee tap.

Whole two three four

Whole notes.

A half note lasts half as long as a whole note—two beats. You practice the half note by saying "half-note, half-note," with each word falling on a pulse.

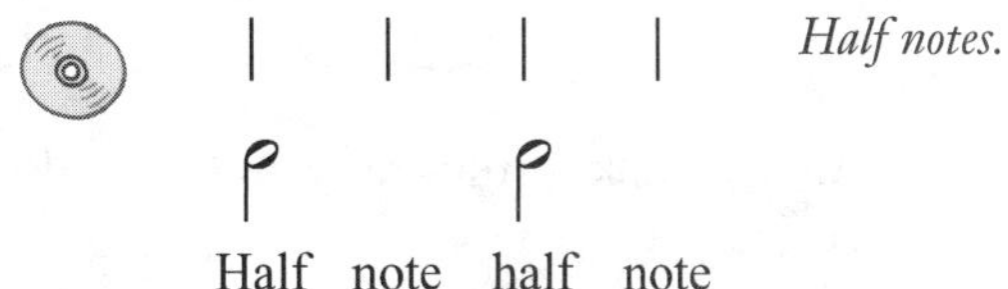
Half note half note

Half notes.

The quarter note is your basic beat. You practice the quarter note by saying "walk" every time you tap your knee: "walk, walk, walk, walk."

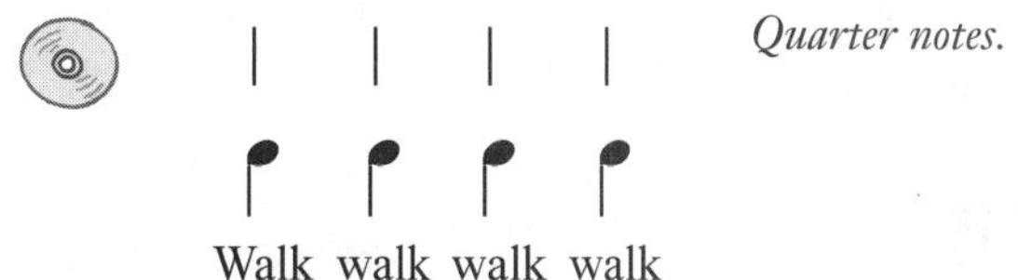
Walk walk walk walk

Quarter notes.

Next up is the eighth note. There are two eighth notes for every beat, so say "run-ning" on every pulse: "run-ning, run-ning, run-ning, run-ning."

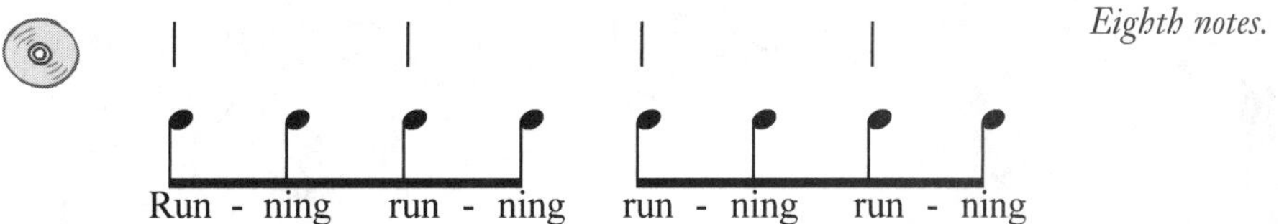
Run - ning run - ning run - ning run - ning

Eighth notes.

There are four sixteenth notes for every beat. You practice sixteenth notes by saying the word "Alabama" on every pulse: "Al-a-ba-ma, Al-a-ba-ma, Al-a-ba-ma, Al-a-ba-ma."

Al - a - ba - ma Al - a - ba - ma Al - a - ba - ma Al - a - ba - ma

Sixteenth notes.

There, by saying just a few simple words, you've learned the most commonly used rhythmic patterns in the world of music! Of course, there are endless combinations of these rhythms, but this gives you a point of reference for further study.

Exercise 12.13

Let's put your newfound rhythmic skills to the test by reading through a few lines of different rhythms. I've given you a head start on this first exercise by writing the "walk, walk, run-ning" words under each note. (For the other rhythmic exercises, you'll have to notate the rhythms yourself as you keep that knee-tapping thing going.)

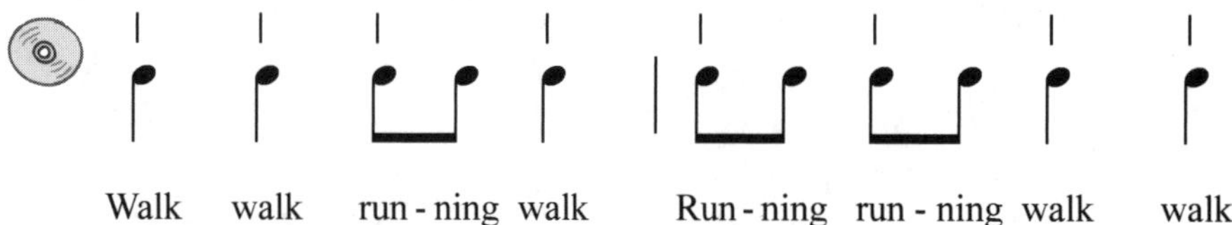
Walk walk run - ning walk Run - ning run - ning walk walk

Exercise 12.14

Exercise 12.15

Exercise 12.16

Exercise 12.17

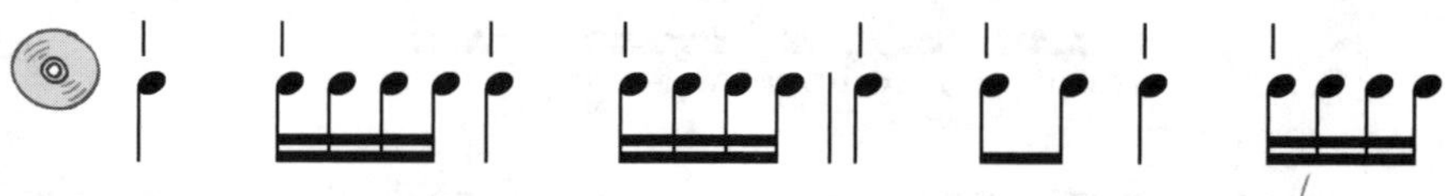

Exercise 12.18

Exercise 12.19

Exercise 12.20

In both this and the next exercise, notice that "running" notes (eighth notes) can be grouped into any number of notes. How the notes are grouped doesn't change their relative speed.

Exercise 12.21

Exercise 12.22: Putting Pitches and Rhythms Together

Now you're ready to translate rhythms into speech sounds in a real piece of music. This exercise uses a Bach Minuet that you're probably familiar with and is divided into two steps.

1. Work through the exercise saying only the rhythms, using the "walk, walk, run-ning" method.
2. Once you've mastered the rhythms, sing the exercise on the Solfeggio syllables in the rhythm that is notated.

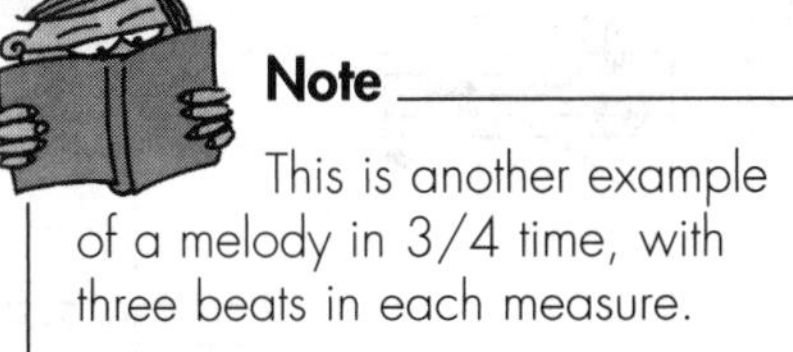

Note

This is another example of a melody in 3/4 time, with three beats in each measure.

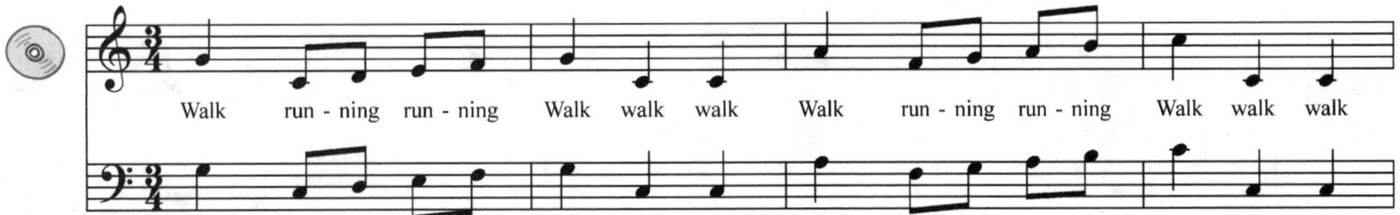
Walk run - ning run - ning Walk walk walk Walk run - ning run - ning Walk walk walk

Exercise 12.23: Name That Tune

When you master the previous exercise, you're putting pitches and rhythms together—which means you're reading music on your own! So let's keep going by sight singing the following mystery tune. See if you can identify it after sight singing all the notes and rhythms. (Hint: Do is D-flat, and the melody starts on So.)

Note

From here on out, you should use the accompanying CD purely as a "check" against how you sing the exercises. The point of these exercises is to develop your ability to sight sing new melodies; if you listen to the CD before you figure it out on your own, you're cheating!

Sight Singing in a Minor Key

All the previous exercises in this chapter have been in a major key. That's fine, but not every song you sing will use the major scale; some songs will be in a minor key.

With that in mind, the next two exercises are both in minor keys.

Exercise 12.24: "Poor Wayfaring Stranger"

This traditional tune is in the key of C minor. That's right—the key signature looks like E-flat, but since it's in the relative minor, the key is C minor—and the Do is on C.

Exercise 12.25: "Erie Canal"

Here's another minor-key melody to practice. I hope it doesn't take you "fifteen years" to learn it!

More Sight Singing Practice

As if the previous exercises weren't enough, here are eight more exercises for you to sight sing. (Watch out for some different time signatures in the last few exercises—not every song is written in 4/4!)

Exercise 12.26

Exercise 12.27

Exercise 12.28

Exercise 12.29

Exercise 12.30

Exercise 12.31

Exercise 12.32

This exercise and the next are both in 6/4 time, where you have six beats in a measure instead of the regular four. It's helpful to think of each measure as containing two groups of three, so that it has a slight waltz feel.

Exercise 12.33

The Least You Need to Know

- Sight singing is the ability to read—and sing—a piece of music without first hearing it played on another instrument.
- You develop your sight singing skills through continued practice.
- You practice sight singing intervals by first "hearing" the interval in your head, and then singing the interval.
- Natural speech patterns (such as "run-ning" or "Al-a-ba-ma") can be translated into actual rhythmic notation.

Part 4

Taking It Further

Once you've mastered the basics, it's time to hone your technique. This part helps you perfect your diction, phrasing, and dynamics—and shows you the best way to practice new songs.

Chapter 13

Diction

In This Chapter

- Learning how to pronounce the basic vowels—in song
- Dealing with diphthongs
- Working with consonants
- Confronting common pronunciation problems

One of the great advantages that we singers have over other musicians is the ability to tell a story or convey strong emotions through the words of a song. Powerful lyrics, whether of loss or happiness, have moved listeners and touched hearts in both personal and profound ways for as long as we've had a developed language.

Singers are fortunate to have this powerful artistic tool—although it carries with it some special burdens that other musicians don't have. Because words are so important, it is the singer's task to learn how to form them correctly so that they can enhance, rather than hinder, a fine musical performance.

The process of proper pronunciation is called *diction*, and that's what we're going to work on in this chapter. We'll look at the two different components of the spoken language—*vowels* and *consonants*—and how to properly pronounce each in the art of singing.

Vowels: The Vehicles of Tone

Since about 90 percent of our singing is on vowels, we're going to look at them first. The five primary vowels—A, E, I, O, and U—are what we call the vehicles of tone because we use them to produce sustained singing tones. (That other "sometimes" vowel, Y, doesn't have its own unique sound; depending on how it is used grammatically, it takes on the sound of the long I or E, and is treated like those primary vowels.)

In his classic book *The Singer and the Voice* (The Scolar Press, 1978), Arnold Rose writes:

"The beauty of the voice and the expression of emotion is heard in the vowel sounds, the intensity and color of which can be varied to a very great extent."

I couldn't agree more; sometimes a simple adjustment of pronunciation by altering a vowel shape in the mouth will make dramatic improvements in the tone being produced.

Shaping the Vowel

When it comes to sounding a vowel, you should try to feel as if your mouth is full of the vowel you are singing. This can also be thought of as keeping your mouth "tall" inside as you sustain the vowel tone.

If this sounds a bit confusing, try this experiment:

1. Say the word "love," just as you would normally speak it. Try to isolate the sound of the O vowel—which probably came out more like "uh." Sustain the spoken "l-uh-v" and visualize the shape of your mouth as you do.
2. Next, on a comfortable but somewhat elevated pitch, sing the word "love" just as you have spoken. Listen to the sustained tone on "l-uh-v" and analyze the shape of your mouth—the position of your tongue and soft palate (velum) and the space between your teeth. Remember what the tone feels and sounds like—because you don't want to go there again.
3. Finally, pronounce the word "love" as if it were "l-ah-v" (*not* "l-uh-v"). There should be a very tall space in your mouth, and you should keep your tongue low and your soft palate high. Now sing it, with the identical "ah" feeling in the sustained vowel. Do you hear—and feel—the difference?

This little exercise is one of the best arguments that I know for holding your mouth right while singing. As is now obvious, the "shape" of the vowel affects the tone.

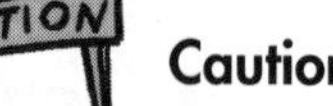

Caution

It's important to remember that the sustained vowels used in singing are pronounced differently than the vowels we use in speech. Old habits die hard, so you'll always have to be on guard where vowels are concerned. More on this later in the chapter.

This simple concept of shaping the vowel, or generally making it "taller," works across the board. When our mouths are open with a low tongue and high soft palate, we produce more open and resonant tones.

Try saying all the major vowels in a sustained and connected manner. Now, on a comfortable pitch, *sing* all the vowels—using the image of the egg between the teeth, from Chapter 9—and you'll feel and hear a dramatic difference in the results. Here's the reason:

When we produce vowels in normal speech, the soft palate is "lazy" and low, cutting off the passageway to the resonators in the mask. Also, as you can see in Figure 13.1, the mouth opening is usually more horizontal than vertical and the space between the back teeth (the jaw hinge) is somewhat tight.

Figure 13.1

The right and wrong ways to sing a vowel.

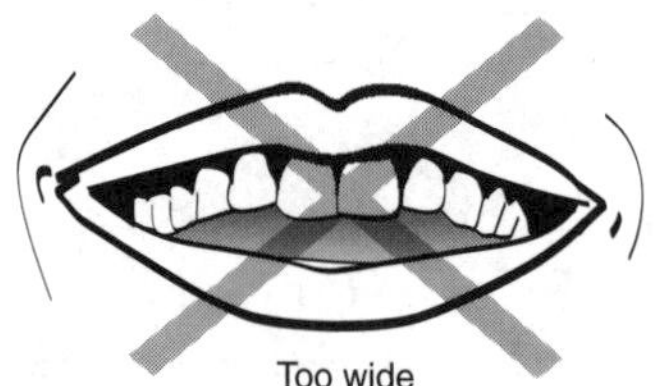

Singing, on the other hand, requires a high soft palate, a vertical mouth position, and an open, relaxed jaw hinge—which means you need to consciously adjust these elements when you're singing.

Finding the Open Jaw

Some students find the open jaw difficult to achieve—so let's work for a minute on finding the open jaw.

Start by placing your fingertips just in front of the little "flaps" of your ears. With your mouth closed and teeth together, apply a little pressure to the area just in front of the flaps to really feel them.

Now start to yawn and feel what happens. The space seems to "cave in" as the jaw hinge opens. (For some reason, this sometimes freaks out young singers; I always get a kick out of the looks on their faces when they perform this little exercise.)

The point here is to understand that in everyday circumstances, we rarely drop the jaw or open the hinge to the degree needed for good tone production. Which means, of course, that you have to unlearn your normal habits to produce a good vocal tone. I suggest that you begin each practice session with this simple physical checkup for the open, relaxed jaw. You can even go so far as to sing your vocal warm-ups with your fingertips in the sunken areas. If you can keep your jaw from closing down, you'll love the results.

Singing the Five Basic Vowels

Now that you've found the open jaw position—and your fingertips are in place to check—it's time to start singing the vowels. Table 13.1 lists all the basic, pure vowel sounds and how they should be pronounced when singing. (You can also hear how they sound on the accompanying CD.)

Table 13.1 Long Vowel Sounds and Pronunciations

Vowel	Sung Like	As In
U	"oo"	"soon"
O	"oh"	"only"
I	"ah"	"I"
A	"eh"	"baby"
E	"ee"	"meet"

Sing through all the vowels, in the order listed, and with the modified pronunciations shown in the table. As you sing each one, try to keep your jaw open, relaxed, and as still as possible.

A funny thing happened when you got to the last vowel, didn't it? All the other vowels can be produced without much movement or closure of the jaw hinge, but the hinge wants to pull together when we produce the long E. Why is this?

The long E vowel is a slippery slope for many singers. The natural tendency is to spread your mouth into a wide horizontal grin, tighten down the hatches, and go "whee." Unfortunately, this isn't the best way to go.

What you should do when singing the long E (in words like "me," "he," "be," and so on) is to gently pull the sides of your mouth into a position more like the "ah" vowel sound, and try to keep the sense of openness in the mouth. The jaw hinge will close a little, which is fine—as long as you don't allow the jaw to clamp together or your lips to widen into a great big grin.

Some teachers overemphasize this "lip pursing" adjustment and their students sound unnatural and affected, so try not to get into any contorted mouth positions to avoid a strident E vowel. You want to produce beautiful sounding vowels—but not at the expense of being understood! The best approach is to strive to sing the word as naturally as possible, without a negative impact on your singing tone.

Singing the Short Vowels

Just as you need to substitute different sounds for long vowels when singing, you also have to change the short vowels from the way you'd typically speak them.

Table 13.2 details the four short vowels, and how they should be pronounced when singing.

Table 13.2 Short Vowel Sounds and Pronunciations

Vowel	Sung Like	As In
i	"ih"	"sit" (with a touch of "e" in the tone—and a slight smile)
o	"ah"	"hot"
e	"eh"	"every"
u	"ah"	"under"

Handling the "Uh"

Breaking old speech habits is really tough to do. Our speech is like a part of our personality; it reflects our geographic and cultural heritage. When we have to change the way we pronounce a word when singing, it's like trying to unlearn everything we've learned since we first learned to talk.

One of the big issues in vocal pronunciation is the "uh" sound. If I had to guess, I'd say that at least three-quarters of the words in the English language are produced with the "uh" substitution for the O and U vowels. Just speak the words "love," "oven," "under," "until," "of," "rub a dub," and on and on … It's easy to see that the "uh" sound is a big player in our spoken language.

The problem is, the "uh" sound is an anathema to good singers. That's because the "uh" sound forces key parts of our vocal mechanism into precisely the opposite position than they should be.

I want you to think about your mouth and soft palate position as you say the "uh" words I just listed. The feeling you get with the spoken "uh" goes against everything you've learned about free and open tone production. Instead, you get a lazy soft palate, a horizontal mouth, and a tight jaw.

So let's just pretend that the "uh" sound doesn't exist when we sing, and alter it to sound more like a nice open "ah." (Remember the "tall" vowels?) Taking this approach, the word "until" becomes "*ah*-ntil," and "under" becomes "*ah*-nder." See how it works?

Note

The uh/ah substitution, like several of the other vowel substitutions, doesn't apply to all styles of music—particularly jazz and country. Learn more about different styles in Part 5 of this book.

Note

Make sure you note the reverse situation in the EW and the OH combination; in these cases, you should pre-form the second vowel sound *before* you initiate the word. For example, when singing "you," always think of initiating the "oo" sound first, pre-forming your lips off your teeth and in a pursed position. Otherwise, you'll end up sounding like a hungry coyote!

Dealing with Diphthongs

When we practice or vocalize, we normally do so on pure vowel sounds—the five long vowels discussed earlier in this chapter. That's because pure vowels provide the best vehicles for sustained, beautiful tone.

Limiting our singing to only these vowel sounds is great for practice, but in the real world, you'll encounter a lot more than just these pure vowels. In the real songs we sing in the real world, few words are made up of only pure vowels; many words contain compound vowels, with two (or more) vowel sounds blended together.

We call these compound vowels—created from two pure vowels—*diphthongs*. (The *di* is for the two vowels; add another to the mix and you get a *tripthong*.)

Table 13.3 shows the most common diphthongs and the stuff of which they're made. The boldface type indicates the pure vowel that should be sustained until the last nanosecond, when you gently add the ending sound (shown in lowercase).

Table 13.3 Common Diphthongs

Diphthong	Made Up of These Sounds	Sounds Like
AY	**EH** + ee	"say"
EW	ee + **OO**	"you"
I	**AH** + ee	"tight"
OH	uh + **OO**	"no"
OW or OU	**AH** + oo	"town" or "mouse"

This completes our look at the role of vowels and how—for better or worse—they sustain our singing tone. Now it's time to look at the "seasoning" of this alphabet soup we call diction—the consonants.

Consonants: The Articulators of Tone

By definition, a consonant is a sound that either partially or completely blocks the stream of breath during phonation. We all know consonants as everything *other than* the vowels.

Understanding Consonants

While vowels seem to flow freely on a stream of breath, the consonants are formed with parts of the mouth we call the *articulators*—our lips, tongue, and teeth. (Other articulators are the hard and soft palate and the glottis.) Vowels tend to open the throat (which is good technique), while consonants seem to get in the way of the tone (which could be bad technique).

This doesn't have to be the case, however; crisp, articulated consonants are the spice of life, and our audiences couldn't understand a word we sing without them. The best thing to do is rely on the beauty of tone, emphasizing the vowels and "seasoning the sound" with the consonants.

Note

We'll look further at the role of consonants and how they impact expression and style in Part 5 of this book.

Voiced and Unvoiced Consonants

It's probably helpful for us to look at two main categories of consonants: *voiced* and *unvoiced*.

Voiced consonants are the ones that make a "buzz" when you produce them. You can hear for yourself by plugging up one of your ears and saying "B, G, L, V." You'll feel the buzz that is produced.

Unvoiced consonants don't do this. Try saying "F, T, K" and you won't hear or feel that same buzz.

Why does this matter? It's simple; voiced consonants assist us in connecting words in a musical phrase, kind of like gluing words together to form sentences. Unvoiced consonants tend to stop the tone or cause a break in the flow of the lyrics and melody. Because of this potential "blocking" effect, we need to emphasize the vowels in the lyrics and use the consonants only as needed to be understood.

Confronting Common Pronunciation Problems

The English language is a confusing mish-mash of words and phrases integrated from several other languages, and pronunciation isn't always logical. For example, why isn't "singer" pronounced like "finger"—and why isn't "phone" spelled "fone?"

Volumes have been written on the rules of pronunciation, and you're free to snooze through as many as you like. I'd rather take a more practical, although less comprehensive, approach—and point out the most common problem areas when it comes to vocal pronunciation.

Thirty years of teaching and thousands of students have pretty much distilled a "top 10 list" of common pronunciation problems. I hope you'll appreciate the following short list of common pronunciation problems as you deal more and more with actual lyrics, rather than just vocal exercises.

Give the Most Weight to the Initial Consonant

Inexperienced singers often emphasize final consonants—particularly final Ts—in an attempt to articulate clearly. The result can be percussive and very unnatural. It's much better to give the most weight to the initial consonant in a word.

The "final T" situation is so common that it deserves a bit more attention. You see, even in classical music Ts tend to stand on their own—whether at the end or in the middle of a word—so you should be careful not to overemphasize them. Don't sing "tha *ti* see" for "that I see"; the consonant and the vowel have to be separated by a slight glottal stroke. You may even have to go so far as to soften the final T to more of a D sound, especially in more popular music.

Watch Which Consonants You Connect

Legato singing requires a sense of melding our words into one continuous line—but you have to be very careful about some consonant connections. Connecting the wrong consonants can turn a specific phrase into two very different words.

Tip

That slight glottal separation between words is also a good idea when singing "your ear!"

For example, the phrase "it's not" has to have a separation between the words so as not to sing "it snot." Another example is inadvertently singing the phrase "I am" as "I yam." (This is called the Popeye effect.)

Thinking back to the "final T" effect discussed in the previous section, it should go without saying that final Ts should never be carried over to any following word that starts with a vowel. (I shudder to think of an untrained choir singing the phrase "might it!")

Don't Hum Your Ns and Ms

It is unfortunately common for singers to sing through a final N or M, elongating the consonant into a kind of hum. This makes a word like "times" sound more like "tahmmmmz," when it should sound like "tahhhhmz."

Note

While it's certainly difficult to argue with his success, Frank Sinatra was one of these inadvertent end-of-word hummers.

While you can produce a hummed pitch on M or N, it's not really considered good technique. You should stick to sustaining the vowel rather than the consonant. (There are some genre-specific exceptions to this rule, which we'll discuss in Part 5 of this book.)

The Extended "Arrrr"

Words with a final R have always been a problem for singers—especially if you're from Texas or parts of the Midwest. The tendency for some singers is to extend the R, so that a word like "far" turns into the rather pirate-like "farrrr." (Arrrr, maties!)

When you encounter a word that ends with an R, take care to extend the vowel, not the ending R. So the word "heart" should be sung as "hahhhht"—*not* "harrrrt"—with just a hint of the final R at the very last moment.

The same goes for words like "river," "mother," and "father." These words should have more of a deep-South pronunciation: "rivah," "mothah," and "fathah."

When we allow the lips to close around the R formation, we call this "chewing the R." This is a tough habit to break, and sometimes I have to go to the extreme of telling my students to feel as if they drop that final R altogether. Our habits being what they are, that R will still show up (believe me on this), even when we try not to sing it. And audiences won't mistake "heart" for "hot" if you slight the R.

Don't Slur Your Rs

Some singers have a problem with slurring their Rs, especially in the middle of words. One way around this is to adopt the classical approach of flipping the R with your tongue, rather than forming it with the lips. In this fashion, "Merry Merry Christmas" becomes a little more like "Medy Medy Christmas." (This is especially true when repeated Rs occur at a fast tempo.)

Don't Drop the Final Consonant

While you don't want to overplay final Ts in words, that doesn't mean you should drop or underemphasize other ending consonants. In fact, you should take care to clearly enunciate final voiced consonants.

For example, you should finish words like "man" or "sound" by allowing the tongue to spring off the roof of the mouth after you produce the N or the D sound. Don't get carried away and sing "maaa-NUH" or "soun-DUH," but *do* release the pressure that's built up from the closed N or the ND. The same applies for the final voiced consonants B, V, and G—as in the words "web," "love," and "big"—although these consonants have a tendency to be a little more percussive by nature in our speech and finish themselves.

M and N are probably the most overlooked consonants in this regard and deserve your special attention when sung at the end of a word.

EW or OO?

It's amazing how many times you'll sing the words dew, duty, consume, student, renew, and (particularly) tune and news. We have come to accept our "dooty" as "stoodents" to "consoom" popular "toons" and the evening "nooz" But when it comes to singing (in a classical style, anyway), your words will have more ring and seem to come alive if you use the diphthong "EW" rather than the dull sounding "OO."

Just remember to purse the lips *before* starting the vowel or you'll be spreading the "nee-yous" when you should be spreading the "nyous." Practice it by saying "you-you-you" with very forward lips, then—without changing your mouth/lip position—add the N.

The Least You Need to Know

- Vowels are used to produce sustained singing tones.
- Sung vowel sounds are different from spoken vowel sounds.

- The five basic vowel sounds are U (sung as "oo"), O ("oh"), I ("ah"), A ("eh"), and E ("ee").
- Diphthongs are composed of two or more blended vowels; singers need to learn to emphasize the initial vowel, adding only a hint of the final vowel at the very last moment.
- There are two types of consonants—voiced (that make a "buzz" when produced) and unvoiced (that don't).
- The most common pronunciation problems involve breaking words or phrases at the wrong places—and giving undue emphasis to hard consonants.

Chapter 14

Phrasing and Dynamics

In This Chapter

- Understanding phrases and form in music
- Discovering the art of vocal phrasing
- Learning how to use tonal shading and dynamics as phrasing tools
- Understanding how rhythmic and harmonic nuances relate to phrasing

There's singing, and then there's *singing*.

You can sing a piece of music and hit all the notes exactly as written, but still have the piece sound "wrong." That's because if all you do is sing the notes you see on paper, the end result is most often flat and emotionless. The best singers take a song and make it ebb and flow, giving it a life and a musicality beyond what was notated. They breathe life into a song through the use of *phrasing* and *dynamics*.

Phrasing and dynamics are elements that separate the women from the girls—or the boys from the men. They're somewhat nebulous things, difficult to describe, really, that when executed properly, make your singing *musical*. In short, it's your individual treatment of a musical phrase—how you make it rise and fall, how you make it *breathe*—that impacts the feeling, the expression, and the musicality of your performance.

Some great examples of how phrasing can affect a performance are the vocal performances of the late, great Louis Armstrong. Pops didn't have a trained, "beautiful" voice (just the opposite, really), but the way he handled a musical phrase was without parallel. Louis' vocal phrasing on standards like "Stardust" and "What a Wonderful World" created a kind of gold standard for every popular singer (and instrumental musician, for that matter) ever since. Even though he wasn't *technically* a great singer, the man could really make a song *sing*.

Before we tackle the concept of phrasing, however, we need to look at the various parts of a piece of music. How you handle a song's pieces and parts determines how you approach the phrasing for the song's performance.

Introducing the Phrase

You already know about beats and measures, which can be likened to the letters and words in a written work. What we're interested in here is something a bit longer and more complete—that part of a song we call a *phrase*.

If a piece of music in its entirety can be compared to a short story, then a musical phrase is like a sentence. If you remember your English (or "language arts") classes back in school, you learned how to construct written paragraphs made up of individual sentences. Well, composers and songwriters do much the same thing when they write songs—they write musical "sentences" called phrases.

Note

The eight-bar phrase isn't a hard and fast rule; you can have phases as short as a single bar or as long as 16 or 32 measures. (In much blues and jazz music, for example, you'll encounter twelve-bar phrases.)

In most pieces of music, a musical phrase is typically eight measures long. You can tell a phrase because it can stand alone and still make sense, musically. In other words, a phrase expresses a single—and complete—musical thought.

Vocally, a phrase can also mean a group of notes that are meant to be sung together, smoothly, in a single breath. This type of phrase is indicated by a curved line over (or under) a group of notes, like this:

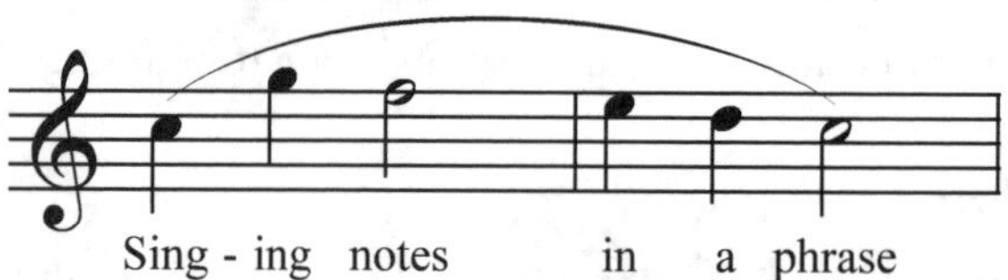

A group of notes sung together in a single phrase.

If phrase marks are included in a piece of music, you can use them to help you map out your breathing during a performance. Take a breath before the start of a phrase, sing the phrase, then take another breath at the end of the phrase. During the phrase, make sure you sing all the notes in a *legato*, or smooth, style, letting each note flow into the next until you reach the end of the phrase.

Discovering Song Form

By now you're beginning to realize that songs and other musical compositions aren't just a bunch of random, unorganized notes that composers write down when the creative spirit moves them. Just the opposite; composers often follow a set of fairly rigid "blueprints" for specific musical forms when they're creating a new song. These blueprints—called the *song form*—define the song's structure by dictating the type and organization of individual phrases to be employed and give the song a logical flow.

As a singer, it's important that you know the song form to gain a better feel for the music you'll be singing. When you have a clear understanding of how the phrases fit together to form a song, you can provide a more sensitive (and hopefully original) interpretation of its parts. After all, the sections of any piece of music are composed with artistic impact in mind, so you will benefit as a performer by understanding the original intent or function of the song's structure.

As you might suspect, there are hundreds of musical forms, ranging from a simple two-part song to a grand and glorious symphony. But for our purposes, we'll look at the musical form used in the popular song, since this form—or something like it—is the singer's most common musical vehicle today.

A typical song is constructed from two or more contrasting and/or repeating sections. (Repetition provides the comfort of familiarity; contrast adds interest.) In the modern popular song, these sections are commonly labeled as follows:

- **Verse.** This is the most common element in the popular song; in fact, some songs contain only verses, with no other elements. The verse is the section that tends to supply the information of the song through the lyrics. It's typically made up of one or two eight-measure phrases—although it can be longer.
- **Chorus.** The chorus typically follows the presentation of one or more verses. Musically, it's generally a bit different from the verse, often using a different chord progression and sometimes hovering around a contrasting tonal center. It can be as short as a four-bar phrase or as long as multiple eight-bar phrases. Melodically, it's typically the most memorable part of the song, containing the "hook" that listeners remember long after. In fact, for most of the songs written before 1950, it's the *only* part that most people even know.
- **Bridge.** The bridge is kind of a break in the middle of the piece. Most bridges sound completely different from the verse and chorus, and are often based on a different harmonic structure; they serve as a kind of "intermission" before you move toward the song's finish. In addition, bridges typically are short; only about eight measures. (That's why a bridge is sometimes called the "middle eight" of a song.)

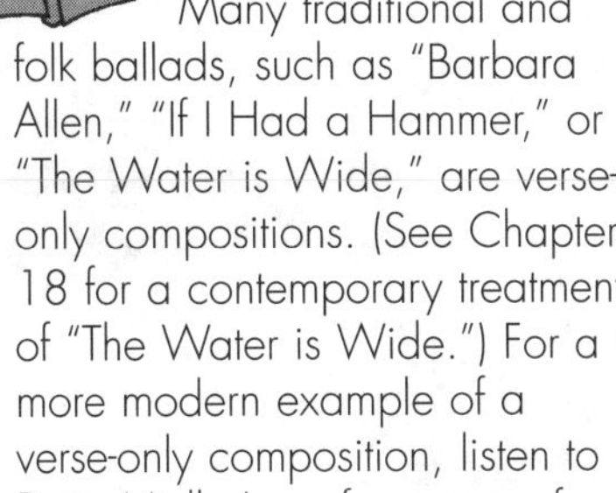

Note

Many traditional and folk ballads, such as "Barbara Allen," "If I Had a Hammer," or "The Water is Wide," are verse-only compositions. (See Chapter 18 for a contemporary treatment of "The Water is Wide.") For a more modern example of a verse-only composition, listen to Bette Midler's performance of "The Rose."

You can diagram a piece of music by assigning letters to each of these three sections. The verse is indicated by the letter A, the chorus by the letter B, and the bridge by the letter C. So if you have a song that includes one verse, a chorus, and another verse, it's diagrammed like this:

A B A

Three-part song form.

If you have a song with two verses, a chorus, a bridge, and another chorus, it's diagrammed like this:

A A B C B

Two verses, a chorus, a bridge, and another chorus.

It's important to know that these A-B-C song forms are often supplemented by a brief introduction (to set the musical mood) and instrumental solos in the middle (using the chords of either the verse or the chorus). Many modern songs don't end precisely at the end of a section, either; some "fade out" over a repeating verse or chorus or have a special ending tacked on to the end of the form.

The Art of Phrasing

Now that you know what a phrase is and how phrases are put together to form complete songs, let's look at what we as singers can do to best represent the composer's creation—or even give it our own "signature." That's right—it's time to talk about *phrasing*.

The art of phrasing involves nuances of tonal intensity, rhythm, dynamics, breathing, melodic and lyrical emphasis—in other words, all the elements of your singing style. You use any or all of these elements when you create your own unique vocal phrasing.

When it comes to phrasing, it helps to compare a musician to a carpenter. Just like a carpenter analyzes a set of blueprints, a musician analyzes the musical score. Both the carpenter and the musician then determine what tools (for the musician, the treatment of the score) are needed to do the job.

Before you develop your phrasing for a particular song, you have to analyze the song itself (which is another reason to learn about those blueprints we call song form). Here's what you need to do:

- Take a look at the song and break it into its component parts. Analyze the song structure, with attention to repeated or contrasting sections within the piece.
- Study the shape and contour of the song's melodic phrases and note the high (or low) points of the melody.
- Evaluate the sense of harmonic movement underlying the melody—in other words, the song's chord changes.
- Identify the important lyrics within each phrase.
- Study the song's phrase lengths, for breath considerations.
- Take a brief look at the song's general stylistic and contextual tendencies.

Once you've got a feel for the song, it's time to develop an approach to phrasing. To do this, you use a specific set of tools—which we'll discuss next.

Tip

Phrasing is also useful in making a mediocre song sound good—or at least better. Not all songs are created equal, after all; you won't always be singing a gem from the pen of a Gershwin or Sondheim. (These songs almost "sing themselves," they're so skillfully composed!) When it comes to making the most of what you're given to sing, good phrasing makes all the difference in the world.

Lyrical Emphasis

The first tool in your phrasing toolbox is lyrical emphasis. What do I mean? Here's an example.

Say this sentence:

"I don't believe a word of what you're saying."

Now, repeat it several times, emphasizing different words each time you repeat it. For example:

"*I* don't believe a word of what you're saying." (This implies you don't, but someone else may.)

"I don't *believe* a word of what you're saying." (This implies you just might consider it.)

"I don't believe a *word* of what you're saying." (This implies you really don't believe anything they're saying.)

"I don't believe a word of what you're *saying*." (This implies you might believe their intent, but not their words.)

You get the idea—how you say or sing something can affect the meaning, depending on the emphasis you place on certain words (lyrics) within a phrase. It's the same thing in music—and not just where lyrics are concerned.

Note

The Italian musical term for increasing the tempo is *accelerando*; the term for slowing down is *ritard*; and the term for playing with a flexible or "loose" beat is *rubato*.

Tempo Variations

A song's tempo greatly affects its mood, which influences the way you phrase your singing. By speeding up (*accelerando*) and slowing down (*ritard*) within a song, you can create a sense of intensity or drama that captures the listener's attention. Taking liberties with the tempo is also a pretty common technique in popular vocal music—especially with those big diva-style ballads.

Of course, the composer had a particular tempo in mind when he wrote the song, but you are certainly free to present your own "re-interpretation" of it. A lot of songs that were originally conceived as up-tempo pieces take on a real poignancy when performed as a ballad. A great example is "Someone to Watch Over Me"; Gershwin originally wrote this as a bouncy, almost flippant dance tune, but later rewrote it as a tender ballad. That change of tempo made all the difference.

Tip

You'll need to plan ahead and mark your breathing places in each song to coincide with the punctuation marks in the lyrics—so as not to break up or interrupt a phrase.

You can hear this for yourself by singing some of your favorite songs at different tempos. Remember that fast songs tend to be sung in a more percussive, conversational style, while ballads require smoother (*legato*) singing. Breath control becomes an issue too; in slow songs, you have long sustained phrases that need to sound smooth and connected.

Articulation and Legato

How we separate or connect the notes of a melody is an important element of phrasing. When you clearly separate the notes in a melody, you're said to *articulate* the notes. When you sing the notes together in a smooth line, you're said to be singing *legato*.

Articulating the Phrase

How do you sing in the more "conversational" style that is required of up-tempo songs? It's simple and somewhat intuitive; all you have to do is pay closer attention to the consonants of the lyrics, making them clear and crisp.

It's natural to make the words in a lyric a little more separated rather than connected, so they can be better understood. Think about it for a moment; you tend to sustain the tone on extended vowels and in ballads because you have time for all those nice, elongated words. But when the tempo is fast, the words seem to fly by, making it even more important to make yourself understood.

I tell my students to feel as much like they are telling a story as singing a song. Just remember that everything—words, breaths, tonal shadings, dynamic changes, and so on—happens faster as the tempo of a song increases. So make sure you have developed a definite game plan for your phrasing when you learn those faster songs.

Smooth Singing for Pop Ballads

As to legato phrasing, that smooth singing typical of today's pop ballads, remember that long notes provide a lot of freedom where phrasing is concerned. Unfortunately, too much freedom can be dangerous.

It's common to hear today's pop divas sing all around an extended note, seemingly playing the game of "I can sing 20 different notes on the same vowel sound!" This type of gospel-influenced embellishment is called a *melisma* and, if used sparingly, can be an effective phrasing tool. If it's overused, however (and I'm not naming any names …) it can be as annoying as a howling coyote on a moonlit night.

Remember that most of the great classic pop singers sang their songs relatively "straight." Think of Barbra Streisand, Judy Collins, Patsy Cline … nary a melisma among them. These great songstresses demonstrated the beauty of a pure melody, without unnecessary embellishments. So feel free to put your original stamp on a legato phrase, but please don't overdo it. When it comes to melismas in pop music, remember that *less is more*.

Rhythmic and Melodic Nuance

Other than in the classical genre, we aren't really expected to sing every note exactly as it appears on the score. Singers commonly change notes or rhythms of a song to convey their own style or interpretation of a tune—which, in a sense, is what phrasing is all about. I'm not talking about real improvisation here, but rather the small changes in the melody or note values that can add spice to the song and make it your own.

A good example of this is when the singer syncopates a tune by breathing on the downbeat rather than singing the note that was on that beat in the score. Here's an excerpt from the classic jazz tune "I Ain't Got Nobody (And Nobody Cares for Me)." In the first example the melody falls as written, firmly connected to the downbeat. In the second example, the melody starts (and continues) on the upbeat, providing a syncopated feel.

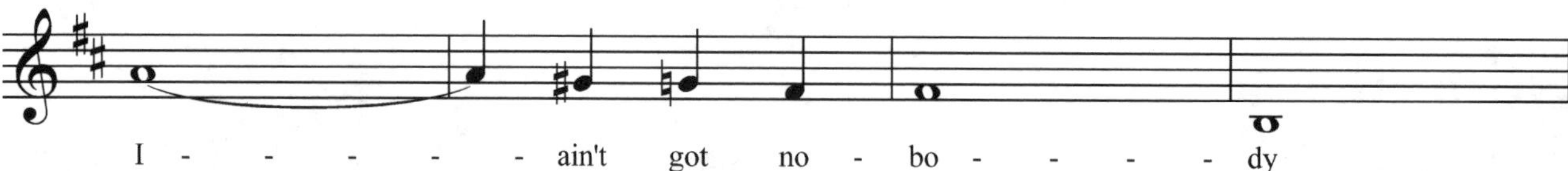

"I Ain't Got Nobody," sung straight.

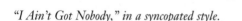

"I Ain't Got Nobody," in a syncopated style.

To hear examples of this type of rhythmic and melodic nuance, check out any album of "standards" sung by the great pop singers of yesterday and today—songs like "Lover Man," "Someone to Watch Over Me," and "I've Got Rhythm." Every singer will have his or her own approach to these songs, which shows how important this type of phrasing is to your individual performing style.

Tonal Shadings

Because music is so much about creating tension and release and since the voice is such an expressive vehicle, you can do a lot with tonal shadings to interject feeling into your singing. By tonal shadings, I mean things like putting more air in the tone, darkening or brightening it, intensifying vibrato, singing with a straight tone, or even adding a little "growl" for emphasis.

Tonal shadings in the voice reflect emotions in a very up-front way, so you should be cautious about their use. You've undoubtedly heard both good and bad examples of all these techniques, so I simply encourage you to listen to as many singers as possible, keeping an "open ear" for the impact they have on the singer's performance. Then you'll know how much or how little you'll want to use them in your own singing.

Note

This type of tonal shading isn't unique to pop music or musical theater; you'll even find it employed in classical opera as the drama of the scene dictates. It's common for the dying diva to color her notes with a gasp or a sigh to better portray her character's dilemma.

Dynamic Contrasts

Dynamics generally refers to the volume level of a piece of music. This can be in the context of a whole song or within an individual phrase. In other words, in the course of developing your phrasing, you can sing a song soft or you can sing it loud—that's the dynamic level.

Applying Dynamics to a Phrase

Dynamic shadings within a phrase are dependant upon the contour and shape of the melody. Sometimes the verbal accents—emphasized words or syllables—will determine the dynamic shading to be used. Either way, it's important for you to look at the tonal contour of the notes within a phrase and find the highest pitch or the most important word. These serve as target points for your singing; they provide clues to where the actual high point or climax of the phase is.

Normally, it's a sound artistic choice to start a phrase smoothly, build to a point of climax (in terms of loudness), then gently end it. I tell students to "set the phrase down gently," meaning to sing the end with less volume or intensity than you used at the climax.

If a fragment of a melody—or even a whole phrase—is repeated, there is often a chance for the singer to create interest through radical dynamic changes. This might mean repeating a chorus or phrase at a soft dynamic the second time it's presented or by reversing that order (going soft to loud). Either way, it's an effective phrasing tool.

> **Caution**
>
> One of the most common mistakes made by singers is to unnaturally "kick" the endings of phrases—usually because they are out of breath. You can avoid this mistake through careful preparation and study of the score. Mark the climax points in your music, and make sure you have enough breath to execute the climax *and* a controlled phrase ending.

Changing Your Volume

As you can see, you don't have to keep the same volume level throughout an entire piece of music. You can sing one phrase loud and another soft, and you can gradually change your volume level over the course of one or more measures—or even a few notes.

Singers often fail to remember a basic rule in music: *Music is motion*. Long notes shouldn't just "hang in the air," but should feel as if they are going someplace.

Long notes should gradually increase in volume (they *crescendo*). Sometimes, it's only a *sense* of increasing volume, but to whatever degree is necessary, you shouldn't allow long notes to die on the vine. Always feel the underlying motion and direction in the line of music you are singing. Make your long notes interesting!

> **Note**
>
> When you gradually increase your volume level, you're performing a *crescendo*. When you gradually *decrease* your volume level, you're performing a *decrescendo*.

Dynamic Markings

It's common for a composer or arranger to dictate the dynamic level intended for a specific song or phrase. This is done by the use of dynamic markings—either full Italian musical terms or common symbols and abbreviations. You should look for these dynamic markings when you first outline a piece of music, so you'll know where the loud and soft sections lay.

To help you recognize the loud and soft of it, Table 14.1 presents the most common dynamic markings found in today's vocal music:

Table 14.1 Common Dynamic Markings

Symbol	Term	Meaning
pp	pianissimo	Very soft
p	piano	Soft
mp	mezzopiano	Medium soft

continues

Table 14.1 Common Dynamic Markings (continued)

Symbol	Term	Meaning
mf	mezzoforte	Medium loud
f	forte	Loud
ff	fortissimo	Very loud

Other Vocal Markings

While we're talking about dynamic markings, let's address a few other musical terms and markings you're likely to encounter in your singing career. As you can see in Table 14.2, these are all Italian terms, and they provide instructions on how to address specific phrases or entire pieces of music.

Table 14.2 Other Common Vocal Terms Markings

Term	Looks Like	Means
crescendo	<	Gradually increase volume
decrescendo	>	Gradually decrease volume
accent	> (over note)	Sing the accented note louder than the surrounding notes
tenuto	– (over note)	Sing a note for its full duration; sing it long
staccato	. (over note)	Sing a note for less than its full duration; sing it short
diminuendo	dim.	Gradually growing softer
sotto voce	sotto voce	In an undertone; whispered
cantabile	cantabile	In a slow tempo; with a broadly phrased vocal line (literally, in a singing style)
legato	leg.	Smooth and connected
ritardando	rit.	Gradually slow down
accelerando	accel.	Gradually speed up
a tempo	a tempo	Return to the previous tempo
rubato	rubato	Expand or contract note values within a phrase

The Least You Need to Know

- A phrase is a discrete musical idea, typically four or eight measures in length.
- A piece of music is made up of multiple phrases, typically organized with a specific structure called a song form.
- Most songs are composed of one or more of the following elements: verse, chorus, and bridge.
- How you perform a specific musical phrase is called phrasing.
- You use the following vocal tools to develop your phrasing: lyrical emphasis, tempo variations, articulation and legato, rhythmic and melodic nuance, tonal shadings, and dynamic contrasts.
- The term "dynamics" refers to the volume levels in a piece of music.

Chapter 15

Learning and Practicing a Song

In This Chapter

- Learning how to mark the score
- Applying your analysis to a song
- Developing a practice plan
- Building your portfolio of music

So far in this book, we've been working to develop your vocal skills—and some of it's been real work! Even though all those vocal exercises are necessary, you're probably saying to yourself about now, "When do I get to *sing*?"

Well, now's the time!

This chapter starts the "good part" of the book, where you get to put all those new skills to real use—in a real song. So warm up those vocal chords, and get ready to sing!

How to Mark Your Music for Learning

Before you can sing, you need to prepare—you don't want to sing "blind" if you don't have to. In this case, preparation means reading through a piece of music beforehand and marking it up to help you sing your part properly.

Sure, you can learn a new song by simply listening to someone else's recording, but that's kind of a secondhand approach. It's better to approach a piece of music from the notes on the written page and then interpret the music in your own personal style—not like someone else sang it. That means you need to know how to read music, but then you already know how important that is. (And if you don't, you're not as serious about singing as you might think you are.)

Over the years, I've devised what I consider an efficient but thorough method for learning new pieces of music. Granted, it takes a little time and effort, but the end result is worth it; the payoff is a real sense of accomplishment and a more sensitive, artistic performance of the music.

Here's how to proceed, using the music for "Shenandoah" as a guide:

How to mark your music—before you sing a note!

Note

The full score for "Shenandoah" is found later in this chapter.

Tip

It's best to make any marks in pencil, since they may change as you become more comfortable with the piece of music.

1. Number each measure of the music for quick reference. It's quite likely that you'll need to refer to specific places in the music as you continue reading, practicing, or working with an accompanist. And you should start your numbering with the first full measure of the main vocal line—not in the introduction.
2. Read the key signature to establish Do. In the preceding example, the song is in the key of D. (Remember—read a sharp key signature as one half-step up from the last sharp.)
3. Write the Solfeggio syllable under each note.
4. Look at the rhythms in the music and determine the note that gets the beat or the pulse. In our example, it's the quarter note (which makes sense, as the time signature indicates we're in 4/4 time). You may want to put a slash mark where each beat falls, over the words.
5. Study the lyrics and decide where you should take your breaths, so as not to interrupt the lyrical or musical phrase. Remember to use the natural punctuation marks as a guide, then mark them on the music.
6. Look at the shape of each phrase. Is there a high point or climax? If so, you should mark it in your score. In the case of "Shenandoah," this first phrase's highest pitch occurs on "A-way" in measure 2. Because it's the highest pitch in the melody, you'll want to indicate it with something like the letters "PC" for "pitch climax." Remember this point in the music as you experiment with style and phrasing.

   The second phrase in our example tends to climax in measure eight—but not because of pitch. Remembering what you've learned about phrasing, can you find the elements that seem to *move* the phrase to the third beat of measure eight? If you noted the repetition of the lyric "a-way," the length of the note, and the harmonic movement underneath it—you're right! (And you're ready to take the next step …)

Taking the Next Step—Singing!

Once you've studied and marked your music, it's time to take the next step—singing it. I realize that you probably already know the folk song "Shenandoah," but I still want you to approach this song as if you had never heard it before. (Besides, there may be some slight differences between this particular arrangement and one you already know, so keep that in mind as you proceed.)

Shenandoah
Traditional
Arr. P. Fulford
Vocal
Piano
Oh
(So)
Shen - an - doah, I long to hear you, A - way, you roll - in
(Do) (Do) (Do) (Re) (Mi) (Fa) (So) (Mi) (Do) (Ti) (La)
ri - ver - - - Oh Shen - an - doah just to be near you, A -
way we're bound a - way, cross the wide Mis - sou - ri (Oh)
rit.
rit.

Reading music is like learning a new language—or worse! Reading a piece of music is almost like reading three different languages at once. You have to read the lyrics, read the pitches, and read the rhythms, all simultaneously. Just how are you supposed to cope with all that?

The answer is to break a piece of music into its component parts. It's up to you to determine which part to start with, since one element may be easier for you to comprehend than another.

The Rhythm

> **Caution**
>
> "Shenandoah" is an extremely simple piece, rhythm-wise. Don't expect every song to be this easy!

For our purposes, let's start by examining the rhythm. Begin by "saying" the rhythm of the melody (out loud), while tapping the pulse that you've marked in your score. Use the "whole, two, three, four," "walk," "running" system you learned in Chapter 12 —unless you can already read rhythmic notation, that is. If you *can* read the proper rhythms, just say those rhythms on a nonsense syllable like "la."

In the example of "Shenandoah," the rhythm of the first two measures of the melody (with the pickup note) sounds like this:

Walk / *Run*-ning, *walk*, (*run*)-ning, *run*-ning / *walk*, *half note*, *run*-ning /

We've italicized the syllable that falls on the beat, indicated tied notes with parentheses, and used slashes for the measure lines.

The Pitches

Now that you have the basic rhythm in your head, it's time to put the pitches in there, too. You can either find Do (D in the case of "Shenandoah") on an instrument or just pick a pitch out of the air—remember, Do is relative.

Now you should practice singing the pitches on the Solfeggio syllables you notated earlier, while trying to recall the rhythms as you do so.

The Lyrics

> **Note**
>
> The techniques presented in this chapter (and throughout this book) are good to get you started, but admittedly won't always serve you in more complex musical situations. Use these tips and suggestions as they are intended—as a practical and useful *beginning* for going as far as you care to go.

The final step is to transfer the Solfeggio syllables to actual lyrics, and congratulate yourself—you've just learned a song without having to listen to someone else sing or play it! You've actually read the rhythms, the notes, and the words—and all at once. So give yourself a big pat on the back; you've actually read the music.

And More ...

As you continue to learn new songs, I encourage you to do your very best to learn them on your own, using the techniques presented here. You can then try listening to recordings of each piece. The time you spend studying a song will help you later when you listen to other singers; you can then focus on particular places in the music that merit your attention.

Developing a Practice Discipline

You've heard the old joke. In the streets of New York City, one man walks up to another and asks how to get to Carnegie Hall. The other man answers: "Practice!"

Whether you dream of performing in Carnegie Hall, on a big rock stage, or in your church's sanctuary, that old joke still applies. It doesn't matter whether you're singing in a karaoke bar or on *American Idol*, if you want to be successful and feel good about your singing, you have to make practice a part of your daily discipline.

There are 24 hours in every day and 7 days in every week; how many of these hours should you set aside for the hard work of practice? The more the better, of course, although it all depends on your personal situation. If you're really serious about improving your voice, you should practice *some* amount every day—a minimum of 20 minutes, ideally.

I can already hear you saying, "But I'm too busy to practice!" You may have a 60-hour-a-week job or, even worse, you may have a 60-hour-a-week job and be a mother of three. Everybody has a hard time fitting practice into their daily schedule, but here are a few tips to make it a little easier to find the time to sing:

- Make it a habit. Vocal practice is a little bit like physical exercise; it gets easier the more often you do it. Just as you carve out time in your schedule for regular workouts or trips to the gym, schedule in *regular* vocal practice time. Once you get into the habit, you're doing it!
- Remember that "practice" is anything you do to promote and develop your singing skills. This means that breathing exercises, vocalises, score study, and even just listening to other singers can—and *should*—be considered practice. Your assignment: Find creative ways to incorporate practice into your busy schedule. You can study your musical score when you're riding in a car or subway. You can memorize lyrics when you're on the treadmill at the gym. You can listen to music all day long on a portable CD or MP3 player. And you don't need a piano or a CD to practice your sight singing or basic rhythmic studies—you can do breathing exercises virtually anyplace. (Just don't get too carried away—or you may actually be "carried away!") It's all practice!
- As for more "conventional" forms of practice, like working with the accompanying CD, or with a teacher, use the reproducible page in Appendix E to track your progress. This simple checklist will help you develop a practical practice plan—with a minimal time investment and maximal results.

Caution

As you get more into it, you may find that you'll want to spend more time practicing—but you want to be careful about overdoing it. I tell my students that three or four 30-minute sessions a week are far more productive than a single two-hour practice session. Singing for that long at a stretch is just too tough on the voice; besides, it's daily repetition that builds skills—not an all-night cram session!

Building Your Portfolio

As you begin to learn more songs, it's a good idea to develop a portfolio of the songs in your new repertoire.

There are many ways to do this. One of the most popular is to keep a notebook of the sheet music for your favorite songs. By keeping all your sheet music in one place, any song is at your fingertips when it's time to practice or perform—plus, it's right there to hand to an accompanist. You should also create (and maintain) a list of the songs in your portfolio on a single sheet of paper that you can provide at auditions. (You never know what they may want to hear!)

Tip

Make sure to clearly mark any special tempo or dynamic changes on the sheet music.

For your own reference, it's a good idea to write down your comments regarding various recordings of songs in your repertoire. You can insert a special page into your notebook for each song. This sheet is also a great place to jot down any other pertinent information regarding the song, such as who performed it and where it

> **Note**
> We'll look a little further into the kinds of songs you need to have in your portfolio in Chapter 24.

came from. (Is it a folk tune? Did it come from a musical?) With the wealth of recorded material out there today, it's easy to forget what artist's rendition you particularly liked (or hated) and which CD you found it on.

Finally, if you have the means, make a recording of three of your best songs in your portfolio and carry a copy with you. It's also a good idea to have just the accompaniment on tape or CD, in case you find yourself at an audition without a piano player.

The Least You Need to Know

- Before you attempt to sing a song, go through and mark your music with breath marks, beat marks, and anything else to help you in your performance.
- To learn a song, break it into its component parts—the rhythm, the pitches, and the lyrics.
- Practice makes perfect, so you should develop a daily practice discipline—at least 20 minutes a day.
- Remember that you can practice breathing and sight singing almost anywhere—you don't always need a piano or CD player nearby.
- Once you've learned a number of songs, create a notebook full of sheet music that you can take with you to auditions and performances.

Part 5

Singing in Style

Different types of music require different vocal techniques. Study this part to learn the ins and outs of choral singing; singing in the classical style; pop, rock, and country singing; jazz singing; and gospel and R&B singing. (And then sing along with all the different types of songs on the accompanying audio CD!)

Chapter 16

Choral Singing

In This Chapter

- Understanding the differences between solo and ensemble singing
- Discovering different types of choral ensembles
- Observing proper rehearsal etiquette
- Learning how to read a choral score
- Practicing an ensemble piece

The only thing that's more fun than singing is singing *with other people*. If one voice alone can sound angelic, many voices together can sound heavenly.

Singing together with other vocalists can be very rewarding, but it's also a challenge. You have to learn how to blend in with the group, rather than stand out as a soloist. You also need to learn how to read a choral score and how to follow a conductor. Neither one is the easiest thing in the world.

This chapter gives you some tips on how to become a valued member of a vocal ensemble—whether that's a barbershop quartet or the Mormon Tabernacle Choir. Read on to learn how to sing in a group and how to fit in with the other singers!

Learning to Fit In

So far in this book, we've dealt with issues like breathing, focus, and diction—all techniques used by fine vocal soloists. When it comes to singing in a choir, these same techniques come into play; good singing technique is good singing technique, whether you're singing solo or in a group. The big difference, then, between solo and ensemble singing is a thing we call *blend*.

Every voice is unique and has its own distinct tone quality, which is a very good thing. However, an overly distinct or unique voice placed in a group can be a very bad thing. When you sing with others, you have to give up a little bit of yourself—musically, that is—in order to blend in with the other voices. The audience wants to hear one smooth vocal whole, not an amalgamation of individual soloists. So you have to learn to fit in to create that whole.

Here's a good way to think of it. Ensemble singers have to be more like the strings on a guitar or the keys (actually the strings) on a piano. Sure, each string or key is a different pitch, but they share a similar tone quality. When chords are played on either instrument, they sound beautiful because their individual strings blend together as a single "voice."

Can you imagine how bad it would sound if just one of the keys on the piano (or strings on a guitar) had the timbre of a pipe organ? It would be as jarring as a choir with one ill-fitting voice that didn't blend with the whole. You and your fellow singers have to work together to create a single voice, a single instrument, a single *choir*.

That's the challenge.

So how do you "blend" your voice into a vocal ensemble? Here are some of the things you need to do:

Tip

Since it's sometimes difficult to hear your own voice when in an ensemble situation, you may need to lightly cover one ear as you sing to better monitor how your voice is sounding in relation to others.

- Listen. Listen. Then listen some more. Listening is critical for all musicians, but particularly so when you're singing (or playing) in an ensemble. Pay close attention to the tonal subtleties of the other voices and try to fit your tone to theirs—not theirs to you.
- Always sing on pure vowels. Everyone in an ensemble has to pronounce the words—particularly vowel sounds—*exactly* the same. We call this "vowel unification," and it's one of the primary means of achieving vocal blend.
- Back off on the volume level. Remember, you don't want to be louder than everyone else in the choir—no matter how beautiful your voice is. You are not in an ensemble to show others how well *you* sing. (And if you think you are, you may not be for long!)
- Surrender your personal singing style—which is sometimes a sticky point. Many singers have gone to great lengths to develop their own singing style. Many singing styles are heavily influenced by today's popular music, and while this kind of style might get you rave reviews at the local karaoke bar, it won't cut it in a choral ensemble. This doesn't mean you have to sing like a voice synthesizer; just leave those vocal "flips" and "scoops" at home when you go to choir rehearsal.
- Be very sensitive and judicious with your vibrato. Yes, vibrato gives your voice color and life, but it can also be one of the biggest stumbling blocks to achieving vocal blend. So when you're singing in a vocal ensemble, use a little less vibrato than you would as a soloist.

Remember, the goal of an ensemble vocalist is to make the ensemble sound good—which means learning to sing like the others in your ensemble. There is much satisfaction to come from creating a pleasing choir sound—but if you want personal recognition, you should pursue a solo singing situation, instead.

Types of Choral Ensembles

The term "ensemble" is a French word meaning "together." There are many different kinds of ensembles when it comes to making vocal music—so let's look at some of the most common.

Trio

A vocal trio is just what it says—three voices. In the classical genre, trio music is typically written for female voices (soprano, second soprano, and alto), although trios in pop music can consist of all female, all male, or mixed voices.

For some good examples of vocal trios in pop music, check out some of these readily available CDs:

- The Andrews Sisters: *50th Anniversary Collection, Vols. 1 & 2* (1990)
- The Dixie Chicks: *Home* (2002)
- The Kingston Trio: *Capital Collector's Series* (1990)
- The Lettermen: *Capital Collector's Series* (1992)
- Peter, Paul and Mary: *The Collection: Their Greatest Hits and Finest Performances* (1998)
- The Roches: *The Roches* (1979)
- Dolly Parton, Linda Ronstadt, and Emmylou Harris: *Trio* (1987)

Quartet

A quartet is a four-voice ensemble. In classical music (and some pop and jazz), the breakdown is standard SATB—soprano, alto, tenor, and bass. Of course, you can have all-female or all-male quartets, like those in barbershop quartets. But the mixed-voice quartet is the most popular.

Regardless of style or voicing, quartet singing demands a lot from its members. However, many singers consider the vocal quartet to be the ultimate ensemble experience.

There are lots of great examples of quartet singing in popular music, as you can tell by listening to any of the following recordings:

- The Mills Brothers: *The Anthology* (1968)
- The Four Freshmen: *Capital Collector's Series* (1991)
- The Nylons: *The Best of the Nylons* (1993)
- Manhattan Transfer: *The Very Best of the Manhattan Transfer* (1994)
- Boyz II Men: *Legacy: The Greatest Hits Collection* (2001)

Also cool are the four- (and more) part harmonies on many of the Beach Boys records, especially *Pet Sounds* (1966) and *Surfer Girl* (1963).

Chamber Choir

A chamber choir is a small choir, normally with 12 to 24 singers, typically performing repertoire from the sixteenth and seventeenth centuries. There are also some fabulous modern chamber choirs that sing everything from Renaissance music to jazz, as noted in the following recordings:

- The King's Singers: *20th Anniversary Celebration* (1990)
- Chanticleer: *Out of This World* (1994)
- Chanticleer: *Colors of Love* (1999)

Note

The term "chamber" comes from the idea that the group was small enough to perform in private residences (chambers) rather than large concert halls.

Madrigal Choir

Another common vocal chamber group is the madrigal choir. The madrigal is a form of choral music that was popular in Europe primarily in the sixteenth century. It is usually sung without accompaniment (a cappella), and its lyrics often deal with human conditions like love or romping in the grass.

The continued popularity of the madrigal is due in part to the theater that surrounds it—the colorful Renaissance costumes, the quaint traditions, and (lest we forget) the food. Chances are, you've either heard about or attended a madrigal dinner during the Christmas holidays. If so, you know how entertaining the madrigal tradition can be.

Madrigal singing itself requires highly developed vocal skills. That's because madrigal music is quite complex, with intricately interweaving vocal lines and constantly shifting harmonies. If you want to listen to some great madrigal singing without the dinner and costumes, check out these CDs:

- The King's Singers: *All at Once Well Met: English Madrigals* (1990)
- Quink Vocal Ensemble: *English Madrigals* (1993)
- John Rutter and the Cambridge Singers: *Olde English Madrigals and Folk Songs at Ely Cathedral* (1990)

Large Vocal Ensembles

We'll call almost any choir or chorus a large vocal ensemble. You may have sung in such a choir in high school or college or in church. These choirs can be of any size and composition—while mixed-voice is most common, there are also many popular all-male and all-female choruses.

Choirs can represent any level of expertise and can embrace a wide variety of music, from the classical repertoire to the latest pop hits. Whether you choose to sing with a school choir, a "glee club," a church choir, a community choir, or a choir that performs with a professional symphony, know that singing with other musicians in a choir is one of the most beneficial and satisfying things you can do as a singer.

Rehearsal Etiquette

Please excuse my enthusiasm for the vocal ensemble format; 30 years of choir directing will do that to you. Still, I hope I've convinced you to check your local paper for choral audition notices, or at least call up your church choir director and get involved in a singing ensemble of some sort.

Once you become a member of a group of like-minded musicians, there are a few points of etiquette that need to be addressed. After all, things work a bit different when you aren't going solo.

Here are some points to keep in mind:

- Always be in your seat or in place before the rehearsal starts. It's very distracting to everyone else when someone comes in late for a rehearsal. If you can't be on time, it's probably better to sit in the back and observe until the conductor offers a break. At the very least, wait to quietly move to your seat between numbers—not during the middle of a song.
- Come prepared. That means practicing your part at home, as much as you need to. (Remember, the conductor is there to rehearse the choir as a whole—*not* to teach you your individual part.)
- Before the rehearsal, number each measure of your score to help you find your place during practice. In addition, bring a pencil along to rehearsal to mark any dynamic changes or breath marks that your conductor may indicate.
- Keep any comments or social chatter to an absolute minimum. The time to socialize is before or after rehearsal, not while you're singing. Also, remember that the appropriate time for questions or comments to the director is before or after the rehearsal, or possibly during a break. Don't interrupt the entire group with your personal observations or problems.
- Be flexible in your musical judgment. In an ensemble situation, things won't always be exactly to your liking; you're just an "employee" here, and the director is the "boss." That means the ultimate artistic interpretation and presentation is the responsibility of the director, and it's your job to implement his or her vision as accurately as possible.

- Do your best to develop positive relationships with other members of the group. Group dynamics have a significant effect on the musical outcome, so always try to be a good team player.

Reading a Choral Score

Music is written a little differently when multiple voices are involved. If you're used to reading a "lead sheet" with solo vocal on one staff and accompaniment (typically piano) on another, be aware that music for a vocal ensemble has to notate multiple vocal lines.

There are two primary ways to notate music for a choir—*closed score* and *open score*. Open score notation, illustrated below, shows the soprano and alto parts on one line, and the tenor and bass/baritone parts on another. (This is similar to the way most hymns in your church hymnal are notated.) In closed score notation the soprano notes generally have the note stems above the note head and the alto notes have their stems below the note head. The same is true for the tenor (above) and bass (below) notation.

Closed score choral notation.

When the individual vocal lines get more complex, you'll see each part notated on its own staff, as shown next. This type of notation is also called SATB, for soprano, alto, tenor, bass.

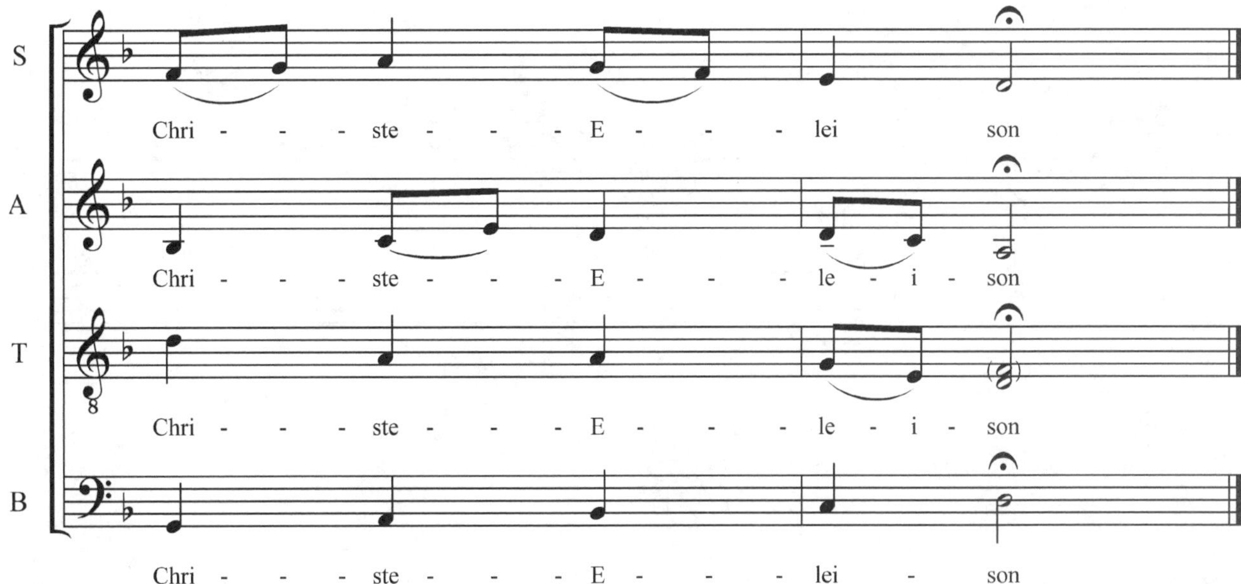

Open score choral notation.

Kyrie

Phyllis Fulford

2
Kyrie

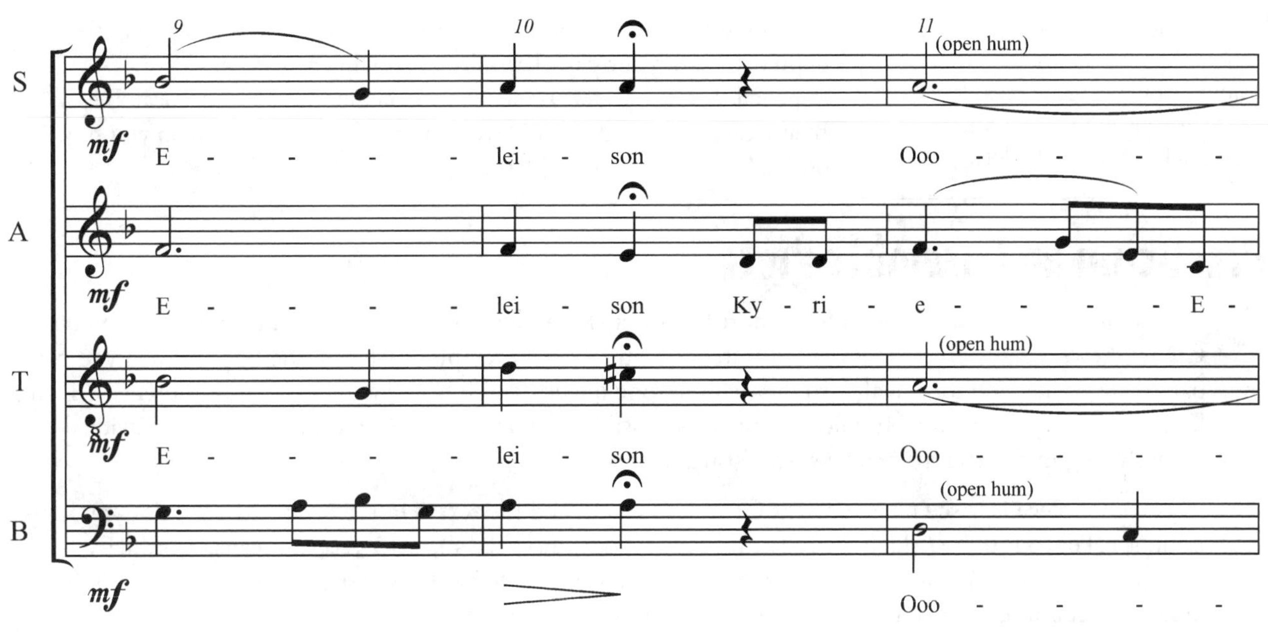
S
A
T
B
9
10
11
(open hum)
mf
E - - - - lei - son
Ooo - - - - -
mf
E - - - - lei - son Ky - ri - e - - - - E -
(open hum)
mf
E - - - - lei - son
Ooo - - - - -
(open hum)
mf
Ooo - - - - -

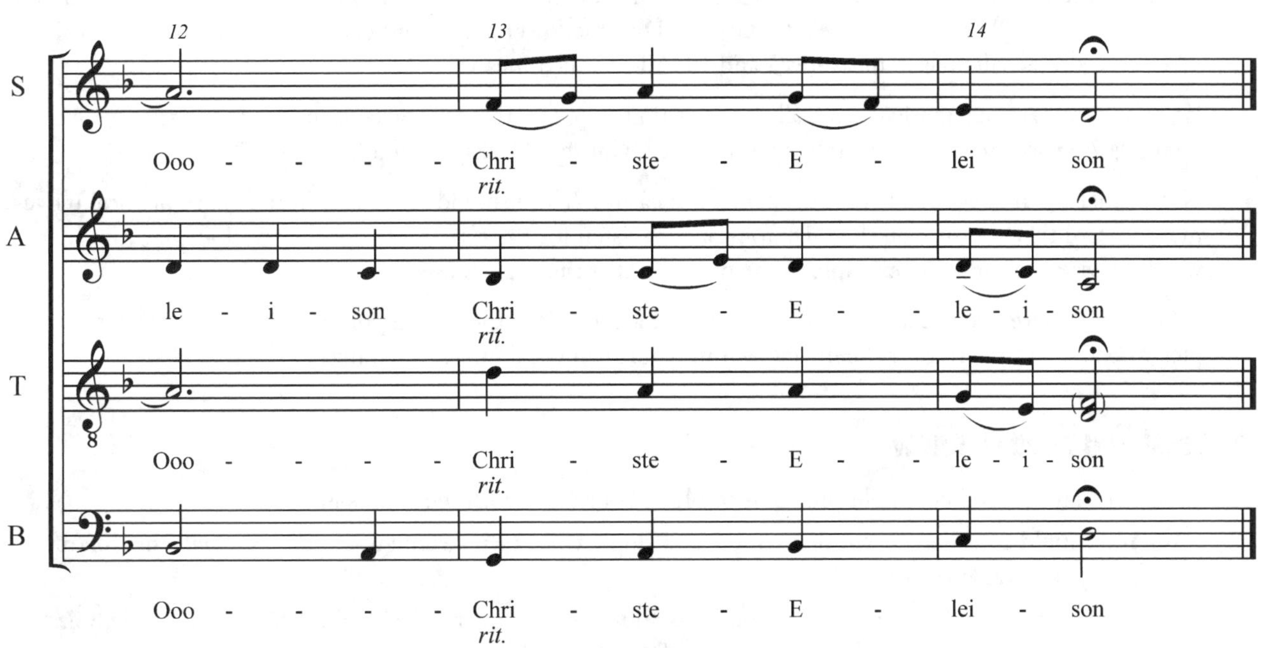
12
13
14
Ooo - - - - Chri - ste - E - lei son
rit.
le - i - son Chri - ste - E - - le - i - son
rit.
Ooo - - - - Chri - ste - E - - le - i - son
rit.
Ooo - - - - Chri - ste - E - lei - son
rit.

Caution

Tenors have it rough. Their parts are written in the bass clef in closed scores and in the treble clef in open scores. If you're a tenor, this means you have to be familiar with both clefs!

Following a choral score is a little more difficult than just reading a lead sheet or other type of solo music. So when you find yourself in an ensemble, it's a good idea to mark your particular voice part in the score, in some fashion. If you own the music, you can use a highlighter to mark your part. If you're borrowing a score, it's better to pencil in small arrows or stars at the beginning of your vocal line. In any case, you want to mark your part on each page to help you stay on track.

Practicing an Ensemble Piece

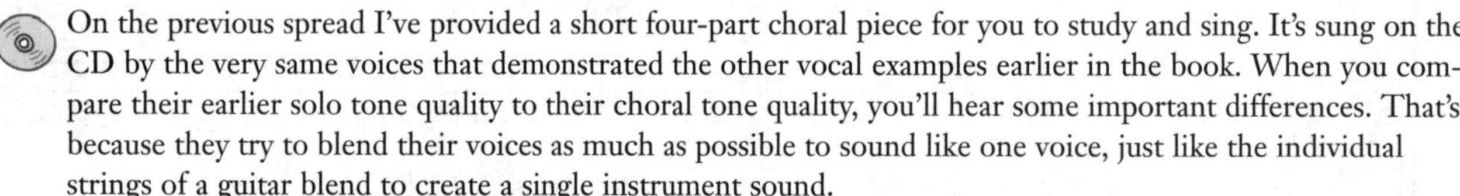

On the previous spread I've provided a short four-part choral piece for you to study and sing. It's sung on the CD by the very same voices that demonstrated the other vocal examples earlier in the book. When you compare their earlier solo tone quality to their choral tone quality, you'll hear some important differences. That's because they try to blend their voices as much as possible to sound like one voice, just like the individual strings of a guitar blend to create a single instrument sound.

This choral piece is based on an ancient Gregorian chant, and the text is in the original Latin. For you non-Latin speakers out there (which is pretty much everybody, these days!), *Kyrie Eleison* means "Lord have mercy," and *Christe Eleison* means "Christ have mercy." The Kyrie has been a regular part of the Catholic liturgy for centuries and is still sung in many church services today.

When you first glance at the score, you'll see that the key signature seems to indicate F Major. Look closer, however, and you'll see that the melody starts on D in the lower voices and ends on D in the soprano voice. There are also accidentals in measures 3 and 10. All of which means …?

If you remember your music theory, all this adds up to the fact that this piece is in D minor—the relative minor of F major. So when you sight sing the piece, you should assign Do to the note D.

Notice that the highest points of pitch come in measure 7. You should be able to hear a sense of vocal movement toward that measure on the CD. You can also listen for the rise and fall of the vocal lines within the words "Kyrie Eleison"—an example of the phrasing that the singers use.

All that said, here's your chance to be a member of a choir. Pop the CD in your CD player and take your pick of parts. Even better: Try them all—within your own vocal range, of course.

The Least You Need to Know

- The key to good ensemble singing is to blend your voice with the others in the choir.
- You should consider the vocal ensemble as a single voice or instrument—not as an amalgamation of wildly individual voices.
- There are many different types of vocal ensembles—trios, quartets, chamber choirs, madrigal choirs, and large choirs, all of which can be musically and socially rewarding.
- When you're practicing your part in an ensemble, it helps to mark your part, using a pencil or highlighter. (This way you won't get lost in the middle of a piece—and start singing someone else's part!)

Chapter 17

Classical and Musical Theater

In This Chapter

- Discovering the roots of the classical style
- Comparing classical singing to musical theater
- Learning how to sing an art song

There are many different types of music, each of which requires a different style of singing. A good country singer sounds different from a Broadway belter, who sounds different from a smooth jazz vocalist, who sounds different from an opera virtuoso, who sounds different from a pop balladeer. Still, good singers of all stripes share the same basic vocal techniques and benefit from the same training and discipline—even if *what* they sing varies wildly from one genre to the next.

The principles of good vocal technique inherent in the classical tradition form the foundation for all good singing, regardless of style. So all the techniques you've been learning as you work through this book apply no matter what type of music you're singing. Good technique is good technique.

That said, it's useful to pay particular attention to classical singing in general—and opera, in particular. A skilled classical singer should have all the technique necessary to sing in any other style, which is why so many serious singers start with classical music and then migrate to other genres.

So let's take a quick look at classical singing and its surprisingly close cousin—the musical theater.

The Roots of Classical Singing

There are three primary types of classical singing:

- *Lieder*, a small recital format where the singer is accompanied by a piano
- Oratorio, a concert format for soloists, choir, and orchestra
- Opera, a theatrical blend of music (in the classical style) and drama

Note

Lieder is German for "songs." The singular of lieder is lied.

Of these forms, opera is the most universal. It gained prominence as an art form way back in 1600 and long ago became the standard by which all other forms of singing are judged.

Now, before you turn up your nose and put down this book, please realize that my intent is *not* to turn you into an opera singer—it's to turn you into a *good* singer, period. You may love opera or you may run for cover at the sheer mention of it, but every serious singer needs to have an understanding of the operatic style. It's that important, whether you like the music or not.

I realize that opera may not be everyone's cup of tea, but at one time it was about the only beverage being served. Opera was definitely the "popular music" of its day, and people just couldn't get enough of it—especially in Europe.

Europeans have had a long love affair with opera. Italy, especially, produced a large number of great operatic composers—Verdi, Puccini, Rossini, and so on. In many ways, opera is to Italians what the NFL is to Americans. It's not that Americans generally dislike opera, we just happen to like our music to be understandable in our mother tongue. (And if the music accompanies a play, we like at least some of the dialogue to be spoken, not sung—which is where American musical theater comes in, as we'll discuss later in this chapter.)

Note

The singing lessons in this book are based on the same techniques studied by classical singers for centuries.

The point is, opera isn't an art form for the elite. In other countries and in other times, opera has been an art form for the people. And, more important to our discussion, it's an art form performed by highly skilled singers—singers who we all can learn from, no matter what type of music we really like.

Opera to Listen To

If you're serious about the art of singing, you should spend some time listening to the great opera singers of our day. Start with sure bets like Thomas Hampson, Bryn Terfel, Placido Domingo, Frederica von Stade, Kiri Te Kanawa, Renée Flemming, or Cecelia Bartoli. These singers are the Tiger Woods of the singing world, each possessing a remarkable mastery of their instrument.

Tip

While today's classical singers are terrific, you should also take a listen to the "vintage wine" of the opera world—singers such as Luciano Pavarotti, Maria Callas, Joan Sutherland, and Beverly Sills.

Here are a few suggestions for your listening library:

- *Il Barbiere di Siviglia* (Rossini's *The Barber of Seville*); Erich Leinsdorf (conductor) with Roberta Peters, Cesare Valletti, Robert Merrill, and Giorgio Tozzi (RCA, 1958)
- *Le Nozze di Figaro* (Mozart's *The Marriage of Figaro*); James Levine (conductor) with Kiri Te Kanawa, Dawn Upshaw, Anne Sofie von Otter, and Thomas Hampson (Deutsche Grammophon, 1990)

- *Bryn Terfel: Opera Arias* (arias from *The Marriage of Figaro*, *Don Giovanni*, *The Magic Flute*, and other popular operas) (Deutsche Grammophon, 1994)
- *The Three Tenors in Concert 1994* (José Carreras, Placido Domingo, and Luciano Pavarotti) (Atlantic, 1994)
- *James Levine's 25th Anniversary Gala* (with guests Bryn Terfel, Renée Fleming, Plácido Domingo, Samuel Ramey, Kiri Te Kanawa, Grace Bumbry, Frederica von Stade, and Anne Sofie van Otter) (Deutsche Grammophon, 1996)

Everything Old Is New Again: The Re-Emergence of the Classical Style

As a voice teacher, I've been very happy over the past few years to witness an increase in popularity of the classical style of singing. This newfound popularity started with the Three Tenors performances and recordings and accelerated with Andrew Lloyd Webber's operatic *Phantom of the Opera*, featuring Michael Crawford and Sarah Brightman. Later, Charlotte Church served as a lovely model for young ladies and Josh Groban made them swoon with his appearances on *Ally McBeal* and *Oprah*. And today, most culturally savvy music lovers own at least one CD by the Tuscan tenor, Andrea Bocelli; he's released five multi-platinum discs to date.

All of these artists have done a stellar job of bringing the classical style of singing to the masses—and bravo to that! Just remember that these artists, as great as they are, aren't the only representatives or the ultimate expression of the classical style. So if you're a Brightman or Bocelli fan, branch out—and listen to some of the true classics I listed earlier.

Crossing Over to Musical Theater

By now you should recognize that the elements of projection, focus, breath control, and articulation are key components in the classical style of singing and that these are obvious techniques exhibited in opera and other classical styles of singing. But there is another, more accessible venue for the classical style of singing. It's called musical theater.

That's right—the Broadway musical is America's answer to European opera. Singing in a musical requires tremendous range, diction, breath control, and dramatic ability—just as the best operas do, but in English instead of Italian. It's a technically difficult singing form that takes years to master, but the top Broadway singers are among the most skilled vocalists performing today.

The Musical Theater Repertoire

Not only does musical theater exemplify the pinnacle of vocal technique, it also provides an almost unlimited repertoire for singers. It's hard to recall any well-known song written before 1960 or so that didn't find its origin in musical theater.

Just take a look at these so-called standards that have been covered by popular singers and great jazz artists for decades. Every one was written for the theater stage: "Embraceable You," "Someone To Watch Over Me," "Summertime," "My Funny Valentine," "Mack the Knife," "All the Things You Are," "Isn't It Romantic?," "The Lady Is a Tramp," "Bewitched, Bothered, and Bewildered," "My Romance," "Send In the Clowns" … and the list goes on and on. These are the best songs from some of the best songwriters of the twentieth century—George and Ira Gershwin, Cole Porter, Irving Berlin, Richard Rodgers and Oscar Hammerstein (and Lorenz Hart), and too many more to mention. When it comes to finding a great song to sing, your search needs to include the repertoire of the American musical theater.

Singing in Musical Theater

Musical theater not only supplies you with a wealth of great songs to sing, it also provides an exciting venue for you as a performer. Most communities have amateur theater groups, many of which stage musicals on a regular basis. Most musicals have large singing casts, so there's probably a place for you somewhere in the chorus. All you have to do is audition.

You'll find that performing in a musical is a richly rewarding experience. You may or may not eventually find yourself in a leading role, but regardless, you will learn a lot about singing and connecting with an audience. Since all singers need to have a bit of actor in them to "deliver" a song, your local community theater is a wonderful place to hone those skills.

When you prepare a song that comes from a musical, you should prepare just as if you were acting the role it was written for. That means you need to research the context of the music—and watch a performance of that musical, if at all possible. Who (what character) sang the song—and why? What is the overall mood or purpose of the song? How does the song advance the plot?

Tip

If you can't get to a live performance of a particular musical, there's always the movie. Many of the best Broadway musicals have been made into movies, and most of these are available on DVD or videotape.

You also shouldn't be afraid to use your imagination. You may find that one particular tone quality is more appropriate than another because it better reflects the personality of the character singing the song. It's even okay if you want to sing the lyrics in the character's onstage dialect.

All of this is acceptable in musical theater—which is probably why it's so much fun for us singers. After all, we all have a little "ham" in us. Body language and facial expression also play major roles in the delivery of these show tunes, so it's a good idea to practice in front of a mirror. If you aren't entertaining to watch, it's very likely that people won't notice your technical abilities.

Listening to Musical Theater

When it comes to the Broadway musical, here are some of the best recordings to listen to, featuring some of the biggest stars of stage and screen—including Julie Andrews, Shirley Jones, Nathan Lane, Gordon MacRae, Mandy Patinkin, Bernadette Peters, and Brian Stokes Mitchell:

- *Camelot* (original 1961 Broadway cast; Sony, 1998 reissue)
- *Carousel* (1956 film soundtrack; Angel, 2001 reissue)
- *Guys and Dolls* (1992 Broadway revival cast; RCA, 1992)
- *Into the Woods* (original 1987 Broadway cast; RCA, 1990 reissue)
- *Kiss Me, Kate* (1999 Broadway revival cast; DRG, 2000)
- *Les Miserables: A Concert at Royal Albert Hall* (10th anniversary performance; Relativity, 1996)
- *Man of La Mancha* (original 1965 Broadway cast; Polygram, 2001 reissue)
- *My Fair Lady* (original 1956 Broadway cast; Sony, 1990 reissue)
- *Oklahoma!* (original 1943 Broadway cast; Polygram, 2000 reissue)
- *Sunday in the Park with George* (original 1984 Broadway cast; RCA, 1990 reissue)
- *West Side Story* (original 1957 Broadway cast; Sony, 1998 reissue)
- *Wonderful Town* (studio recording conducted by Simon Rattle; Angel, 1999)

Singing an Art Song

Now let's take a step back from the Broadway stage and learn a little *lieder*—a vocal solo in the classical style. For your practice, I've selected a beautiful but simple art song by Johannes Brahms. (Yeah, he's the same guy who wrote that famous lullaby, along with a lot of other lasting works.) The song, "Below in the Valley," appears at the end of this chapter.

Lieder is an important art form for serious singers. Classical singers have made *lieder* by Brahms, Schubert, Schumann, and other great composers the meat and potatoes of their repertoire for over a century.

The original text of "Below in the Valley" is in German, but I've provided a modern English translation that captures the tender feelings behind the lyrics. The original German lyrics are shown in the second half of the score, in case you want to sing along in the native language.

When you listen to this song on the CD, note how clearly our singer, Dr. Mitzi Westra, enunciates the text, both in the English and the German versions. She follows the notation and the words precisely as written, and each note is sung "straight," without any scoops or flips in the voice. The simplistic beauty of the song stands on its own without the need for vocal embellishment; variety and emphasis are achieved through dynamic shadings and subtle phrasing. This, in a nutshell, is the essence of the classical art song technique.

Note

One of the difficulties in translating a foreign text is keeping the meaning of the original words intact while substituting new words that follow the rhythms of the melody. Since the melody and the lyrics share center stage in art songs, it's always better to sing them in the original language, if you can.

The Least You Need to Know

- All good vocal technique comes from a classical foundation.
- The three primary types of classical singing are lieder, oratorio, and opera.
- Opera is a theatrical combination of classical singing and drama.
- Musical theater is extremely similar to classical singing—and requires the same depth of technique.

Below in the Valley

English translation by
Phyllis Fulford

Johannes Brahms

2
Below in the Valley
8
9
10
11
keep
too
12
13
14
1:Da - - - un - ten im Ta - le läuft's Was - ser so
2:Sprichst all - weil von Lieb', - - - sprichst all - weil von
15
16
17
18
trüb und i kann dir's nit sa - gen, i hab' di so
Treu', und a bis - se - le Falsch - heit is au wohl da -
19
20
21
22
lieb
bei!

Chapter 18

Pop, Rock, and Country

In This Chapter

- Discover the differences between classical and popular singing
- Learn how to be a pop or rock singer
- Find out how country singing differs from pop and rock singing
- Learn how to sing a big pop ballad

If you want to make it really big in the music business, you have to be a popular singer—that is, a singer of what is typically called popular music. There are many different types of popular music, but the most popular today are pop, rock and roll, and country.

Many aspiring popular vocalists hear their favorite singers on the radio and say, "I want to sing just like that—why do I need to learn all that classical stuff?" That's a fair question, and one not always easily answered. When you hear some popular singers—especially in the rock genre—you don't hear a lot of classical training. But then again, many popular singers are extremely well trained, and you can tell the difference. If all you want to do is scream at the top of your lungs in a garage band, then you probably don't need to read any further. But if you want to be a *real* singer—pop, rock, country, or whatever—then you need to train your voice. At its best, popular music is every bit as demanding as classical music; if you want to be a singer's singer in your chosen style, you'll need to train for the part.

Popular vs. Classical Singing: What's the Difference?

The truth of the matter is that a good popular singer needs to be as well trained as any classical singer. That's because popular singing isn't all that different from classical singing. In fact, the major difference between classical and popular singing is one of diction, not of technique. You can find a lot of popular singers with terrific classical technique; what's different is how they use that technique, in service to the popular song.

Put another way—most classically trained singers have little or no trouble crossing over to popular music. Untrained popular singers find it quite difficult to sing in the classical style.

Understanding Popular Singing Styles

That's not to say that classical singing and pop singing are identical; they're not. One thing that distinguishes popular from classic singing is the importance of the lyric. Popular music places a tremendous emphasis on the interpretation of the text—more so, in many cases, than on the melody. Many popular singers, in interpreting a song, follow the dynamics of speech rather than strictly following the melody. Their voices are often lower-pitched, in more of a talking than a singing style. (Think Bob Dylan here.)

Caution

When you're listening to your favorite pop and rock singers, don't confuse the singer with the song. It's often the song itself or the particular recording that you like, regardless of the singer's talent or technique. Let's face it; popular music is often more about entertaining than it is about singing, so it's easy to confuse a great production with great singing.

This conversational style is made possible by the use of the microphone. Dramatic vocal and musical stylings are achieved by using varying amounts of breath or nasality in the tone. Because the microphone (and the accompanying sound system) supplies the volume, the singer doesn't have to concentrate on intensity, focus, or projection—just the words and the tune.

Other popular singers pull out all the stops, using a full voice across the registers and a clear, classical tone. This type of singing is most common among so-called pop divas, who like to show off their vocal technique whenever possible. These divas' propensity to embellish a melody, while derived from the gospel tradition, is not dissimilar to the vocal embellishment in Italian opera. They're apt to use melismas, mordents, turns, slurs, rubato, and other embellishments, even when not written into the music, in order to "personalize" their performances.

Tip

To hear a great example of gospel-influenced vocal enhancement, listen to Chaka Khan singing "My Funny Valentine" on the *Ultimate Divas* CD (1999)—a terrific performance.

Still other popular singers embrace rock and country's R&B roots by introducing African-American blues phrasing into their singing. These singers tend to bend and slur their notes in imitation of old-time blues singers; they're also apt to sing in a head voice and fuzz their diction. (This is true of a lot of male hard rockers, and even a lot of blues-influenced Brits—including Mick Jagger and Van Morrison.)

As you can see, what we call popular music is actually lots of different types of music, sung by lots of different types of singers. While some singers eschew the sound associated with classical singing technique, others wield their technique like a proud sword. In popular music, it's as much about a singer's personality as it is about his or her technique.

Using the Microphone

The one thing all popular singers have in common, however, is the microphone. It's the microphone that enables the popular singer to focus more on the lyrics and less on projecting to the last seat in the auditorium. Learning how to use a microphone is an extremely important part of learning how to be a popular singer; the best vocalists know how to use the microphone to achieve all manner of vocal effects.

Of course, the microphone is a sensitive device that amplifies what it hears. In this manner, it exposes both good and bad vocal technique. So a poorly trained singer can't expect his voice to suddenly sound better when he uses a microphone; good singing will come through, with or without a mic.

Note

Learn how to use a microphone in Chapter 23.

So the bottom line is this: The best training for singing pop, rock, or country music is to first learn to sing in a classical style. Everything you learn in a classical vein can then be applied to your later pop efforts.

Singing Pop and Rock Music

Pop music and rock and roll are two different but closely related genres. True pop music (not "popular" music) is derived from the musical theater tradition and the "standards" of the pre-1950s era—the music of Gershwin and Porter and their ilk. Rock music, on the other hand, is born of the rhythm and blues tradition and is more raw and gritty than its more cultured pop cousin. The two styles are interrelated, however, with most of today's pop having a rock and roll beat, and much current rock music having definite pop sensibilities.

Singing either type of music, of course, requires similar technique. Read on to learn how to adapt a classical technique to the pop and rock genres.

How to Sing Pop and Rock

Singing pop music isn't that far removed from singing Broadway musical tunes, which you learned back in Chapter 17. A solid background in classical singing will serve you well, as long as you adapt your technique to work well with a microphone.

Singing rock and roll can be a bit different. Good vocal technique still holds, but you have to modify your phrasing to sing *around* the other instruments. There's no way your voice can out-sing a screaming lead guitar, so you have to learn to place your voice in between the other instruments.

With some significant exceptions, most pop and rock vocalists are baritones, tenors, and altos; you seldom hear deep basses or high sopranos on hit recordings. The exceptions are notable and primarily female—witness the vocal histrionics of Mariah Carey and Patti LaBelle, as well as several of their younger imitators.

It's not uncommon to hear falsetto in the male voice, however. The falsetto can be especially powerful when singing a ballad—just listen to the great Smokey Robinson and you'll know what I mean. Many of the current boy bands throw falsetto in from time to time, as well; it's also a technique employed by some heavy metal screamers (Led Zeppelin's Robert Plant, for example) and a number of groups from the disco era (most notably the Bee Gees).

Nasality is more accepted in pop singing than it is in classical singing or musical theater. Singing nasally can give an edge or character to your voice that might be attractive (or necessary) in certain situations. It's typical to sing in a head voice for normal or low volume, or in a chest voice when you need to really belt it out. (This is similar to musical theater singing, actually.) Just make sure you use little or no vibrato—keep it clean, keep it clear, and don't worry about that raised soft palate.

When you're singing pop or rock (pop, especially), you often need to convey a dramatic expression through your song interpretation and delivery. That means you have to "act" the lyrics. If you're singing a dramatic, emotional song, you should call on all the expressive techniques in your arsenal, such as tonal shadings and dynamic contracts, to assist you in your presentation of the song.

Sing, Don't Scream

Some rock singers like to scream. Screaming is actually a natural reaction to singing in a loud environment. You're up on stage, surrounded by drums and amplifiers and whatnot, and you can't hear yourself think, let alone hear yourself sing. When you can't hear yourself, your natural reaction is to sing louder. And louder. And louder, until you're screaming at the top of your lungs.

While this might have worked for Janis Joplin, it's probably not the best thing for you—or your poor vocal cords. The thing is, if you have a good sound system, you don't have to scream to be heard over the band. That's why you have a microphone. Use the microphone, and work with your sound technician to make sure you're at the top of the mix that gets sent to the audience.

You should also work with your sound guy to make sure you get a good sound sent back to *you*, via monitor speakers or in-ear monitors. You have to be able to hear yourself while you're singing, and then resist the urge to sing louder than is natural. Let the sound system do the amplification for you, and don't try to out-sing the amplified instruments. Doing otherwise has unnecessarily cut short the careers of many an aspiring young singer.

Great Pop and Rock Singers

Most pop and rock singers are more about style than technique. That is, there's no one "right" technique for singing pop and (especially) rock; there's plenty of room to develop your own personal style. Imagine Sarah McLachlan and Alanis Morissette (Canadians both) singing the exact same song. Sarah will sing it softly in a slightly breathy head voice, while Alanis will belt it out in a rough and raw chest voice. Both interpretations are valid, but the individual styles build on entirely different vocal techniques.

While it's okay to learn by listening, you shouldn't try to overly imitate popular singers. You're not the singers you hear on CD or the radio—no matter how much you might like a particular singer, you need to establish your own vocal style.

> **Caution**
>
> Remember, many of the popular and rock vocalists you hear on the radio are untrained. That means they'll often do things with their voices that aren't quite Hoyle—things that can actually damage their voices over time. If it hurts when you try to imitate a specific singer, don't do it!

That said, here's a short list of the some of the better vocalists in the pop and rock arenas. Listen and enjoy!

Jon Bon Jovi

Jon Bon Jovi is the front man for Bon Jovi, a heavy-metal outfit with power pop leanings. (Some critics define their sound as *pop-metal.*) He's also one of the better singers in the genre, capable of displaying some honest-to-goodness vocal technique when called for.

Here are some of the CDs that best represent Jon Bon Jovi's vocal performances:

- *Slippery When Wet* (Bon Jovi, 1986)
- *Destination Anywhere* (1997)

Celine Dion

This Canadian chanteuse broke into the U.S. market in 1990 and has been a superstar ever since. She has a remarkable voice and is capable of singing in a variety of styles; she's especially effective singing big pop diva ballads, such as the theme to the movie *Titanic.*

Here are some of the CDs that best represent Celine Dion's vocal performances:

- *All the Way: A Decade of Song* (1999)
- *A New Day Has Come* (2002)

Gloria Estefan

Gloria Estefan was one of the biggest singing sensations of the 1980s, and (along with her group, Miami Sound Machine) helped to bring Latin-influenced music to mainstream America. She's also capable of wringing the emotion out of a big pop ballad and of tackling more traditional pop material.

Here are some of the CDs that best represent Gloria Estefan's vocal performances:

- *Greatest Hits* (1992)
- *Hold Me Thrill Me Kiss Me* (1994)

Whitney Houston

The daughter of gospel/R&B great Cissy Houston and the cousin of Dionne Warwick, Whitney Houston certainly had the genes to be one of the greatest female pop stars of all time. Her 1993 cover of Dolly Parton's "I Will Always Love You" became the best-selling single in rock history, and she had a terrific career going until some poor personal and career choices greatly affected her musical output. But focus on her early work and you'll hear one of the great singers of the modern era, as exemplified on the following CDs:

- *Whitney Houston* (1985)
- *The Greatest Hits* (2000)

James Ingram

Sometimes the mark of a talented singer is who he sings with. This is definitely the case with James Ingram, a talented baritone who has made a career of singing on other people's albums, without an accompanying success in his solo career. He's enjoyed considerable success, however, singing duets with other popular singers, from Patti Austin to Linda Ronstadt.

To hear the best of James Ingram, listen to these CDs:

- *The Greatest Hits: The Power of Great Music* (1991)
- *Forever More* (Love Songs, Hits & Duets) (1999)

Billy Joel

Best-known as the "piano man" and a versatile songwriter, Billy Joel is also a master singer, capable of varying his delivery to suit the material. And anyone who saw him sing "New York City Serenade" with Tony Bennett knows he has the chops to hang with the best.

Here are some of the CDs that best represent Billy Joel's vocal performances:

- *The Stranger* (1977)
- *Greatest Hits Vol. 1, 2 & 3* (2000)

Elton John

Like Billy Joel, Elton John is a great piano player, terrific songwriter, and versatile vocalist. He can belt his way through a rock song or croon his way through a ballad; he has certainly sung his way through a variety of material in his 30-year career.

Here are some of the CDs that best represent Elton John's vocal performances:

- *Madman Across the Water* (1971)
- *Greatest Hits 1970–2002* (2002)

Kenny Loggins

Kenny Loggins is a sensitive singer/songwriter with a mellow tenor voice. Here are some of the CDs that best represent his vocal performances:

- *Celebrate Me Home* (1977)
- *Yesterday, Today, Tomorrow: The Greatest Hits* (1997)

Paul McCartney

Sir Paul McCartney is a musical icon—and a terrific singer, to boot. His sweet choir-boy tenor was at the front of many of the Beatles' greatest hits; he's also sung his way through a staggering number of post-Beatles hits.

Here are some of the CDs that best represent Paul McCartney's vocal performances:

- *The Beatles 1* (The Beatles, 2000)
- *Wingspan: Hits and History* (2001)

Smokey Robinson

Motown legend Smokey Robinson is a soul singer extraordinaire—and an expert at the floating falsetto vocal. Here's a list of CDs that represent his best vocal performances:

- *20th Century Masters—The Millennium Collection: The Best of Smokey Robinson* (2000)
- *The Ultimate Collection* (Smokey Robinson and the Miracles, 1998)

Linda Ronstadt

From the mid-1970s to the mid-1980s, there was no bigger female singer than Linda Ronstadt. Since then she's expanded her repertoire to include big band swing (with the Nelson Riddle Orchestra), roots bluegrass (with Dolly Parton and Emmylou Harris on the *Trio* album), and traditional Mexican music.

Here are some of the CDs that best represent Linda Ronstadt's solo performances:

- *Heart Like a Wheel* (1974)
- *Round Midnight* (with Nelson Riddle and His Orchestra, 1986)

Barbra Streisand

Barbra Streisand is a legendary vocalist who is comfortable singing either musical theater or popular songs. She's lit up the concert stage for almost 40 years, and her voice is as strong today as it was when she first debuted.

Here are some of the CDs that best represent Barbra Streisand's more pop-oriented performances:

- *The Barbra Streisand Album* (1963)
- *Stoney End* (1971)
- *The Essential Barbra Streisand* (2002)

Note

When you're listening to pop singers, don't forget the singers of the previous generation (Frank Sinatra, Tony Bennett, Rosemary Clooney, et al) and their modern-era pop/jazz counterparts (including Diane Krall, Liz and Ann Hampton Calloway, and Norah Jones), as discussed in Chapter 19.

James Taylor

It's hard not to like James Taylor. He's a sensitive songwriter with a pure tenor voice and a disarmingly casual ease of delivery; listening to JT live is a true delight for singers and nonsingers alike.

Here are some of the CDs that best represent James Taylor's vocal performances:

- *Sweet Baby James* (1970)
- *Hourglass* (1997)

Singing Country and Folk

To the casual listener, country music sounds a lot different from pop or rock and roll. Many of the same vocal techniques apply, however—especially if you can get past the rural twang seemingly part and parcel of the Nashville sound.

What Makes Country Country—and Folk Folk

Singing country music is a little like singing rock and roll. You tend to avoid the use of vibrato and head voice as you "talk" your way through the lyrics. In addition, scoops or flips into pitches are commonplace and appropriate to the style.

What's a little different is the diction; country music implies a rural orientation and a bit of a southern accent. Final Rs tend to be chewed or sung through, and the vowels are much more closed than open and rounded as you find in the classical style. The rural edge in the dialect comes from a slightly set jaw, which produces a more nasal tone. (Note, however, that modern country recording artists tend to play this down as it tends to reflect a more "hard core" country sound, more like bluegrass music—which has a narrower audience appeal than mainstream country music.)

Beyond that minor difference, it's easy to understand why so many country vocalists have crossed over to the pop and rock charts—and vice versa. Two of the biggest pop singers today are Shania Twain and Faith Hill, both of whom are firmly entrenched in the country tradition. And this isn't a new phenomenon; artists like Glen Campbell, Charlie Rich, Kris Kristofferson, and even Bob Dylan have had hits on both sides of the fence.

Then there's folk music. Country music today has roots in traditional bluegrass, Brill Building pop, and the folk music of the 1960s. Artists like Nanci Griffith, Alison Krauss, and Tish Hinojosa fit in both the country and folk camps—or maybe in neither. Pure folk music differs from country in that it actually embraces a more traditional vocal approach, typically with a purer vocal tone and less regional diction. (Although this, too, differs from singer to singer.)

In any case, the best country and folk singers have wonderful vocal technique and should be on the listening list of any serious singer.

Great Country and Folk Singers

Yes, there are many country and folk singers who are great performers but lack classical vocal training. We'll ignore those performers here. Instead, let's look at a dozen or so of the best country and folk singers of the past 50 years, in terms of vocal technique.

Glen Campbell

Glen Campbell started out as a studio guitar player, was chosen to replace Brian Wilson in the touring version of the Beach Boys, and ultimately went on to crossover country/pop success—thanks to his clear tenor voice and to his unerring choice of material. Here are some of the CDs that best represent his solo vocal performances:

- *Galveston* (1969)
- *The Glen Campbell Collection (1962–1989): Gentle on My Mind* (1997)

Patsy Cline

Patsy Cline was a pure singer, with a voice as clear and distinct as a piece of the finest crystal. Unfortunately, she died young and didn't make a lot of recordings; here are some of the CDs that best represent her vocal legacy:

- *Twelve Greatest Hits* (1988)
- *The Ultimate Collection* (2000)

Judy Collins

When it comes to 1960s folk singers, Judy Collins is *the* voice. Her pure, sweet soprano elevated many a song of the time and continues to charm audiences today.

Here are some of the CDs that best represent Judy Collins' vocal performances:

- *Who Knows Where the Time Goes* (1968)
- *The Very Best of Judy Collins* (2001)

Vince Gill

Vince Gill is a great singer who just happens to sing country. His smooth voice has just a touch of gospel/R&B styling, and he has the technique to handle even the most difficult musical passages.

Here are some of the CDs that best represent Vince Gill's vocal performances:

- *I Still Believe in You* (1992)
- *The Key* (1998)

Emmylou Harris

Emmylou Harris is one of those performers who's part country and part folk and part something else. Her vocal integrity and remarkable gift for phrasing have marked her career since the early 1970s.

Here are some of the CDs that best represent Emmylou Harris' solo performances:

- *Pieces of the Sky* (1975)
- *Anthology: The Warner/Reprise Years* (2001)

Faith Hill

Along with Shania Twain, Faith Hill is one of the biggest country stars of the 1990s and a huge crossover artist in the pop market. Here are some of the CDs that best represent her vocal performances:

- *Take Me As I Am* (1994)
- *Faith* (1998)

k.d. lang

k.d. lang started out as an alternative country artist but later embraced adult contemporary pop. Her considerable vocal talents include an amazingly pure tone and a unique power and depth in the middle and lower registers.

Here are some of the CDs that best represent k.d. lang's more country-oriented performances:

- *Shadowland* (1988)
- *Absolute Torch and Twang* (1989)

Patty Loveless

Patty Loveless represents the neo-traditionalist trend in country music today. Her style embraces the honky-tonk and bluegrass traditions, with a voice that wouldn't sound out of place on the pop charts (with different material, of course).

Here are some of the CDs that best represent Patty Loveless' vocal performances:

- *On Down the Line* (1990)
- *Mountain Soul* (2001)

Kathy Mattea

Kathy Mattea was named Female Vocalist of the Year by the Country Music Association in 1989 and 1990. Her warm alto voice belies gospel and folk influences, and she's proven to be an excellent interpreter of quality material.

Here are some of the CDs that best represent Kathy Mattea's vocal performances:

- *A Collection of Hits* (1990)
- *Lonesome Standard Time* (1992)

Steve Wariner

Steve Wariner, while definitely a country singer, has a voice with a rich and nuanced quality that wouldn't be out of place on the pop charts. (He's also one heck of a guitar player, having studied with the great Chet Atkins.) Here are some of the CDs that best represent his vocal performances:

- *Burnin' the Roadhouse Down* (1998)
- *Ultimate Collection* (2000)

Trisha Yearwood

Trisha Yearwood started out as a demo singer, then found work as a background vocalist for Garth Brooks, who promised if he became successful, he'd help her career. He did—and he did—and Trisha became a star. She's one of the most gifted contemporary pop vocalists today, a powerful interpreter with a silky-smooth tone.

Here are some of the CDs that best represent Trisha Yearwood's vocal performances:

- *Trisha Yearwood* (1991)
- *Where Your Road Leads* (1998)

Singing a Pop Ballad

On the next page, you'll find the music for a song called "The Water Is Wide." This is a traditional tune that makes for a great pop or country-pop ballad.

The Water is Wide

Arr. Fulford/Miller

Traditional

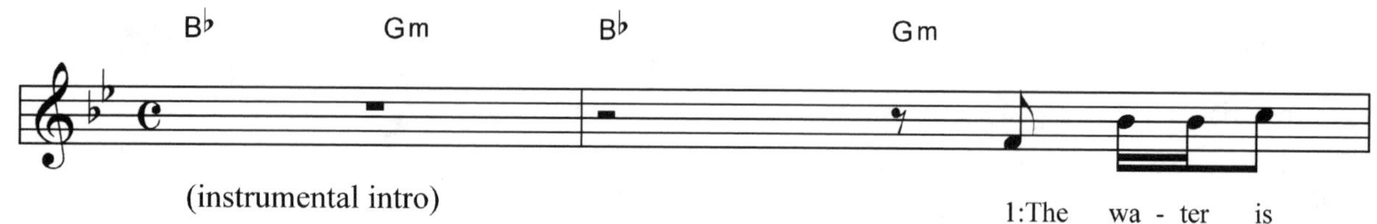
B♭ Gm B♭ Gm
(instrumental intro)
1:The wa - ter is

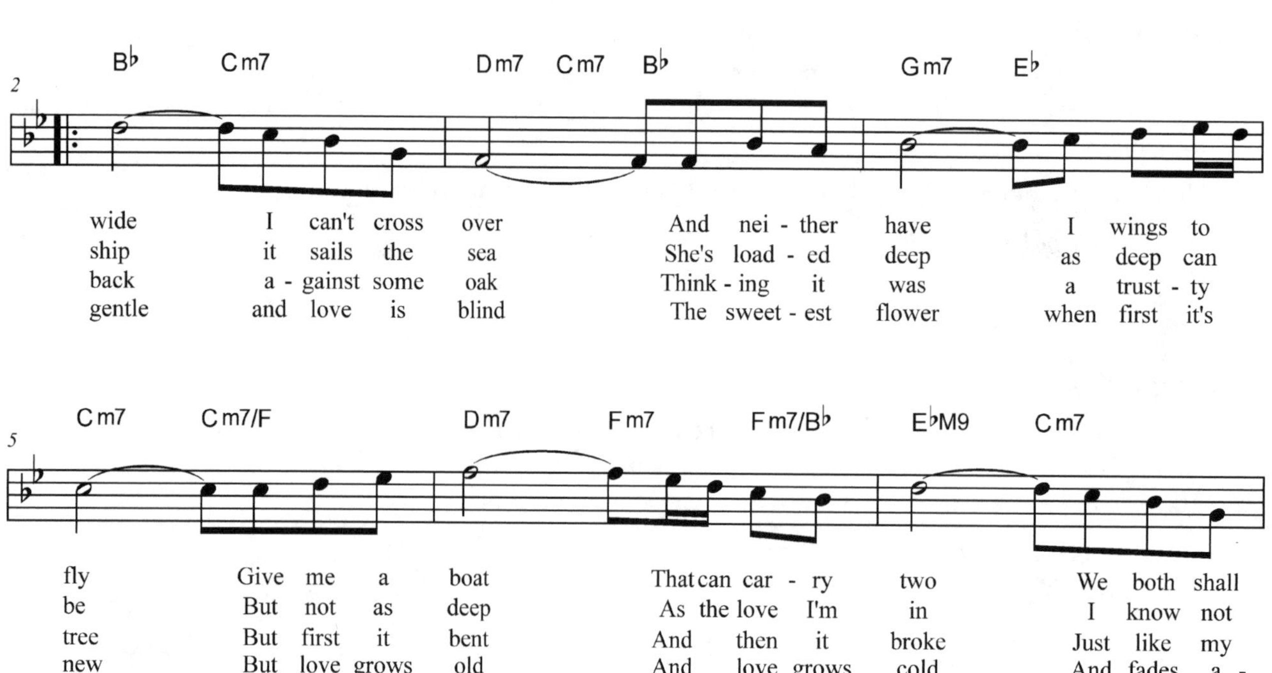
B♭ Cm7 Dm7 Cm7 B♭ Gm7 E♭
wide I can't cross over And nei - ther have I wings to
ship it sails the sea She's load - ed deep as deep can
back a - gainst some oak Think - ing it was a trust - ty
gentle and love is blind The sweet - est flower when first it's
Cm7 Cm7/F Dm7 Fm7 Fm7/B♭ E♭M9 Cm7
fly Give me a boat That can car - ry two We both shall
be But not as deep As the love I'm in I know not
tree But first it bent And then it broke Just like my
new But love grows old And love grows cold And fades a -

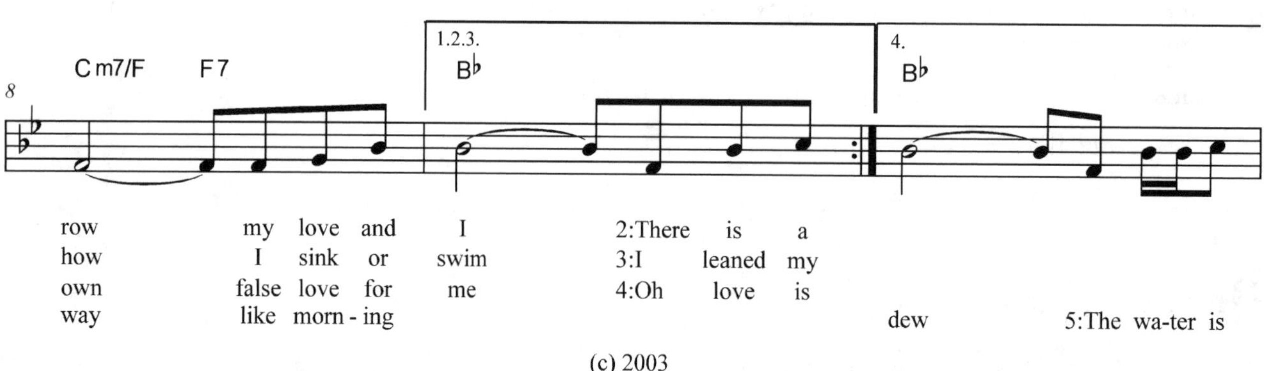
Cm7/F F7
1.2.3.
B♭
4.
B♭
row my love and I 2:There is a
how I sink or swim 3:I leaned my
own false love for me 4:Oh love is
way like morn - ing dew 5:The wa-ter is

2
The Water is Wide
11
B♭ Cm7 Dm7 Cm7 B♭ Gm7 E♭
wide I can't cross over And nei - ther have I wings to
14
Cm7 Cm7/F Dm7 Fm7 Fm7/B♭ E♭M9 Cm7
fly Give me a boat that can car - ry two We both shall
17
Cm7/F F7 Gm7 C7 Cm7 Cm7/F
row my love and I We both shall row my love - and

20
B♭ Cm7 D♭M6 E♭ E♭/F B♭
I - - - - - - - - - - - - - - -

Our version of "The Water Is Wide" is presented in what is called a *lead sheet*. As you can see, a lead sheet contains the melody, lyrics, and chords of the song; it doesn't contain the full instrumental arrangement. If you do any professional singing, you'll see a lot of lead sheets, as this is how most popular vocal music is presented.

The CD accompanying this book contains two versions of this song. The first is a full production, including lead vocals; the second is the background instrumental only, so you can sing along with it. You should probably listen to the version with vocals first, to get a feel for this arrangement, then proceed to sing it on your own.

This arrangement of "The Water Is Wide" is typical of many pop ballads, in that it builds from a simple and subdued beginning to a big climax, then settles down to a softer coda. Since "The Water Is Wide" is all verse (no chorus), you repeat the main melody over and over, building volume and emotional intensity from verse to verse—with a break for a guitar solo between the third and fourth verses. If you *don't* build emotionally throughout the verses, the song will come off rather flat and boring; it's to your benefit to make each succeeding verse bigger and more emotional than the one before it.

When you listen to "The Water Is Wide," note how our vocalist, Joe Brown, doesn't always sing the melody as written. Joe takes some liberties with the rhythm, and (in a few places) the pitch, via the occasional ornamentation. This personalization of the melody peaks on the fourth vocal verse, when he wrings all the emotion he can out of the lyrics. If you have the technique (and the confidence), you can turn this into a real diva moment; this is your chance to show everyone what you've got!

The Least You Need to Know

- Popular singing uses many of the same vocal techniques as classical singing.
- In both rock and country music it's okay to sing with conversational diction and vowel shapings, and even some nasality or breathiness is stylistically acceptable.
- When singing pop, rock, and country, the words are often more important than the melody.
- Many pop singers display tremendous vocal technique, to the point of using various vocal "tricks" to embellish the melody.

Chapter 19

Jazz

In This Chapter

- Understanding what jazz is
- Learning jazz vocal technique—and improvisation
- Discovering the great jazz singers
- Learning to sing a jazz tune

All music is demanding, in its own way. The music we call jazz is uniquely so in that it requires the singer or instrumental soloist to create new melodic lines during the course of a live performance—what we call *improvisation*. And in order to improvise, a performer must have a firm grounding in music theory and be familiar with all manner of scales and chords.

The payoff for all this extra training is freedom—the freedom to create your own music within the confines of the jazz song. No other type of music offers this degree of freedom, which is why jazz is so appealing to many intelligent, well-trained vocalists.

It's impossible to teach you how to sing jazz in just a few short pages; for most jazz vocalists, it's a life-long pursuit. What I can do, however, is tell you what makes a jazz tune jazz, describe the unique qualities of jazz vocal technique, and present you with a list of great jazz singers to listen to and learn from. And, as a bonus, I'll even give you a jazz tune to practice on your own—and listen to, on the accompanying CD.

What Jazz Is

Some people might define jazz as music with improvised solos. While most jazz does include improvisation, so do many types of music—and I'd be hard-pressed to define Phish or Eric Clapton as jazz musicians.

Others might define jazz as music with a swing beat. While some jazz does have a definite swing, much big band swing music from the 1940s and beyond isn't strictly jazz—it's just popular music with a swing beat.

No, jazz is something else. It's a complex music, but with flexible-enough parameters to include both smooth ballads and frantic bebop. Jazz can be played over a swing beat, a rock beat, a funk beat, or a Latin beat. It can be played by a solo pianist or by a big band or orchestra. And it can be sung by all manner of vocalists, from the sultry stylings of Diana Krall on one end to the inventive vocalese of Jon Hendricks on the other.

At first blush, jazz appears to be the polar opposite of classical music. Classical music is all about playing notes on paper as precisely as possible, where jazz uses written music only as a jumping-off point for further musical exploration.

And, truth to tell, jazz and classical music have a nice rivalry going. Many classical singers don't believe that jazz singers have the discipline or the technique to sing properly. Similarly, jazz singers often believe that classical singers only follow musical "rules" and lack any musical creativity. There is some truth to both statements, but both musical forms go beyond these simple stereotypes. The reality is that classical singers do a lot of interpreting of the written music, and that most jazz vocalists have tremendous technique backed up with a lot of formal music training.

Jazz vs. Classical Music

Perhaps the best way to describe the differences between the classical approach and the jazz style of singing is to look at the way the music is presented or interpreted.

Classical music is careful to represent the music on the page as closely as possible. Classical singers are carrying on an established tradition, similar to the tradition of oratorical speech. Abraham Lincoln gave a large number of great speeches that are still read and studied today; these speeches contain many grand and often eloquent words and provide a unique look at who Lincoln was as a person. Similarly, classical music represents a composer and who he was at the time he wrote a piece of music. Classical singers are studying and representing that composer—and because of this, they are very careful not to modify the music, so that it is preserved as originally written over the course of time.

If classical music is a speech, jazz is a conversation—and a conversation is much more intimate and personal than a speech. In a conversation, the topic may start in the same place, but where you end up is less certain. The same is true for jazz singing. The song always starts the same, but each performer puts their individual personality into the song—its melody, rhythm, harmony, and feel.

This idea of a conversation is important in jazz. Jazz singing should be a conversation between the singer and the instrumentalists, as well as a conversation between the singer and the audience. This is where many of the ideas surrounding jazz singing come from.

The Jazz Form

The form of a typical jazz song is designed to encourage improvisation. A jazz tune is typically presented in a set form that repeats many times. Typical jazz forms have 12, 16, or 32 measures (often called *bars*) that make up a chorus. Repetition of the chorus provides the opportunity for the improvisation that is a crucial element of jazz.

The vocalist is usually able to sing through the song more than once. You will start to hear this more as you listen to jazz recordings. Singers will often sing once through the song and then wait while the instruments improvise for several choruses. Then the singer will come in and sing the song again.

It sounds a little complicated on paper, but once you start to listen, it becomes much more clear.

Jazz Vocal Technique

Where your body is concerned, jazz singing is similar to traditional or "classical" singing. Everything from your throat down uses the same technique as more traditional singing. You must still breathe correctly and use a good alignment. The way you use your mouth and your resonators is the only real physical difference when it comes to singing jazz.

Back in Chapter 3, I described classical singing as singing with an egg turned up in your mouth. That was to help you remember to utilize all of the space you could by keeping your soft palate raised, your jaw hinge open, and your tongue low. The same concept applies in jazz, but you should think more of singing with the egg turned on its side. You still need a raised soft palette, relaxed jaw, and relaxed tongue, but your soft palette doesn't need to be quite as high. The relaxed soft palate results in a more forward placement and a slightly brighter and more conversational tone.

Tip

Unlike in classical singing, in jazz a microphone is not just recommended, it's pretty much a requirement. As a jazz singer, you need to get used to using a microphone and to how your amplified voice sounds; this will affect the sound you project to the audience. (Learn more about using a microphone in Chapter 23.)

Other than these slight differences, vocal jazz technique is very similar to classical singing technique. The thing that really distances the two is the way in which the singer approaches and presents the music—which we'll discuss next.

Tone and Diction

This is one of the topics that can start to set apart classical and jazz singers. It's actually a sore spot for some, but it doesn't need to be.

As you recall from Chapter 13, classical music is sung on pure vowels with what is often called Italian diction. There are lots of rules on how to sing each vowel properly and how all the consonants should be pronounced.

Jazz uses a different type of diction; you should pronounce words in jazz the way you would say them in a conversation. This doesn't mean that you shouldn't sing on the vowels or that you should mumble the words. The principles of good singing don't change; you must still sing the words and pronounce them so they are understandable.

Vowels

Singing on vowels is absolutely necessary in all forms of music, but there are two major differences between jazz vowels and classical vowels. The first has to do with vibrato. As you know, vibrato is the natural vibration that occurs in your voice when you sing. In jazz singing you want to sing most of the time with a straight (no vibrato) tone. It's also desirable to put a little more air in the tone—again, more like conversation than the sharply focused classical sound. While vibrato is encouraged in classical singing, it's usually only used in jazz to add color, warmth, or intensity to a sustained tone. A jazz vibrato is also generally much lighter than a classical vibrato.

The second difference is in the way you pronounce your vowels. Classical singing avoids singing on any sound that is not a pure vowel. (So you substitute "eh" for "ay," for example.) This has the effect of making certain words sound very different when they are sung as opposed to being spoken. When you're singing jazz, however, the words should be sung as close as possible to the way you speak. This means that you will sing lots of sounds that don't fall into the pure vowel category—but by doing this, you'll discover the more conversational style of performance that is jazz.

Consonants

Consonants are also used differently in jazz. In classical music, consonants are most often pronounced in a hard, crisp manner. Hard Ts, Ds, and the like are the norm. In jazz these letters are actually de-emphasized.

Tip

If you want to hear some great sustained Ms and Ns, listen to some old Frank Sinatra and Mel Tormé recordings. Nobody did sustained consonants better than the Chairman of the Board and the Velvet Fog!

Let's look at an easy example. Say the word "football." If you're like most people, you didn't make a hard "T" sound. Now say "football" again, but this time put a good, hard T in the middle of the word. That choppy sound just doesn't work in the conversation of jazz music—which is why you should de-emphasize hard consonants when singing jazz.

Another difference between the classical singing style and jazz singing is in the use of voiced consonants. In classical music, the sustained vowel reigns supreme. Jazz, however, takes the opportunity to sing on some of the consonants. Ms and Ns are regularly held out to help emphasize a word. At times, even hard (unvoiced) consonants are overemphasized to give a sense of percussion.

You should note, however, that all of these decisions are made by the performer; every singer has a different approach to these issues. As you can see, in jazz it's not the rules of the classical tradition that govern the performance, it's the singer's own personal interpretation of the music. That's what makes jazz so challenging and satisfying—for both the singer and the listener!

Melodic Embellishment

We first discussed melodic embellishment in Chapter 14. The concept may sound complicated at first, but it's pretty simple once you get into it.

Melodic embellishment is the act of changing some of the notes in a melody. Contrary to classical music, in jazz the singer is actually encouraged to sing notes other than the melody. There are a few rules that go along with this freedom, however.

First, you should demonstrate that you actually do know the melody. This means that you should sing enough of the song exactly as it is written so that anyone listening can recognize it. Many beginning jazz singers make the mistake of going straight to the embellishment without demonstrating that they know the original tune. Wait until you've built a little reputation before going too far out on an "improvisational limb"!

Second, the further you go in the song, the further you can get from the melody. You are generally allowed the most flexibility when you sing the last chorus.

Third, use the song's underlying chord structure to inform your melodic embellishment. One way to approach this is to "outline" all the chords in the song by singing each note of each chord, in both directions (ascending and descending). For example, if you look at the sheet music and see a C Major 7 chord, you would sing the four notes of the chord (C-E-G-B) like this:

Singing the notes of a C Major 7 chord.

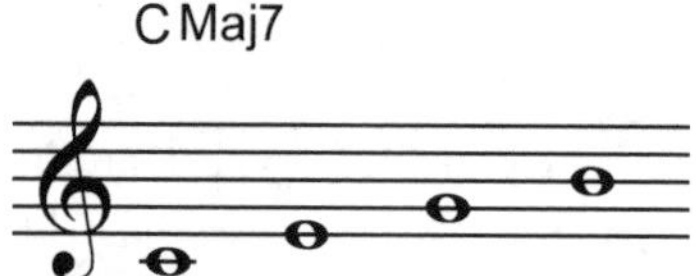

Naturally, to sing all the notes in a chord means you have to *know* all the notes in the chord—which requires a good grounding in music theory. You started on this process in Chapter 10; if you're serious about singing jazz, you'll need to continue studying chord construction, chord changes, and scales.

Follow these rules and you can embellish to your heart's content—as long as it sounds good!

Rhythmic Variation

Rhythmic variation is something else we discussed in Chapter 14. Remember how, in the classical style, all the notes should be performed as written? The same is true for rhythm; all the note values in classical music should be performed exactly as written.

Jazz is different. In jazz, you're encouraged to modify the rhythm of the song to make it more your own. This idea, like melodic embellishment, is based on improvisation; you can play around with a tune's rhythm just as you can with its melodic line.

Another way to introduce rhythmic variation in a jazz tune is through the use of *back phrasing*. This is where you sing the same melody notes that are written, but you sing them later than you're supposed to.

For example, let's assume that the music calls on you to sing your first note on beat 1 of the first measure. If you want to back phrase that portion of the song, you might wait until beat 3 of the measure or even beat 2 of the second measure! You would then adjust the rhythm of the song to end that musical phrase in the correct place, as shown below.

I'll wish you a Mer - ry Christ - mas

A simple melody sung straight …

I'll wish you a Mer - ry Christ - mas

… and then back phrased.

Once you start listening to examples of a song you are preparing, it is easy to hear how back phrasing is done. The more experience you get, the further "back" you can start.

However you phrase the rhythmic line, it's important to keep the song in a conversational rhythm. You should sing in a manner that is more similar to speech, and use the rhythm to emphasize the words that you think are important in the song.

Sometimes composers do not do a good job of this on their own. Other times, the composer has done a fine job of emphasizing the correct word, but you want to deliberately introduce a different phrasing. That's the beauty of jazz; you're free to make whatever changes you want.

Of course, variations in rhythm and melody can occur together. But when you're first starting to sing jazz, you should probably stick to one at a time until you're more comfortable with the form. Just remember to always keep track of where the melody is supposed to be, so you don't get lost somewhere in the middle of a long embellishment.

Note

The opposite of back phrasing is *front phrasing*, which is used only sparingly in jazz. Front phrasing means to start a line before the music tells you. This technique is much more difficult than back phrasing, however, and should not be attempted until the easier technique is mastered.

Character

There's one more thing to consider when you're deciding how you want to sing a jazz song. That's the fact that the best jazz music has a character, a persona, that defines the performance.

Tip

Many jazz singers can sing the original written melody in their head while they sing their own version of the song out loud. This will also help you keep track of the form and know when you are supposed to come in.

When you're determining the character of your performance, remember that many jazz standards come from old Broadway or Hollywood musicals. You can easily research the plot of the musical to find out why the person is singing the song and to whom it's being sung.

Even songs that don't come from musical theater have their own unique point of view. Giving adequate thought to the song's intention or character will really enhance your performance, so don't overlook that aspect of the music. It's your responsibility to make the song speak to your audience—and you can't do that unless it speaks to you, first.

Improvisation

Improvisation is probably the scariest word for most people who want to sing jazz. You may have heard those instruments playing incredibly fast, the singers singing those funny do-be do-be syllables (what jazzers call *scat singing*), and wanted to run in the opposite direction.

Never fear—you're not alone.

Note

The art of improvisation can take years to master, and a thorough discussion of the subject can fill the pages of a book twice this big. For that reason, we're not covering improvisation in depth in this chapter. See Appendix D for books and training materials that focus on teaching improvisation to jazz vocalists.

Very few singers start out as accomplished improvisers. Fortunately, you don't have to improvise to sing jazz. There are many great jazz singers who don't do a lot of improvising. However, they all learn to improvise as they continue to learn jazz music.

Improvisation is a tricky technique to master. If you want to learn to improvise, the best thing to do is to listen to all of the jazz you can and seriously consider taking some lessons from a trained jazz vocalist. You should also check out the artists at your local jazz club and ask about jazz programs at your local high school or college. Many schools offer classes in improvisation, where singers can learn right along with instrumental soloists.

And above all, practice. When it comes to jazz improvisation, there's no substitution for doing. Take advantage of any situation that lets you perform live in a jazz setting. You may hit a few wrong notes, but even the wrong notes are worth their weight in gold where improvisation comes in—it's those wrong notes that help you determine the *right* notes to sing!

Great Jazz Singers

If you want to learn to sing jazz, the most important thing that you can do is listen, listen, and then listen some more. It's imperative that you listen to as much jazz music, and to as many solo artists, as you can.

And don't limit yourself to only singers. You can learn a lot about phrasing and improvisation from the great jazz instrumentalists, from Charlie Parker to Miles Davis. Tony Bennett once said that all the great jazz singers learned phrasing and execution from the consummate jazz artist, Louis Armstrong—a trumpet player!

Today's technology gives you a tremendous advantage over singers from earlier generations. Remember that the only "classrooms" for jazz in the 1920s and 1930s were the dance halls and clubs across our nation where the hot jazz bands of the time played. Instrumentalists and singers had to travel for days, under pretty dire conditions, just to listen to and learn from other artists. Today, all we have to do is pick up one of a thousand great CDs—or better yet, spend a few hours online—to experience the greatest jazz musicians of all time.

As you listen, you'll discover some common jazz techniques and hopefully, some things that make each artist unique. So let's take a quick look at some of the best jazz vocalists of this or any era—and recommend some CDs for you to listen to.

Pure Jazz Singers

The jazz fraternity can be a tad insular. Hardcore jazzers will gush over what they call "pure" jazz musicians, while heaping loads of disdain on so-called "smooth jazz" artists—or, even worse (in their minds) pop artists pretending to play jazz. For that reason, we're dividing our list of jazz vocalists into those "pure" artists without obvious pop pretensions and those popular singers with a jazz bent.

This first bunch of singers should meet the requirements set forth by any jazz purist. We'll proceed (roughly) from the oldest to the newest, emphasizing those singers who can hold their own when it comes to embellishment and improvisation.

Louis Armstrong

The granddaddy of all jazz singers was better known as a trumpet player. Louis Armstrong (b. 1901 d. 1971) not only defined the vocabulary of jazz with his Hot Five and Hot Seven ensembles, he also created the jazz vocal. Although not a classically trained singer (I'm not going to comment on his tone quality!), "Pops" introduced a unique approach to popular song that merged elements from instrumental jazz with "straight" singing. Interestingly, he was also the first singer to "scat sing" on record.

Here are some of the best of Louis Armstrong's vocal recordings:

- *Ella and Louis* (with Ella Fitzgerald, 1956)
- *Sings Back Through the Years: A Centennial Celebration* (2000)

Billie Holiday

Billie Holiday (b. 1915 d. 1959) melded jazz, pop, and blues into a highly emotional style. She gave highly stylized readings of traditional pop songs, rephrasing both the melody and the beat like a horn soloist.

Here are some of the best of Billie Holiday's many recordings:

- *Lady Sings the Blues* (1954)
- *Lady Day: The Best of Billie Holiday* (2001)

Ella Fitzgerald

Ella Fitzgerald (b. 1917 d. 1996) is considered the First Lady of Song and one of the finest jazz singers of all time. Ella is a lady who could really swing and knew how to scat, but could still "sell" a straight pop song. Whether you're listening to her sing Gershwin or "trade fours" with the best instrumental soloists of her day, every performance is a delight—and one to learn from.

Here are some of the best of Ella Fitzgerald's many recordings:

- *Sings the George and Ira Gershwin Songbook* (1959)
- *The Complete Ella in Berlin: Mack the Knife* (1960)
- *Something to Live For* (1999)

Note

Make sure you check out the albums Ella did with Louis Armstrong, listed in Louis' discography.

Joe Williams

Joe Williams (b. 1918 d. 1999) was a big band singer with a smooth baritone voice. Perhaps best known for his work with Count Basie, Williams later sang with other big bands and numerous small groups—and even became a regular on *The Cosby Show*.

Here are some of the best of Joe Williams's many recordings:

- *Count Basie Swings, Joe Williams Sings* (1955)
- *Every Day: The Best of the Verve Years* (1993)

Jon Hendricks

One of Jon Hendricks's (b. 1921) unique talents is the ability to write coherent lyrics to the most complex instrumental jazz solos—an art known as *vocalese*. Whether singing solo or with the vocal group Lambert, Hendricks, and Ross, Hendricks's vocals were as close to pure jazz as you could get, and highly influential to the next generation of bebopping jazz vocalists (such as Al Jarreau and the Manhattan Transfer).

Here are some of the best of Jon Hendricks's many recordings:

- *Sing a Song of Basie* (Lambert, Hendricks, and Ross, 1957)
- *Boppin' at the Blue Note* (1993)

Shirley Horn

Shirley Horn (b. 1934) didn't hit big until she was well into her 50s, but she is definitely a talent worth waiting for. She's an especially fine ballad singer with her low, haunting voice. Some of her best recordings include:

- *Close Enough for Love* (1988)
- *You're My Thrill* (2001)

Sarah Vaughn

Sarah Vaughn (b. 1924 d. 1990) ranked with Ella Fitzgerald and Billie Holiday in the upper echelon of female jazz singers. The combination of a wide range, controlled vibrato, and wide expressive abilities (including a supreme mastery of scat singing) let Sassy do almost anything she wanted to do with her incredible voice.

Here are some of the best of Sarah Vaughn's many recordings:

- *Sarah Vaughn with Clifford Brown* (1954)
- *Sassy Swings the Tivoli* (1963)
- *Verve Jazz Masters: Sarah Vaughn* (1995)

Mel Tormé

Mel Tormé (b. 1925 d. 1999) was a pop singer who really knew his jazz. The "Velvet Fog" was an accomplished composer and arranger, in addition to being a talented drummer, occasional actor, *and* a popular singer. (Among his many accomplishments was co-writing the holiday classic, "The Christmas Song;" he also personally arranged most of the songs he sang.) As a singer, Tormé was a baritone with great control and a solid scatting style, a real joy to listen to.

Here are some of the best of Mel Tormé's many recordings:

- *Sings Fred Astaire* (1956)
- *The Best of the Concord Years* (1999)

Al Jarreau

Al Jarreau (b. 1940) is a Grammy-winning vocalist with an engaging style. Capable of singing jazz, pop, and R&B, Jarreau employs his own unique brand of vocalese. In addition to his jazz work, he has also had pop hits with "We're In This Together" and the theme from the *Moonlighting* television show.

Here are some of best of Al Jarreau's jazz-oriented recordings:

- *Look to the Rainbow* (1977)
- *The Best of Al Jarreau* (1996)

Bobby McFerrin

Bobby McFerrin (b. 1950) is one of the most distinctive singers in popular music today. An active educator, his vocal style ranges from pop to jazz to classical. He's known for his a cappella performances and recordings, including the hit song "Don't Worry, Be Happy."

Here are some of the best of Bobby McFerrin's jazz-oriented recordings:

- *The Voice* (1984)
- *Beyond Words* (with Chick Corea, 2002)

Kevin Mahogany

Kevin Mahogany (b. 1958) is a swinging jazz vocalist in the tradition of Joe Williams. He has a smooth baritone that's equally at home on an up-tempo swing tune as it is on a smooth ballad.

Here are some of the best of Kevin Mahogany's many recordings:

- *Songs and Moments* (1994)
- *My Romance* (1998)

Karrin Allyson

Alternately sultry and saucy, Karrin Allyson (born in the 60s) is a great young scat singer who can also sing her way around a jazz ballad. She's also a bop-based improviser with near-flawless diction, and is quickly earning a strong reputation in the jazz world.

Here are some of the best of Karrin Allyson's recordings:

- *Sweet Home Cookin'* (1993)
- *Ballads: Remembering John Coltrane* (2001)

Kurt Elling

Blending vocal jazz, bebop, and beat poetry, Kurt Elling (b. 1967) employs a unique scat style to complement his more traditional Sinatra-style croonings. Elling's superb voice control lets him imitate many different horn instruments; he's simply one of the most innovative vocalists performing today.

Here are some of the the best of Kurt Elling's recordings:

- *Live in Chicago* (2000)
- *Flirting with Twilight* (2001)

Jane Monheit

Jane Monheit (b. 1978) is one of the highest-touted young singers of the new millennium. She burst onto the scene with the support of some of the finest of today's jazz musicians; her voice is near flawless, and she's as comfortable with a mid-tempo swing tune as she is a ballad.

Here are the best of Jane Monheit's recordings to date:

- *Never Never Land* (2000)
- *In the Sun* (2002)

Pop Singers in a Jazz Style

Beyond these pure jazz singers, there is another group of singers who sing in a jazz style, even though they don't do a lot of improvising. These artists—many of whom came to prominence during the big band era—are better defined as popular singers in the swing style. They employ many jazz vocal techniques (including jazz-style diction and rhythmic and melodic embellishment), but don't often take that next step into true jazz improvisation.

These singers are perhaps easier to listen to—and to learn from—than some of the hardcore jazz singers listed previously. After all, you can't help but relax to a great Frank Sinatra or Tony Bennett CD!

Frank Sinatra

Frank Sinatra (b. 1915 d. 1998) truly was the Chairman of the Board—one of the most important singers of the twentieth century. Sinatra was a terrific interpreter of great songs, capable of selling a song with a passion that other singers could only dream of. He was truly a one-of-a-kind singer.

Here are some of the best of Frank Sinatra's many recordings:

- *Songs for Swingin' Lovers!* (1955)
- *Only the Lonely* (1958)
- *Classic Sinatra* (2000)

Tip

Nat's daughter, Natalie Cole, is a talented pop/R&B vocalist in her own right.

Nat "King" Cole

Nat "King" Cole (b. 1917 d. 1965) was an extremely popular singer of pop ballads, as well as an inspired swing pianist. His smooth vocal style created a number of pop music hits, including "Mona Lisa," "The Christmas Song," "Route 66," "Nature Boy," and "Unforgettable."

Here are some of the best of Nat "King" Cole's many recordings:

- *Greatest Hits* (1994)
- *The Unforgettable Nat King Cole* (2000)

Peggy Lee

Miss Peggy Lee (b. 1920 d. 2002) was a popular performer for almost six decades. She covered songs by the Tin Pan Alley greats and the best songwriters of the rock generation, including the hits "Lover," "Fever," and "Is That All There Is?" She was a bold interpreter, equally adept at blues, jazz, and pop.

Here are some of the best of Peggy Lee's many recordings:

- *The Complete Recordings 1941–1947* (1999)
- *The Singles Collection* (2002)

Tony Bennett

Tony Bennett (b. 1926) is a true American treasure, delighting audiences since the early 1950s. He sings tried and true standards in a warm, husky tenor, and his phrasing is jazz-like and spontaneous. Bennett is a true popular singer of the old school who has racked up numerous hits over the years, the most recognized being his signature tune, "I Left My Heart in San Francisco."

Here are some of the best of Tony Bennett's many recordings:

- *Jazz* (1967)
- *The Essential Tony Bennett* (2002)

Rosemary Clooney

Rosemary Clooney (b. 1928 d. 2002) rose to fame in the 1950s with a string of pop hits like "Come On-A My House," "Tenderly," and "This Ole House." Not a true jazz singer, she was an excellent lyric interpreter with fine timing and intelligent phrasing.

Here are some of the best of Rosemary Clooney's many recordings:

- *Rosie Solves the Swingin' Riddle* (1960)
- *Songs from the Girl Singer: A Musical Biography* (1999)

Nancy Wilson

Nancy Wilson (b. 1937) is a jazz vocalist who successfully crossed over into the pop, R&B, and adult contemporary markets. Her voice is particularly suited to lush romantic ballads.

Here are some of Nancy Wilson's best recordings:

- *Welcome to My Love* (1968)
- *Anthology* (2000)

Diana Krall

Canadian Diana Krall (b. 1964) is a sincere jazz-influenced singer and an impressive jazz pianist. Her 1998 album *When I Look In Your Eyes* won a Grammy for Best Jazz Vocal Performance, and was the first jazz album in 25 years to be nominated for Album of the Year. Her smooth style appeals to a crossover audience of pop music lovers and jazz purists the world over.

Here are some of the best of Diana Krall's recordings:

- *All for You* (1995)
- *The Look of Love* (2001)

Harry Connick Jr.

Harry Connick Jr. (b. 1967) is a crooner in the Sinatra tradition (and a solid jazz pianist) who came to fame singing the standards-infused soundtrack to the movie *When Harry Met Sally*. He has a comfortable style and a nice way with a phrase and is equally comfortable accompanying himself on piano or singing with a big band.

Here are a few of Harry Connick Jr.'s most popular recordings:

- *Come By Me* (1999)
- *It Had to Be You: Best of Harry Connick, Jr.* (1999)

Norah Jones

Norah Jones's (b. 1979) debut album shot her to the top of the pop and jazz charts. The daughter of Ravi Shankar, she won *Downbeat* magazine's Student Music Awards for Best Jazz Vocalist and Best Original Composition in 1996. Her vocal style blends smooth jazz, blues, country, and folk and is equally appealing to jazz lovers and pop music fans.

At the time of this book's publication, Norah Jones has released just one CD—but it's a terrific one, winner of eight Grammys, including Best Pop Vocal Album and Album of the Year:

- *Come Away With Me* (2002)

Learning a Jazz Song: "I Ain't Got Nobody (And Nobody Cares for Me)"

When it comes to singing a song in the jazz style, you need to really study it before you sing a note. This means learning the specific notation of the melody as it is written—not just copying the recordings you've heard. When you sing jazz, you should use all the recordings that you've heard as a resource, but you shouldn't try to copy a particular singer's exact style or phrasing.

After you learn the melody exactly as it appears on the sheet music, you should then learn the chord changes. These are the basic harmonies that the instruments will be playing while you are singing. Of course, you have a great advantage if you can play a little piano or guitar because so much of your vocal styling will be dependent on the underlying harmonic structure of the song. You should do everything you can to learn about the harmony as well as the melody of a tune.

Now we come to the big exercise in this chapter, a real honest-to-goodness jazz song for you to sing. This song is "I Ain't Got Nobody (And Nobody Cares for Me)," a real classic written way back in 1916 but updated for the current century with more modern chord changes. You can practice the song from the sheet music included here, or listen to it (with and without vocals) on the accompanying CD—as performed by an actual jazz trio.

> **Note**
>
> This comes back to the idea that jazz is improvised and distinctly yours. For example, a lot of people have already heard how Nat "King" Cole sings "Route 66." That's all fine and dandy, but what they want is to hear how *you* sing the song.

There are some things to note before you start practicing this song. First, this song is performed with a swing beat—even though the rhythms on paper look like straight eighth notes. This is typically how swing music is notated on paper. The composer or arranger writes straight eighth notes, but these notes are interpreted in a rolling triplet rhythm. So if you see two eighth notes in a row, they're performed like the first and last notes of an eighth-note triplet, as shown here:

Interpret straight eighth notes in a "swing" triplet rhythm.

In addition, the melody should be taken as more of a guide than a dictate. That means you can play around with the melody, shifting the rhythm around, changing and embellishing the pitches, whatever it takes to make it your own. On the CD the song is run through twice. The first pass is relatively straight, while the second time through the vocalist (who is also your author) does a bit of scat improvisation. Feel free to do your own scatting when you sing along.

You should also note that the backing trio is playing slightly different chords than what are written on your sheet music. Actually, they're variations of these basic chords, with more inventive extensions and substitutions. This is also common in jazz; the individual musicians have the freedom to reharmonize the song to fit their personal playing styles.

With all that in mind, it's time to start singing—and swinging. All you have to do is play back the CD track without vocals, and you'll be singing along with your very own jazz ensemble!

The Least You Need to Know

- Jazz is a musical form that encourages freedom on the part of the performers, in terms of melodic and rhythmic embellishment.
- Pure jazz music also encourages soloing and improvisation, on the part of both vocalists and instrumental musicians.
- Jazz vocal technique is similar to classical technique, with the exception of a less-raised soft palate and a more conversational style of diction.
- The great jazz singers—from Louis Armstrong to Jane Monheit—are masters of phrasing and improvisation.

I Ain't Got Nobody
(And Nobody Cares for Me)

Arranged by Fary/Fulford/Miller

Music by Chas. Warfield
Words by David Young

2
I Ain't Got Nobody
33
B♭ Gm C7 F7
1.
B♭
no - bo - dy cares for me
2.
37
Dm7 G7 Cm7
me No - bo - dy cares for me
41
E♭m7 A♭7 Cm7 F7 B♭
Lone - ly as I can be Won't some - one care for me

Chapter 20

Gospel and R&B

In This Chapter

- Discovering the history of gospel music
- Finding out how to sing in the gospel style
- Understanding soul and R&B singing
- Learning to sing a gospel song

The last musical styles we'll look at are those most associated with African American culture—gospel and rhythm and blues. Vocally, these styles are quite similar; musically, the difference between the two styles is the difference between singing for your soul in church and singing *with* your soul in a club or on the concert stage. Both types of music require solid vocal technique and the ability to embellish your performance with melodic ornamentation and improvisation. (Think Aretha Franklin, here.)

So if you're ready to sanctify, raise your voice in praise and start singing!

Singing Gospel

There are three distinct forms of gospel music, all coming from similar religious roots. There is *Southern gospel* (sometimes called *mountain gospel* or *country gospel*), which grew out of a white rural tradition and inspired early rockabilly performers, including Elvis Presley and Carl Perkins. There is *black gospel*, with its roots in the African American church, which inspired the development of rhythm and blues and soul music. Then there's *contemporary gospel*, which describes much of today's Christian pop music.

All three types of gospel offer emotionally charged music wedded to religious lyrics, although the music itself differs dramatically between the forms. The singing style you use for Southern gospel, for example, is similar to how you'd sing classic country music. Contemporary gospel singers, on the other hand, employ modern pop singing technique. But it's black gospel that most of us recognize as the decidedly distinctive musical form—and that requires the most dramatic vocal technique.

The History of Gospel Music

Gospel music developed in the early part of the twentieth century, primarily in the southeastern part of the United States. The music was of the Protestant church, but not necessarily *from* the church—that is, while the performers were primarily Bible-believing people, the music wasn't the outgrowth of a particular church organization. Instead, the roots of gospel music were in Sunday school hymns, camp meeting spirituals, and the melodies and harmonies of the popular music of the time.

Black gospel music truly came into its own in the 1920s and 1930s, thanks to the compositions of Thomas A. Dorsey and the performances of Mahalia Jackson, Sallie Martin, and other great singers. Dorsey set out to write songs that would incite the spirit and inspire people to dance and shout; his songs, such as 1932's "Take My Hand, Precious Lord," became standards in the gospel community and helped to define the genre.

Southern gospel developed somewhat independently of black gospel. This style of gospel had its roots in the Appalachian mountainfolk of Kentucky, Tennessee, Virginia, and North Carolina. Sometimes called "hillbilly" music, Southern gospel has the same religious fervor of black gospel, but with more of a bluegrass or rural blues feel. One of the primary pioneers of Southern gospel was James D. Vaughan, who created the first major white sacred quartet.

It was black gospel music, however, that had the biggest influence on both secular and nonsecular music. Black gospel inspired the rhythm and blues and soul music of the 1960s and beyond, as well as the early rock and roll music of the 1950s and 1960s. It also inspired today's contemporary gospel music, which blends traditional gospel stylings with secular pop and soul music in the service of decidedly nonsecular lyrics.

How to Sing Gospel

When I'm asked to describe a typical gospel vocal performance, the words I tend to use are *energetic*, *intense*, and *dramatic*. Gospel is a sanctified style of singing that tries to express, in music and words, an extremely spiritual experience.

Singing Black Gospel

When you're singing black gospel music, you have to remember that it's a style that borrows heavily from the rural blues tradition. Black gospel music is typically sung by a choir, with individual singers taking solo roles. The music is usually tossed back and forth between the choir and the soloist in a call and response format, with the soloist embellishing the melody for greater emphasis. These embellishments can be quite virtuosic, performed with wild emotion in an attempt to express the spiritual ecstasy the music was meant to evoke.

The embellishment of a gospel melody may take the form of jazz-like improvisation, or of classical forms of embellishment, such as grace notes, trills, turns, and melisma. Less-traditional embellishment is also common, such as moans, wails, shouts, cries, gliding pitches, or spoken interjections. This type of embellishment typically increases as the emotional intensity of the performance increases.

Another way gospel singers increase the intensity of their performances is to employ sudden changes in vocal register or dynamics. They'll also breathe between words or in the middle of phrases, or deliberately produce breathiness or airy tones.

Singing Southern Gospel

Singing Southern gospel is a little different from singing black gospel. With Southern gospel, you have to remember that it draws on the bluegrass and folk music traditions of Appalachia and adjust your vocal style accordingly.

Southern gospel singing is characterized by a very forward, pinched, high nasal tone. Melodies are often harmonized in open fourths and fifths, moving in parallel. This results in a somewhat archaic sound, which makes sense when you realize that its roots go all the way back to the ancient folk music of Scotland, Ireland, and England. Vocal lines tend to be choppy and are sung with a technique of "falling off" the pitch, for dramatic emphasis. (Think Bob Dylan, here.)

Tip

If you want to listen to some great Southern gospel singing, along with a little "old timey" bluegrass, check out the soundtrack to the movie *O Brother, Where Art Thou?* The movie and the soundtrack have done wonders to popularize this type of bluegrass and Southern gospel music.

Singing Contemporary Gospel

Then we have contemporary gospel, which is much like singing pop or rock and roll—but with a little black gospel and soul thrown in. It's an updated, somewhat polished version of traditional gospel, typically sung to a rock or pop beat. Much contemporary gospel sounds like contemporary urban music, with sweet soul vocals punctuated by virtuosic vocal embellishments.

To sing contemporary gospel, start with a solid pop vocal technique. Then you can add melodic embellishments, as necessary.

Great Gospel Singers

The best way to understand gospel music is to listen to it. To that end, here's a list of great gospel vocalists and groups for your listening pleasure, in all three forms of the genre.

Shirley Caesar

Shirley Caesar, known as the First Lady of Gospel, started singing when she was 10 years old. She performed with the Gospel group the Caravans in the 1960s, then left to pursue a solo career. She has an energetic performing style, often shouting to the Lord for her messages to be received. Some of Shirley Caesar's best recordings include:

- *The Best of Shirley Caesar with the Caravans* (1966)
- *The First Lady of Gospel* (2000)

The Five Blind Boys of Mississippi

The Five Blind Boys first sang together in the 1930s, as the Cotton Blossom Singers. They made their first recording as the Blind Boys in 1946 and soon became one of the most popular gospel groups in history. Some of the best recordings include:

- *The Original Five Blind Boys* (1959)
- *The Best of the Original Five Blind Boys of Mississippi* (1981)

Kirk Franklin

Kirk Franklin came to prominence in the mid-1990s, bringing a new vitality (and a new audience) to contemporary gospel. (He was also the first gospel performer to have a video played on MTV!) His best CDs include:

- *Kirk Franklin and the Family* (1993)
- *The Rebirth of Kirk Franklin* (2002)

Larnelle Harris

Larnelle Harris is a contemporary gospel singer with classical voice training. His power-packed vocal cords contribute to his reputation as one of the industry's top pure singers. Mr. Harris's most popular CDs include:

- *The Father Hath Provided* (1987)
- *The Best of Ten Years Vol. 1 & 2* (1991)

The Dixie Hummingbirds

The Dixie Hummingbirds were a pioneering force behind the modern black gospel quartet sound. They began their career in the late 1930s and continued to perform (with replacements) well into the 1990s. (The Hummingbirds also sang backup on Paul Simon's 1973 hit "Loves Me Like a Rock.") Some of their best CDs include:

- *Live* (1976)
- *20th Century Masters—The Millennium Collection: The Best of the Dixie Hummingbirds* (2000)

Edwin Hawkins

Edwin Hawkins (and his choir, the Edwin Hawkins Singers) was one of the pioneers of contemporary gospel music, infusing traditional black gospel music with R&B-influenced production values. He's best known for his 1969 crossover hit, "Oh Happy Day," and for his group's background vocals on Melanie's 1970 hit, "Lay Down (Candle in the Rain)." The most popular Edwin Hawkins recordings include:

- *Let Us Go Into the House of the Lord* (1968)
- *Oh Happy Day!: The Best of the Edwin Hawkins Singers* (2001)

Mahalia Jackson

Mahalia Jackson was one of gospel's first superstars, bringing black gospel music to a worldwide, multiracial audience from the 1930s through the 1960s. Her fame carried her far and wide; she sang at John F. Kennedy's presidential inauguration and at Dr. Martin Luther King Jr.'s funeral. Her energetic and emotional style reflects the influence of both revival singing and classic blues singers, such as Bessie Smith. Some of her best recordings include:

- *Bless This House* (1956)
- *Gospels, Spirituals & Hymns* (1991)

The Mighty Clouds of Joy

The Mighty Clouds of Joy is one of contemporary gospel's most popular groups. The group was formed in the mid-1950s and recorded their first album in 1960. They were the first black gospel group to add bass, drums, and keyboards, and were well known as showmen in concert. Some of the best recordings include:

- *The Best of the Mighty Clouds of Joy* (1973)
- *Live and Direct* (1997)

Sandi Patti

Known as "the Voice," Sandi Patti is one of the biggest stars of contemporary Christian music. Her repertoire ranges from gospel standards to pop ballads, and she's noted for her powerful, flexible voice—and her ability to climb effortlessly to a high C. You can hear her voice to best effect on these CDs:

- *A Morning Like This* (1986)
- *All the Best … Live* (2001)

Clara Ward

Clara Ward and the Ward singers were extremely popular in the 1940s and 1950s. They toured regularly with Reverend C.L. Franklin, and Clara served as a mentor and inspiration to the Reverend's daughter, Aretha. Some of her best recordings include:

- *Down by the Riverside (Live at the Town Hall, NY)* (1958)
- *Meetin' Tonight!* (1994)

Singing R&B and Soul

The music alternately called R&B (rhythm and blues), soul, urban, or hip hop is a secular derivation of black gospel music. This is the sound that defines African American music in the last half of the twentieth century, combining the emotion of the blues, the spirituality of gospel, and the melodies of pop with a driving, rock-solid beat that makes you want to get up and dance.

The History of Soul Music

The immediate predecessor to today's soul and urban music was 1950s rhythm and blues. Back then, the music industry was extremely segregated, with separate top-40 charts for black artists and white artists. While white popular music was stagnating with bland artists like Pat Boone and Patti Page, the black music charts were rockin' and rollin' with the soulful sounds of LaVern Baker, Ruth Brown, and Chuck Willis.

One of the first artists to merge R&B with pop and gospel—and thus appeal to both black and white audiences—was Ray Charles, with his 1954 hit "I Got a Woman." He was followed by such innovators as Jackie Wilson, Sam Cooke, and James Brown, all of whom appealed to audiences of all races. The 1950s also saw the rise of doo-wop music, with its wonderful close-harmony singing and echoes of gospel jubilee quartets. This music led directly to the girl group pop of the early 1960s (with groups like the Shirelles, the Ronettes, and the Crystals) and then to the Motown sound of the mid- and late-1960s. At the same time, a harder R&B sound came from Stax and Atlantic Records, with artists like Aretha Franklin, Otis Redding, Wilson Pickett, and Sam and Dave providing a more gospel-influenced brand of soul.

Note

The 1960s also saw the rise of the "white soul" singer, as typified by England's Dusty Springfield. Listen to her legendary *Dusty in Memphis* record to hear how, in the hands of the right singer, soul music can transcend racial boundaries.

The 1970s saw the evolution of the smoother Philadelphia sound, which was then supplanted by the grittier rap and hip hop music of the 1980s and the 1990s. Unfortunately, there's not much to be said about rap and hip hop singers, since these musical styles feature semi-spoken rhymes, rather than traditional melodies and vocals. It's classic soul music—and the relatively new genre of urban contemporary—that captures our hearts and souls with the emotional performances of its supremely talented singers.

How R&B and Soul Differ from Other Types of Singing

In many ways, singing R&B and soul is a lot like singing pop music, but with gospel inflections. That means using your best pop technique but adding melodic embellishments as called for.

You'll note that some soul singers sing with a very wide smile. This closes down your resonators, giving your voice a more sharply focused (piercing) bright tone that hits the audience like a laser beam. This technique also helps to eliminate vibrato from your voice, which produces the kind of clean, clear tone associated with many classic soul singers.

Great R&B and Soul Singers

There have been so many great soul singers over the past 50 years that it's difficult to compile a short list for you to listen to. That said, here's some of the best of the best over the years, performers that definitely should be part of your listening regimen.

India.Arie

India.Arie is the best of a new group of young female singers in the classic R&B/soul tradition. She's only released two CDs to date, but they're both keepers:

- *Acoustic Soul* (2001)
- *Voyage to India* (2002)

Ruth Brown

Ruth Brown was the premier female R&B singer of the 1950s, with a strong-yet-seductive vocal style. (She was such a superstar that Atlantic Records was known at the time as "the house that Ruth built"—and they weren't talking about the Babe.) She was inspired by the great jazz singers of the 1940s—Sarah Vaughan, Billie Holliday, Dinah Washington—and she in turn influenced Aretha Franklin and the other great soul singers of the 1960s. Listen to these recordings to hear the best of Ruth Brown:

- *Ruth Brown* (1957; re-released in 1999)
- *The Best of Ruth Brown* (1996)

Ray Charles

Ray Charles was one of the musicians most responsible for popularizing R&B music in the 1950s and for developing the genre of soul music. His vocal style isn't technically perfect, but he has one of the most emotional and easily identifiable voices of any style. Here are some of Ray Charles' best recordings:

- *Birth of Soul* (1991)
- *Ultimate Hits Collection* (1999)

Sam Cooke

Along with Ray Charles, Sam Cooke was one of the prime inventors of what we now call soul music. Cooke got his start singing gospel with the Soul Stirrers, then adapted his music to a smoother style that appealed to both black and white audiences of the 1950s. His best recordings include:

- *Live at the Harlem Square Club, 1963* (1963)
- *Greatest Hits* (1998)

Kenneth "Babyface" Edmonds

Kenneth Edmonds—better known as "Babyface"—is a multi-talented singer, producer, and songwriter. His own recordings in the 1990s helped to rejuvenate the R&B tradition of the smooth, sensitive, urban crooner. Babyface's most popular CDs include:

- *The Day* (1996)
- *A Collection of His Greatest Hits* (2000)

Aretha Franklin

Aretha Franklin *is* the Queen of Soul. Her roots are in gospel, and her singing is infused with gospel spirit and technique. Her hits are legend: "Respect," "Chain of Fools," "(You Make Me Feel Like) A Natural Woman," and dozens more. It's safe to say that Aretha defined soul music in the 1960s for both black and white audiences; she has served as an inspiration for generations of younger singers, from Whitney Houston to Mariah Carey to Christina Aguilera. For the best of Aretha, listen to these CDs:

- *I Never Loved a Man the Way I Loved You* (1967)
- *Lady Soul* (1968)
- *Queen of Soul: The Atlantic Recordings* (1992)

Al Green

Al Green was the first great soul singer of the 1970s. He incorporates large dollops of black gospel into his electrifying performances, complete with sanctifying moans and wails. In the mid-1970s he abandoned his singing career for the ministry, but has since returned to the performing and recording scene and remains as vital as ever. Al Green's best recordings include:

- *Let's Stay Together* (1972)
- *Take Me To the River* (2000)

Patti LaBelle

Patti LaBelle grew up singing in a Baptist choir, and in 1960 teamed with Cindy Birdsong (later of the Supremes) to form a group called the Ordettes. With the addition of Nona Hendryx and Sarah Dash, the group was rechristened Patti LaBelle and the Blue Belles and had several hits throughout the decade. In the 1970s Patti went solo (and disco, with the hit "Lady Marmalade"); she enjoyed considerable success in the late 1970s, 1980s, and on into the 1990s. Her best recordings include:

- *Winner in You* (1986)
- *Greatest Hits* (1996)

The Staples Singers

The Staples Singers is a family group: Pops, daughters Mavis and Cleotha, and son Pervis (later replaced by another daughter, Yvonne). They started out singing pure gospel, then crossed over to soul and pop in the 1970s and beyond; their many hits include "I'll Take You There" and "Respect Yourself." To get a feel for the Staples Singers, listen to these recordings:

- *Be Altitude: Respect Yourself* (1972)
- *The Best of the Staples Singers* (1990)

Luther Vandross

Luther Vandross started as a background singer in the late 1970s, and later became a solo hit on the urban contemporary charts. He has an elastic tenor voice that exudes a confident sexuality. His best recordings include:

- *Any Love* (1988)
- *The Ultimate Luther Vandross* (2001)

Note

If you're interested in R&B vocalists, you should also check out those pop singers with a heavy soul bent, such as Smokey Robinson, Whitney Houston, or even Mariah Carey. See Chapter 18 for more.

Singing a Gospel Song

Now we'll give you a chance to test your gospel singing technique, with a tune I'm sure you're well familiar with—"Amazing Grace." It's sung on the CD by the talented Mary Moss; listen to how she embellishes the melody, lending heart and soul to a highly emotional performance.

When you sing the song, don't try to replicate Mary's performance; instead, make the song your own. Start as straight as you like, then start playing with the melody, adding as much syncopation and ornamentation as you can muster. Pretend that you're in church, singing in front of a congregation, and let the spirit work for you!

The Least You Need to Know

- Gospel music evolved from the rural Protestant church in the first part of the twentieth century.
- There are three types of gospel music: Southern gospel, black gospel, and contemporary gospel.
- Black gospel music influenced the development of rhythm and blues, soul, rock and roll, and contemporary gospel music—and continues to influence pop singers today.
- To sing in the gospel or soul styles, start with solid classical or pop vocal technique and add a variety of melodic embellishments.

Amazing Grace

Words by James Newton
Traditional Melody

G G7
1.A - - - - - - ma - - - zing - grace! How
(2.'Twas -) grace that - taught my
3 C D9 G Em7 A9
sweet the sound that - saved a - wretch like -
heart to fear, and - grace my - fears re -
7 Am7 D7 G G7
me! - - - - - - - I once was - lost, but
lieved - - - - - - How pre - cious - did that
11 C G D7 Em A7 G/D D7
now - am - found, was - blind but - now I
grace - ap - pear, the - hour I - first be -
1. 2.
15 G G
see - - - - - - - 2.'Twas
lieved! - - - - - - -

Part 6: The Next Steps

Are you ready for the big time? You will be when you follow the advice in these final chapters. You'll learn how to take care of your voice, how to find a voice teacher, how to sing on stage and in the studio, and how to ace the audition and follow your dreams!

Chapter 21

Taking Care of Your Voice

In This Chapter

- Uncovering the medical causes of vocal problems
- Learning how to deal with vocal misuse and abuse
- Understanding the warning signs of vocal abuse
- Discovering how to take protective measures

Every singer—or, for that matter, every person who relies on their voice to communicate—knows the frustration of a voice that won't work. Our voices are housed in perhaps the most delicate and susceptible part of our anatomy—the upper respiratory system. All that delicate mucous lining is constantly exposed to bacteria, viruses, and a host of environmental allergens. Add to that mix the endless opportunities for vocal overuse or abuse, and you can see that the human voice takes quite a beating every day—and that constant exposure and abuse can create both short- and long-term vocal disorders.

How is a singer to survive and keep his or her instrument in top working condition? The first step is pretty obvious—you have to keep your whole body in the best physical condition possible. This means getting plenty of rest, regular exercise, and eating well. But even when you take all these precautions, there will still be times when those germs or allergens will wreak havoc on your voice.

What it comes down to is that you need to understand how all these factors affect your singing, and know what you can do to better protect your voice—so as not to do real damage to your precious instrument.

What Causes Voice Disorders?

It's often difficult to determine the underlying cause or causes of voice disorders; there are so many factors that can come into play. Complicating this situation is the fact that, frequently, there are multiple causes to any given vocal problem.

For example, a person may develop bad vocal habits as a result of an existing medical condition—or a medical condition may result from bad vocal habits. In this situation, it's hard to determine which came first—the chicken or the egg; all you know is that you have a problem and you need it fixed.

There are all manner of vocal disorders. Some are functional, some are stress-induced, and some even have psychological causes. In general, though, the majority of voice disorders fall into five major categories, listed here in decreasing order of frequency:

- Infectious and inflammatory conditions
- Vocal misuse and abuse
- Benign and malignant growths
- Neuromuscular diseases
- Psychogenic conditions

We'll look at each of these causes separately.

Infectious and Inflammatory Conditions

We're all familiar with these guys. When we're talking about inflammatory conditions, we're talking about sinus infections, sore throats, the common cold, and allergies. While your doctor is the only one who can properly diagnose and treat these problems, there are a few commonsense measures that can be taken to help diminish their effect on your singing voice.

Dealing with a Cold

Probably the worst thing about singing with a cold is that you feel miserable. The good news is you're unlikely to permanently harm your voice to sing when you have a cold—although, on the whole, it's not really advisable.

If you feel you must sing while you have a cold, there are two key points to remember. First, call on your very best technique to help you elevate your voice. (Sometimes you'll feel as though you actually sing "over" the congestion). Second, remember that you don't sound as bad to others as you do to yourself.

The bottom line is that you probably aren't going to feel much like singing anyway, so why push it? Better to get lots of rest and take in all the fluids that you can manage—which means drinking lots and lots of water. Water is one of nature's best expectorants and it thins all that nasty phlegm so you can get rid of it faster. Also, don't overlook the importance of water as a preventative measure. Moist mucous membranes are more resistant to infection than dry ones, so drinking lots of water may help you ward off that cold or sinus infection in the first place.

Tip

Try adding a tablespoon of apple cider vinegar and a bit of honey to a large bottle or glass of water. It may not taste good, but it will help soothe and heal a sore throat without drying it out.

Along the same lines, warm herbal teas can ease scratchy throats and even help loosen excessive phlegm. However, you should avoid teas with caffeine, as caffeine will dry you out—as will alcohol.

Another thing *not* to do (that others might tell you *to* do) is suck on a lemon. I don't know where this so-called "remedy" got started, but I wish it hadn't. While the vitamin C you get from the fresh lemon is good, the lemon's acidity is very harsh and constricting on your delicate singing apparatus. Better to get your vitamin C from other sources and let water do the job of busting up that phlegm.

To help cope with wintertime dry air (caused by lower temperatures and furnace use), some singers find it helpful to employ the use of a humidifier. While this is helpful in keeping the mucous membranes moist and resistant to invaders, it carries some special considerations of its own—mainly dealing with the spread of mold and bacteria. Make sure to keep your humidifier squeaky clean and to throw out any remaining water and clean the bowl between each use. You could find yourself in worse shape if you're careless about humidifier cleanliness—especially if you are allergic to mold!

Head colds are, at the least, annoying and uncomfortable—but not permanently injurious to your singing voice. If the cold is in your throat, however, and is causing symptoms associated with laryngitis (the inflammation of your larynx), then you might as well hang it up for awhile. Rest your voice and visit your doctor to see if any prescription medication is needed. Nobody wants to hear you sing in that condition anyway, and you certainly shouldn't attempt to practice when it could jeopardize the health of your vocal cords in the long run.

Using Over-the-Counter Medications

When it comes to fighting a cold or the flu, you're no doubt familiar with the various over-the-counter medications that are available. You're probably *not* familiar with the effects of these medications on your voice. Here's what you need to know:

- Avoid medications that have drying side effects, such as some antihistamines. They give temporary relief but tend to make secretions more difficult to expel. These medications work by drying out the mucous membranes (including the vocal folds), which could result in further irritation. (In addition, most antihistamines tend to make you drowsy.)
- Look for medications that are pure decongestants, such as pseudoephedrine, and stick to single-ingredient medications. This way, you'll only take that medication you really need. The fact is, some "multi-symptom" medications may actually cause some further irritation—as well as overmedicate you, in general.
- Over-the-counter nasal sprays can be dangerous—primarily because they're mildly addictive. I've seen too many singers develop a dependency on these sprays. In my nonprofessional opinion, the only truly safe nasal spray is a simple saline solution, which you can buy in any pharmacy. (Warm salt water can also safely ease sore throat pain, when gargled.)
- The local anesthetics found in throat sprays or lozenges can temporarily relieve sore throat pain—but by doing so, sometimes give you a false sense of well being and enable you to overuse a voice that should be allowed to rest. The lesson here is to be careful not to mask what your body is trying to tell you; when your throat is sore or scratchy or your voice is hoarse or breaking, it's time to call in professional help.

CAUTION

Caution

When it comes to dispensing medical advice, I'm a pretty good singer. For professional answers to your specific medical questions, consult with your personal physician.

Dealing with Allergies

Having two or three colds a year isn't all that uncommon, especially if you travel a lot or work around a lot of people. But if you have respiratory problems on a more frequent basis, or if you're plagued by recurring sinus problems, coughs, chest tightness, or even shortness of breath, then you may have undiagnosed allergies—or even asthma.

Allergies can cause swelling of the sinuses and nasal lining, which favors the development of infections. If you try to sing under these conditions, you'll often try to compensate for lack of breath or clarity of tone by resorting to some unhealthy practices—that can quickly become bad habits.

With this in mind, it's definitely worth it to make an appointment with an allergist who can diagnose and treat your condition. If you ignore your allergies, continued demands on the larynx under adverse conditions can lead to vocal cord nodes and polyps. The good news is that allergies, while annoying, can be controlled with proper medical attention—and some of the cure is now available as over-the-counter medication.

Vocal Misuse and Abuse

When you're troubleshooting vocal problems, medical conditions are only part of the story. It's also possible that the problems you're having with your singing voice are caused by the way you use your speaking voice.

How to Abuse Your Voice

People who speak in a pinched or high-pitched voice—or in an exaggerated breathy speaking voice—place a lot of unnecessary tension on the vocal cords and the larynx. I've seen this a lot among teenaged girls who think that their "little girl voice" is cute or sexy. It very well may be, but speaking in that type of voice can actually do harm to their singing voice. The healthiest speaking voice is one in the mid-range (neither too high or low pitched) and one that allows a natural, comfortable flow of air over the vocal cords.

Ironically, some of the most abused voices are those of public school music teachers. These poor souls (trust me, I know) have to sing all day with their classes, or—even worse—attempt to speak over all that classroom clamor.

Music teachers, of all people, should know better.

And it isn't just music teachers. Many classroom teachers and sports coaches find themselves overusing their voices on a regular basis—and this daily overuse and abuse, year after year, takes its toll.

As a cautionary tale, I'll relay what happened to me. When I was a very young and overexuberant elementary music teacher, I developed vocal *nodes*—tiny callous-like "bumps" on the vocal cords. My speaking and singing voice became raspy and, at times, certain words couldn't be phonated at all. I went to a voice specialist who prescribed complete vocal rest for three weeks. (That's not talking at all for almost a month, if you can imagine that!) I followed his advice to the letter and, fortunately, the nodes disappeared. (Other singers aren't so fortunate; the presence of vocal nodes often requires surgery.) It was an early wake up call to me, emphasizing the fragile nature of the vocal mechanism and the necessity of its conservation and care.

This same warning goes for avid sports fans who get caught up in the moment and yell or scream at ball games—or for rock singers who try to scream their way over all the amplified instruments in the band. You can do a lot of damage in a short amount of time, so try to be cautious and use some common sense in any loud situations. This goes for sporting events, rock concerts, nightclubs, and even loud parties and restaurants. Don't let a moment of wild abandon cause a lifetime of vocal damage!

Smoking, Drinking, and Drugs

It goes without saying that smoking and drinking can harm your health and, particularly, your voice. While most singers realize the harmful effects of smoking, there are still a lot of singers who think drinking won't hurt them. Drinking in moderation, perhaps, causes little harm, but excessive use of alcohol not only impairs your judgment and motor skills, it also dehydrates your mouth, your voice, and your entire system.

Unfortunately, there's a long history of great musicians who are also drug and alcohol abusers. Read a biography of most any great jazzer or rocker, and you're likely to read the sad story of a life that was cut short by substance abuse. Some tragic examples that come to mind are Billie Holiday and Janis Joplin (vocalists), Bill Evans (pianist), Charlie Parker (saxophonist), and Keith Moon (drummer).

While it's tempting to idolize these individuals and their lifestyles, you have to remember that the creative accomplishments they made were *in spite of* their drug and alcohol use—not because of it. One can only imagine the contributions these great musicians could have made had they lived a normal life span!

Don't kid yourself that drugs or alcohol will spark your creative genius or give you that performer's "edge"—because they won't. Please excuse the moralizing, but you're gambling with your health and your musical career every time you exchange the natural high of a really solid musical performance for the short-lived, artificial high of drugs or alcohol. You need all your faculties to execute your fine-honed musical skills; ceding control to drugs or alcohol makes it that much harder to do what you need to do as a singer.

Physical Problems

The other three causes of voice disorders are all physical:

- Benign and malignant growths, which can include various types of lesions in the vocal tract, such as vocal nodules, granulomas, papillomas, and even cancer
- Neuromuscular diseases, including vocal cord paralysis, movement disorders, and degenerative conditions, such as atrophy of the vocal cords and Parkinsonism
- Psychogenic conditions, in which some sort of psychological trauma causes a loss of voice

These physical maladies are much too involved for us to discuss here. Suffice to say that if you have a physical problem with your throat or lungs, you need the attention of a qualified physician—ideally one who has experience with singers. If worse comes to worst and you require any type of throat surgery, definitely seek out a surgeon who specializes in vocal disorders common to singers. You don't want a less experienced surgeon cutting at your "instrument"; it is unfortunately all too easy to incur damage that can permanently affect your singing voice.

Warning Signs of Vocal Fatigue or Illness

How do you know if your voice is going south? It isn't always that easy to tell.

While you might think otherwise, a tired, overused voice isn't always hoarse. A hoarse voice is a definite warning sign that something is wrong, but you can be doing plenty of damage to your voice without inducing the onset of hoarseness—which means that there are other signs you want to be aware of.

One sign of pending problems is if your vocal range narrows and notes that were once easy for you become difficult. If this happens to you, you must give your voice the rest and attention it needs to recover its former range.

If you find your voice seeming to "cut out" on you when speaking or singing, you could be experiencing the warning signs of vocal nodes. The presence of vocal nodes requires immediate medical attention—and rest.

The onset of vocal fatigue is often signaled by a slight, dull ache around the area of the larynx. It's as if your voice is saying, "Enough—I need a rest!" If and when this happens, don't ignore the message; avoid all unnecessary speaking or singing and rethink your practice sessions for a while. You can study a piece of music or work on memorization without ever singing a note. You can also listen to recordings or watch concert tapes while your voice is getting its much needed rest.

For any of these symptoms, rest and hydration are necessary. If this doesn't do the trick, you should seek medical help. Remember—the voice you have is the only voice you'll ever be given.

Staying Healthy

Of course, an ounce of prevention is worth a pound of cure. What exactly can you do to keep your voice in tip-top shape—and avoid these sort of vocal problems?

My best advice is to pay attention to the do's and don'ts in the following list—and, above all, use common sense!

- DO drink plenty of water.
- DON'T drink alcohol in excess—and don't drink at all when you're on stage or in the studio.
- DO drink warm herbal teas.
- DON'T drink any tea, coffee, or soft drink that contains caffeine.
- DO eat a balanced diet, low in sugar and low in dairy products.
- DON'T do drugs—period.
- DO practice Yoga or similar exercises.
- DON'T forget to keep your head warm in cold weather. Consider wearing ear muffs or putting cotton in your ears when you go out in extremely windy or cold conditions.
- DO make cardiovascular exercise a regular part of your daily routine.
- DON'T take over-the-counter cold, sinus, or allergy medication without first consulting your doctor.
- DO buy a portable steamer with a face mask and use it for 20 minutes before you appear onstage or in the studio.
- DON'T smoke—and avoid smoky rooms. (This includes all types of smoke, including fireplace smoke.)
- DO rest your voice regularly, especially if you sing aggressively. As a guide, take one day off for every three days of performing, or two days off for every five days of performing.
- DON'T talk too much—it wears down your vocal cords. (The same goes for talking too loud—or screaming at sporting events.)
- DO try to cough quietly, if you have to cough. Take a deep breath and use your diaphragm—not your larynx—to expel needed mucous.
- DON'T hang out in dusty environments, if you can avoid it.
- DO place a warm wet towel around your neck after a performance, and don't speak for 10 minutes afterward.
- DON'T try to sing higher or lower than is comfortable.
- DO gargle with warm water containing ½ teaspoon each of salt and baking soda.
- DON'T sing if it hurts—or if it hurts to swallow.
- DO get plenty of rest, especially the night before a performance.

Follow these tips—as well as all the other advice throughout this book—and you'll be a healthier singer from the start!

The Least You Need to Know

- Voice disorders can be caused by infections, misuse and abuse, benign and malignant growths, neuromuscular diseases, and even psychogenic causes.
- Never ignore warning signs like hoarseness, chronic coughing, narrowing of range, "achy" throat, or sporadic loss of voice. Seek medical attention if conditions persist.
- Avoid drug use or excessive alcohol use.
- Avoid overuse of your speaking and singing voice—rest it when it becomes fatigued.

Chapter 22

Finding a Teacher

In This Chapter

- Understanding why taking lessons is important
- Finding out about different types of voice teachers
- Discovering what to look for—or avoid—in a voice teacher
- Learning how to get the most from your voice lessons

You're serious about improving your voice.

You've purchased this book and, one hopes, have diligently read all the chapters (so far) and worked through all the exercises. You've pledged to practice every day and are checking out the different styles of singing available to you. You may even harbor ambitions of pursuing a professional singing career.

But if you're really serious, the next thing you'll do is close this book and pick up the phone.

That's because you need to find a voice teacher.

Why Take Lessons?

It doesn't matter how dedicated you are or how good this (or any other) book is. If you're serious about becoming a really good singer, you need someone to help you achieve that goal—a coach, a mentor, a trainer.

In short, a voice teacher.

Nothing—I repeat, *nothing*—can replace the one-on-one exchange that occurs between two human beings in actual voice lessons. A good voice teacher can help you progress beyond the exercises in this book and work directly with your own particular vocal gifts or limitations. Feedback from an objective voice teacher is necessary for your vocal development; you need someone to tell you what you're doing right and what you're doing wrong, and to help do more of the former and less of the latter. That's something no book or CD can do, not even this one.

Can you become a singing sensation without formal lessons? It's possible. But your success will be more likely if you have someone helping you along the way, pushing you when you need to be pushed and helping you out when you need help. That's what a good voice teacher does and why you'll progress further and faster when you have one.

A good voice teacher can help you in many different ways. Let's look at just a few ....

Regularly Scheduled Lessons

Everyone has a difficult time trying to fit all the demands of today's hectic lifestyle into their schedule. Unfortunately, musical practice often takes a back seat to other, more pressing responsibilities. However, if you have a weekly or bi-monthly voice lesson scheduled—one that you know you have to pay for—then you're much more likely to make time to prepare for that lesson. Which means, of course, that you'll probably take your vocal practice sessions more seriously.

Remember, if you're going to improve, you have to practice. The specter of an upcoming lesson is a good incentive to start working the old vocal cords!

Someone to Hear You

Having someone to listen to how you're singing is absolutely necessary if you're serious about your craft. That's because you can't really hear how you sound to others. You may think you're producing a nice focused tone with a lot of resonance when, in fact, your tone may sound thin or unsupported to another set of ears. The same goes for pitch, diction, vibrato—the whole ball of wax. You need that other set of ears to listen to the way you really sound—and your voice teacher will fill that role.

Expansion of Your Repertoire

Be honest. Left to your own devices, you'd only sing those songs you know—and like. There's a lot more music out there than you know about or might volunteer to sing. You need a dispassionate third party to suggest additional songs and help you expand your musical repertoire.

A private voice teacher can introduce you to a whole new world of music. Look to your voice teacher to suggest songs that are particularly suited to your individual vocal range and abilities. You'll learn a *lot* of new music from a good voice teacher—and learning new songs is both fun and instructional.

Networking with Other Singers and Musicians

There is no better way to link up with other singers and musicians than through a good private teacher. Some teachers hold group classes in addition to their private lessons, so you'll have to the opportunity to compare your progress to that of other singers. In addition, your teacher probably knows other musicians in the area, so if you need to hook up with a piano player or even a full band, your teacher is a good first person to ask.

If your teacher is well connected to the local music scene, he or she will, from time to time, be asked to recommend a student for some gig. It may be singing for a wedding, local theater production, or even a recording session. If you're on your teacher's "A list," it's possible you might get the call. Your teacher knows that a little real-world experience is a great way to supplement your regular vocal lessons.

Development of Other Musical Skills

If you're fortunate enough to find a voice teacher who has a solid background in keyboard or music theory, you can ask to have those skills incorporated into your voice lesson. The more you know about music in general, the more grounded you'll be as a singer; if you have the opportunity to learn keyboard or guitar or general music, take it.

I always encourage my students to develop their ear-training skills, basic keyboard abilities, and understanding of elementary music theory. By adding these tools to their musical toolkit, they can truly call themselves *musicians*—not just singers. We set time aside in each voice lesson to work on those kinds of things. Remember—the development of these nonsinging skills will make you a better singer and give you an advantage over others who don't have the same training.

The Teacher as a Resource for Further Study

A private teacher, particularly one who is connected to your local educational institutions, will be in the know about local classes, workshops, conventions, and concerts that can greatly enhance your study of singing. The most informative and educational venues are often the least advertised, at least to the general public. Your teacher can keep you informed about opportunities that you would never read about in the local paper—which gives you a leg up on anyone studying voice in an isolated situation.

Types of Voice Teachers

When you're hunting for a voice teacher, here's something you need to know—not all voice teachers are created equal. It's very important for you to understand some of the differences that exist so you can find the teacher who best fits your individual needs.

The Voice Teacher

Voice teachers fall into two general categories. The first we'll refer to as just that—a voice *teacher*. This is a person who can help you develop your vocal technique, addressing all aspects of your singing voice from breath control to placement and focus. The voice teacher should have a thorough knowledge of singing technique and should be able to model that technique for you.

Most college-degreed voice teachers will have a solid background in vocal pedagogy (the science of teaching) and classical vocal techniques (the basis for all good singing). They should have a clear understanding of the physical makeup of the singing mechanism and should be able to quickly diagnose any physical adjustments needed to improve your singing tone.

A skilled voice teacher can take you from ground zero to your maximum potential. You'll work on tone quality, breath support and control, articulation, diction, and all the techniques we've addressed in this book. Just don't expect any quick fixes; like most everything of value, the development of a fine singing voice takes much practice and much time.

Note

Sometimes it may be as simple as identifying an incorrect tongue position or a lazy soft palate, but a thorough knowledge of how the voice works is necessary to identify and correct any kind of singing problems.

The Vocal Coach

The second type of voice teacher is the *vocal coach*. A vocal coach functions in a slightly different fashion than a voice teacher—much like the ways a classroom teacher is different from a professional sports coach.

In fact, you might want to think of a vocal coach as a *musical* coach because they normally work with people who can already sing well. (It's just like the way a pro basketball coach works with players who already know the fundamentals.) Once you've learned the musical fundamentals, there is still the need for a vocal coach to keep you on track and developing throughout your subsequent singing career.

The role of coaching assumes that excellent vocal technique is already in place. The coach primarily provides constructive criticism on phrasing, musical and dramatic interpretation, and language clarity.

The vocal coach may or may not be an exceptional singer herself, but she must be able to provide insightful feedback to the singer she's coaching. I've coached professional singers who far surpass my vocal abilities, but they still needed a trusted musical evaluation of their delivery. Even great opera singers continue to work with a vocal coach—someone who can listen to them and be a trusted and sensitive second set of ears.

Caution

Even though you'll eventually need a trusted practice partner—someone to rehearse with and provide much needed feedback on your repertoire—you shouldn't confuse a vocal coach with an accompanist. An accompanist generally plays the piano (or organ or guitar) for the singer and isn't expected to critique the singer's performance, as a vocal coach would. Learn more about accompanists in Chapter 23.

What to Look For—or Avoid—in a Voice Teacher

Finding a voice teacher is not an easy task—especially if you live outside a major metropolitan area. In a community of 35,000 people or so, you may find five or six piano teachers, two or three guitar teachers, and even a drum instructor or two, but you're lucky if you find a single (qualified or not) voice teacher.

Put simply, good voice teachers are few and far between.

Where to Find a Good Voice Teacher

I've never understood why good voice teachers are hard to find, even though they obviously are. It may have to do with the fact that there are a limited number of people who have both the vocal and keyboard skills to cover all the bases during a voice lesson. Since you need someone to accompany you during your voice lessons, that means your voice teacher not only needs to sing, she also needs to play the piano. (Unless you want to drag a piano player to your lessons, of course!) Finding an individual who can both sing and play (and teach, of course) narrows the field quite a bit.

Of course, if you live in a major metropolitan area or near a university with a strong music department, you'll have a lot more qualified teachers to choose from. That's just simple supply and demand—the more potential students, the more teachers who tend to be available. (Although if there are lots of other vocal students around, you may find yourself competing for schedule time with the very best teachers.)

Note

While finding a teacher is pretty much a local matter, there are a few websites that can help you locate teachers in your area. In particular, check out MusicStaff.com (www.musicstaff.com) and the National Association of Teachers of Singing Voluntary Teacher Database (www.nats.org/teacherfind.html).

That said, where do you look for a qualified voice teacher? As I just mentioned, if you have a university, college, or even community college in your town, start there. College-level music schools employ a lot of teachers who (typically) have college or post-graduate degrees in voice (or perhaps music education) and are well grounded in proper vocal technique. If you don't live near a recognized music school, look to junior high and high school choral directors (who will also typically have music degrees) or to the choir directors of your community's best church choirs.

I tend to warn people against enrolling at independent performance studios, which often cater to young singers wanting to be "Broadway Babies." In smaller communities, particularly, these operations can be more about fluff than substance, and they tend to develop belters rather than real singers. But there are some legitimate performance studios, particularly in larger cities, that employ highly skilled (and, in some cases, well-known) teachers and offer first-rate vocal training. Make sure you check out the credentials of the staff so that you understand what you're paying for—and what you hope you'll be getting.

Questions a Voice Teacher Should Ask *You*

A good voice teacher wants to ensure that the two of you are a good match. Just as you're checking out the teacher, the teacher should also be checking you out, to find out a little about your background, your previous training, your ambition, and just about you personally. Look for a teacher who, on first meeting, asks a lot of questions about you, such as:

- Why are you looking for a voice teacher?
- What do you hope to accomplish?
- What style(s) of music interest you?
- What previous training or singing experience have you had?
- Do you read music or play piano?

When you find an inquisitive teacher, you know that teacher wants to make the teacher/student experience work for you.

Questions *You* Should Ask a Voice Teacher

Of course, the teacher shouldn't be the only one asking questions. Here's a short list of things you might want to ask of a prospective voice teacher:

- What is your professional singing experience?
- What is your teaching experience?
- Did you study how to teach—and if so, where?
- What kind of musical styles do you teach?
- What is a typical lesson like?
- What kind of practice should I expect?
- How often will we have lessons?
- What other learning experiences can you provide—such as group classes, keyboard training, or theory skills?
- Who are some other students you've taught?

This last point is important. You need to get the feel of a teacher before you commit to a regimen of training. Talk to some of the teacher's other students and listen to what they say. For that matter, ask if you can have a trial lesson before you commit; there's nothing like first-hand experience to see if a teacher is a good fit for you.

Another good way to evaluate a voice teacher is to listen to his or her students. If the students sound like clones of each other, think twice about pursuing lessons with that teacher.

You see, good technique is good technique, but every individual voice does—and should—have its own unique quality. A skilled voice teacher will help you develop your personal sound within the context of solid singing technique. You don't want a teacher who takes a cookie cutter approach. Don't settle for vocal cloning; look for a teacher who can work with your own individual talents and desires.

Along the same lines, you want to find a teacher who is sympathetic to your musical goals and to your likes and dislikes. If you really, really, *really* want to be a country singer, you probably won't mesh with a teacher who lives and breathes opera and holds other musical styles in disdain. Yes, good vocal technique is good vocal technique, but at some point you'll need a teacher who is well steeped in the particular style you've chosen to pursue. Not that you won't learn anything from a less sympathetic teacher, but it certainly helps when you and your teacher are on the page about what you want to do and where you want to go.

Voice Teachers to Avoid

A good voice teacher will have a respect for varied styles of singing and won't try to use a cookie-cutter approach to your voice. Run from any teacher who insists that you try to sound a particular way or forces you to produce a sound that feels uncomfortable or unnatural!

On the same note (no pun intended), never study with a teacher who is chronically hoarse or has a voice that sounds unpleasant to you. Trust your ears and your heart; you'll know if they can't walk the walk. If its obvious that they can't, go someplace else.

You should also run from any teacher who spends more time singing in your lesson than you do. This may sound crazy, but it's not all that uncommon. After all, it's your lesson, not hers—you should be doing the bulk of the singing!

Getting the Most from Your Voice Lesson

Since voice lessons with a good teacher are expensive—anywhere from $20 to $50 a lesson—it behooves you to get the most from each lesson. Since it's your precious time and money we're talking about, let me offer some tips on how to maximize the time you spend with your voice teacher.

The most obvious and important thing you can do to get the most from your private lesson is to practice. This may sound fairly obvious, but it's important to remember. After all, you don't just have to learn and sing songs during practice, you also have to work to improve specific aspects of your vocal technique. Your practices consists of many different parts, including vocal exercises, breathing exercises, listening to yourself and others, score study, and the like. You won't accomplish much if you skip five days and then try to cram it all into a once-a-week marathon practice session. (And that kind of concentrated intensity isn't good for your voice, either!)

In addition to your normal practice and lesson routine, it's a good idea to keep a lesson notebook. In it you can note suggestions from your teacher, list assignments, or even jot down special problem areas in your music. Keep all your music with your notebook, as well as a cassette tape. You may want your teacher to record exercises or accompaniments on the cassette for you to practice with during the week. The idea is to keep everything in one place and to have it with you at every lesson. It will really make a difference in the effectiveness of your study.

The Least You Need to Know

- One-on-one voice lessons are essential to improving your vocal technique.
- Beginning vocal students study with a voice teacher; more advanced students (and professional students) typically study with a vocal coach.
- When you're looking for a voice teacher, check out the music schools of any local colleges or universities or the music departments of your local junior high and high schools.
- Look for teachers who address your individual needs and goals.
- Avoid voice teachers who apply a cookie-cutter approach or who do more singing than listening.

Chapter 23

Singing on Stage—and in the Studio

In This Chapter

- Learning how to present yourself on stage
- Overcoming stage fright
- Learning how to use the microphone
- Understanding studio singing

You're probably well accustomed to singing by yourself—in your room, in the shower, or in your car. Singing professionally is a bit different, however, in that you'll be singing out in the real world—on stage in front of an audience or in the studio recording tracks for a CD.

Singing on stage or in the studio is what it's all about. Both situations require you to use all that vocal technique you've been practicing for so long—but also require additional skills. You have to learn how to use a microphone, how to play to an audience, and how to best apply your vocal skills in a studio setting.

For most singers, singing on stage or in the studio is a lot of fun—once you've learned the ropes, that is!

Singing on Stage

Performing on stage is the "just do it" part of singing. Part of just doing it is learning how to present yourself as a professional, confident singer in front of a live audience. That audience might be your church congregation, pals in your local pub, or even a television audience watching you compete on the latest *American Idol*-type show. The important thing to remember is to always, under any circumstances and in any venue, give your very best performance. You owe it to yourself, your audience, and the music to be nothing less than the best you can be.

So let's look at some of the tricks of the trade you can use when performing on stage—in front of a live audience, with no retakes!

Be a Boy Scout: Be Prepared!

The first rule of performing on stage is a simple one—*be prepared*. This may sound like the Boy Scout motto, but it's particularly applicable to the art of live performance.

Singing in front of an audience, with no possibility of retakes, is one of the most rewarding—and one of the most frightening—things you can do in your singing career. When you sing, you open your soul in a very personal and intimate way to others. This is the reward. The frightening part is that live performance leaves no room for error; if you screw up, everyone in the audience will hear it.

When you play an instrument on stage, that instrument provides a physical comfort zone between you and the audience. This isn't the case when the instrument is *you*. When you're singing on stage there's nothing to shield you from the audience, except perhaps a microphone. So, perhaps more than any other musician, it's important for the singer (you) to be as prepared as possible beforehand—*just in case*.

This means you have to know the music, inside and out. You have to have a "Plan B" in place if you happen to tense up and forget the lyrics. You have to know what to do if the accompanist goofs up, or if the band goes off in an unrehearsed direction. Basically, you have to be prepared for *anything* to happen.

All of this speaks for the need to improvise. Not the jazz type of improvisation, of course, but rather the ability to go with the flow and adapt your planned performance to whatever circumstances dictate. The best improvisation is based on thinking through various alternatives beforehand.

For example, what do you do if you sing the big high note and the crowd erupts in spontaneous applause? You need to know, beforehand, whether you continue to sing through the big ovation or whether you stop and acknowledge the audience's praise. On the other hand, what do you do if you reach for that high note—and you miss it? Do you back up and try again or soldier on as if nothing has happened? Or what do you do if you wake up that morning with a cold—or just aren't in tip-top shape, vocally? Do you cancel the gig or try to alter your delivery to compensate?

You have to think about these things, in addition to knowing your music backward and forward. After all, if you're not prepared, who knows what will happen?

Put Your Best Foot Forward: You're Only as Good as You Look

How you look onstage has a whole lot to do with how you are perceived by the audience. That may not be particularly fair, but it certainly is the truth.

When you step out in front of that audience, it's important for you to look your best—but within the context of that particular performance. Both the style of music being performed and the venue will determine what is appropriate dress.

Grunge and alternative rock aside, grooming and cleanliness are more attractive than the alternative. You see a lot of extreme fashions in the music world today—floppy hats, big jackets, down-to-there hip huggers, and even the occasional dead swan—but you should use some common sense and a little restraint when you're deciding on what to wear.

Tip

On the other hand, if your goal is to be a big rock or hip-hop star, the more flamboyant you dress, the better. (And if you're singing country, don't forget the rhinestones and the cowboy hat!)

For more traditional gigs, you don't want to draw attention away from your actual singing with a glitzy or revealing outfit. Guys should invest in a dark suit or a tux, and gals should have at least one simple but elegant dress. Black is the traditional color of choice among musicians because it provides a neutral and uniform visual backdrop for the music. In other words, it doesn't compete for attention, and it allows the listener to focus on aural rather than visual stimuli. In addition, dark colors look great under lights and tend to highlight your face—which is very important for a singer.

Walk the Walk: Carry Yourself with Confidence

How you carry yourself onstage is important. If you have an air of confidence—but not arrogance—your audience will be drawn into that perception.

You should walk onto the stage with your best posture and demeanor. Acknowledge the audience with a pleasant smile or nod, then get down to business.

It may sometimes be appropriate to say a few words as a means of introduction or background for the song you are about to sing. If so, say your peace—but keep it short! Granted, talking to the crowd is one way to connect with your audience, but the most effective way is through your musical performance. Keep your personal comments to an absolute minimum—it can get pretty cheesy pretty fast.

Tip

Want to see how you really come across onstage? Have a friend videotape your performance. Anything that makes you wince when you watch the playback probably made the audience wince, too.

Do the Hand Jive: Arm Movement on Stage

It may sound funny, but what to do with your hands is a very common concern among singers. Obviously, if you're using a microphone, you have your answer—for one of your hands. But what about that other hand—or those times when you aren't holding a mic?

If you're standing close to a piano, it's okay to lightly place one hand on the instrument. Just don't grip it as if your life depended on it—it's not a lifeboat. Also, don't lean on the piano; besides looking a little slouchy, it'll put your body out of alignment for proper breath support.

It's best to simply stand straight and tall and let your arms fall naturally at your sides. Do *not* hold your upper arms tightly against the sides of your chest; this comes across as weakness. (We tend to keep our upper arms close against our bodies when we're protecting or shielding ourselves.)

Depending on the context of the performance, *slight* hand gestures may be appropriate—and even quite effective—as long as you use them sparingly. For example, if you're singing at a traditional gig, like a wedding ceremony, you shouldn't gesture at all. But if you're fronting the band at the wedding reception, that's a different ballgame. A general rule of thumb is that the more classical or traditional the venue, the less need for dramatic gesturing.

Note

Review proper posture in Chapter 7.

When you make a hand gesture, start the gesture before you sing a phrase. We humans typically react with motion before we react with our voices, so if you sing before you gesture, it will appear unnatural to your audience. In addition, make sure that the gesture matches the part you're singing; a grand gesture on an intimate passage will definitely appear out of place.

If you're a soloist reading from a musical score during your performance, you should carry the score on and off stage in your *upstage* hand. (That's the one farthest away from the audience.) When you present your song, hold the score about chest level, as if you were serving hors d'oeuvres from a tray. You can then use your other hand to steady the music and turn pages as needed. Keeping the music at chest level is important; it helps you maintain an erect posture and establish eye contact with your audience.

If you're singing in a musical or a musical review, you'll need to take a very different approach to your singing onstage. Here you have to assume more of an "acting" role; you're not simply a conduit for the sound, you're expected to be an entertainer! In these settings, hand gestures, physical movement, and body language are all appropriate—and necessary—performance techniques.

Note

Learn more about musicals in Chapter 17.

You have similar concerns when singing with a rock or country band. When you're singing with a band, you're not out there by yourself; you're part of a group that you need to interact with. It's okay to get a little theatrical and "act" the part of the lead singer; it's important that you do whatever is necessary to connect with the audience. That might mean putting on a bit of an attitude, or jumping on top of a speaker cabinet, or flirting with the lead guitarist. It's all an act, so let your inhibitions down and have some fun!

The Only Thing You Have to Fear Is Fear Itself: Overcoming Stage Fright

If the thought of standing by yourself in front of an audience of strangers scares the bejeezus out of you, you're not alone. Many performers—even established pros—get the dreaded stomach butterflies before they go onstage. Fortunately, stage fright doesn't have to paralyze you. In fact, some performers welcome the slight "edge" it creates, and use it in their performances.

The challenge is to get psyched up for your performance without letting the fear keep you from singing. Here are some tips that the pros use to "sing through" the stage fright and give a great performance:

- **Don't get self-absorbed:** Put aside personal concerns and concentrate on the music; let the music be your center. The music really is bigger than all of us, and the true artist has an almost reverent respect for his particular art form. If you let the music fill your mind and spirit, you won't be as apt to develop a bad case of nerves.
- **Relax:** I know it's easier said than done, but you need to do whatever it takes to physically relax—short of using drugs or alcohol. If you feel jittery, breathe slowly and deeply to slow down your heart beat; stretching also helps. And don't forget the positive effects of Yoga when you're dealing with a bad case of nerves.
- **Warm up your voice:** Never, never go out on a stage and try to do it cold. The physical activity involved in vocal warm-ups tends to calm and focus your thoughts—as well as ready your vocal cords.
- **Embrace the edge:** You can use the adrenaline rush associated with stage fright as a positive physical reaction, not a negative one. Welcome the rush and make it work *for* you and your performance, rather than allowing it to negatively build on itself. It takes a lot of discipline to change your attitudes and perceptions, but it can become quite a freeing experience.
- **Be prepared:** I can't say it enough—you have to be prepared. Nothing can surpass solid technique and comprehensive preparation when it comes to developing confidence and overcoming stage fright. Armed with these powerful tools, you'll be able to shift to autopilot (or carry on with muscle memory) if you find yourself momentarily paralyzed by an unexpected bout of stage fright.

Help Your Helper: Working with an Accompanist

One of the real unsung heroes in the performance arena is the accompanist. A singer's accompanist is typically a pianist, and that person can make or break your onstage performance.

When you find a wonderful accompanist, treat them like royalty. Meet and try to exceed their requests for monetary compensation, if you can. Acknowledge them after a performance with a simple and discreet nod or hand gesture. Don't assume that practice time with them comes free. And when it comes to practice time, don't expect the accompanist to teach you the song; you should have a clear concept of delivery and style beforehand and should be able to communicate all that to the accompanist before you start to work on a number.

It's important that you provide clearly marked music for your accompanist. It doesn't hurt to use a yellow highlighter to mark tempo changes or repeat signs—anything that might be missed in the heat of performance or in the low onstage lighting. In addition, any deviations you plan from the published score should be clearly marked on the sheet music. Always inform the accompanist of the tempo by either singing a bar or two for them or by snapping the beat for a few measures. Songs are rarely sung or played note for note from the score; the fine accompanist appreciates your advance instructions as to performance style and tempo.

Using the Microphone

One of the key tools in a singer's toolbox is the microphone—especially if you're singing pop, rock, or country music, or working in a recording studio. You need to get used to using a microphone, as well as how your voice sounds when mic'ed.

Onstage, the microphone (and attendant amplification) lets you be heard over other amplified instruments, without straining your voice. It can even enhance your natural resonance or allow you to "float" those high notes in a very intimate and easy way, while still being heard. But used incorrectly, the microphone can amplify bad technique or distort an otherwise good singing voice.

It's important, then, to learn a little about this important tool and how to use it both onstage and in the recording studio.

Choosing a Microphone

In many instances you'll have no choice over the type of microphone you'll be using. (That will be the choice of the sound reinforcement personnel or the studio engineer.) If you *do* have the choice of which mic to use (if you're starting your own band, for example), you need to know a little about the different types of microphones available—and which are best for your specific purposes.

Naturally, you want to use a high-quality microphone; the cheap $20 mic you find at Radio Shack just won't do justice to your fine singing voice. It's a simple fact—if you put a great singer on a bad microphone, they won't sound good. (Conversely, the best microphone in the world won't make a bad singer sound better; the end result confirms the concept of "garbage in, garbage out.")

For most singers, you're best to stick with a *dynamic* microphone. Dynamic mics work on almost any sound system without special setup. The more expensive *condenser* microphones you find in a recording studio are typically more sensitive but require a separate power source (either a battery or something called *phantom power*). Dynamic microphones don't require any extras, and are easier for the occasional singer to use.

Tip

You can keep your shopping simple by sticking with the live sound standard for singers, the Shure SM58. This microphone is relatively inexpensive (under $125) and incredibly durable. You may also want to consider microphones from AKG and Sennhauser, who make good inexpensive vocal mics similar to the 58.

It's possible that you'll find yourself tempted by the many *wireless* microphones currently on the market. Despite the cool factor, wireless mics are typically more trouble than they're worth—unless you're planning a Britney Spears-like multimedia extravaganza. In addition to their added expense (a good wireless mic starts at $300), they're harder to connect to most sound systems and often have problems with radio frequency interference. If you feel you *must* have a wireless microphone, be sure to talk with a knowledgeable person ahead of time.

Proper Microphone Technique

How you sound onstage or in the studio depends on proper microphone technique. Here are some tips on how to use the microphone to best capture your vocal abilities:

- **Put your mouth on the metal:** Almost all microphones have what is called a *proximity effect*. The closer you are to the microphone, the more low-end sound the microphone picks up—which makes your voice sound warmer. So if you want a warm, intimate tone, sing close to the mic.

> **Caution**
>
> If you don't have a good live sound person to manage the proximity effect, singing too close to the microphone can cause you to overpower the rest of the musicians.

- **Vary the distance:** Keeping the proximity effect in mind, the distance you hold the microphone from your mouth should vary with the dynamic level of your voice. When you're singing in full voice, pull the mic away from you a little bit. For those really soft, intimate vocal moments, you can hold the mic much closer—and take advantage of the proximity effect. Just don't rely on the microphone to provide your control and support on soft passages or you'll find yourself going flat. And remember that putting too much volume through the microphone's sensitive pickups can cause an overload and create feedback and distortion.
- **Keep the mic aligned:** When you're moving onstage with a hand-held microphone, think of the mic as an extension of your vocal pathway. When you turn your head or body, keep the mic aligned with your voice. Be careful not to hold the mic in one position as you turn your head, or you'll get a real uneven and unprofessional result.
- **Hold the mic in the middle:** Most microphones are made to balance fairly well when held in the middle of the shaft. This is the correct place to hold the mic, regardless of what you see on MTV. (You'll see a lot of singers put their hands over the ball of the mic, even though this affects the microphone's sound—and neutralizes the proximity effect.)
- **Don't switch the microphone from hand to hand:** Pick a hand and stick with it. Shifting the microphone from hand-to-hand makes you look nervous, like an amateur. Figure out which hand is most comfortable for you and sing with the microphone in that hand 90 percent of the time.
- **Adjust the stand—ahead of time:** In a situation where the microphone is on a stand, make sure the height adjustment is just right for you—*before* you begin to sing. We've all witnessed the annoying distraction of the singer who constantly adjusts and fiddles with the stand during the performance; try not to be guilty of that yourself. In addition, you may think it looks cool to tightly grasp the mic stand during your performance or to swing it about while you're singing, like the big rock stars do. Well, it may look cool, but it also affects your sound; unless you're more interested in the show than the music, leave the stand alone and concentrate on your singing.
- **Watch out for popping air and consonants:** Consonants like "p," "b," "k," "s," and "t" can cause an explosive "pop" that is much too percussive to be pleasant. Most microphones are very responsive, so you'll need to soften or modify your articulation to avoid this type of popping. You can also minimize popping by pointing the microphone toward your chin. This puts the mic out of the direct explosive bursts of air from your mouth.

Singing in the Studio

Singing in the recording studio is a lot like singing live, but without the audience. To be a hit in the studio, a you need the same vocal and microphone skills you use onstage—if not more so.

Reading Counts!

In addition to all your other skills, if you want to make it as a studio singer, you have to know how to read music. In fact, the sharper your reading skills, the more successful you'll be. Studio musicians are expected to be able to sight read all manner of charts, and may even be called on to improvise as needed. A studio is not the place to learn your part; with rates well in excess of a hundred dollars an hour, you have to be ready to produce on the spot.

Use the Mic—and the Mix

You won't find a handheld microphone in the studio. Instead, you'll find very expensive mics specially designed for recording, typically hanging down from an overhead boom. Sometimes the mic will have a windscreen in front of it, as shown here, to help reduce popping and sibilance. You'll be instructed to stand a specific distance from the mic and to keep that distance. (If you tend to weave back and forth when you sing, you'll hear about it from the engineer!)

Note

This photo was taken during the recording session for this book's CD; more pictures are available on the web, at www. molehillgroup.com/sessionphotos.htm.

Singer Brad Brock laying down some vocal tracks in the studio; note the headphones and the really big microphone, complete with windscreen.

In most instances, the instrumental tracks will be recorded before you come in to sing. You'll be given a set of headphones, and you'll listen to a mix of the previously recorded instruments. Working with headphones is sometimes trying; it's hard to hear yourself sing when you have the instrumental mix feeding into both ears. For this reason, many singers only wear half the headphone, leaving one ear uncovered so they can hear themselves, too.

Tip

You can ask the engineer to adjust the mix in your headphones, to emphasize or deemphasize particular instruments or vocals.

Sing It Over—and Over, and Over ...

Whether you are recording demo tapes or jingles, you have to be willing and able to do numerous takes of a particular song—or part of a song. This repetition sometimes requires a level of patience to rival Job. The producer or the recording engineer will probably have a particular sound in mind, so you have to be flexible and accommodating in your performance. You also have to put the same energy and life into every take, even if you've sung that same darned chorus a hundred times already.

Here's something else that might seem strange, at first. If you do a lot of studio work, you'll often find yourself singing just *parts* of a tune. You might sing the whole song through a few times, then be called back to "punch in" a particular measure or line. That's because it's easier to fix a few bad notes than it is to rerecord an entire song. This is often facilitated by the use of a *click track*, which is like a metronome that clicks steadily in the background. You use the click track to keep a steady tempo, take after take.

Along the same lines, it's quite common to record one voice or instrument at a time, rather than live as a group. This makes it easier to punch in individual parts later on and gives the producer more control over the recording. (If this seems weird to you, think how the poor drummer feels, thumping along all by himself in the drum booth!)

Don't Be Surprised by What You Hear

You seldom hear vocal tracks that don't have some sort of processing performed on them. By processing, I mean those special effects that make a voice sound unique on a recording—everything from reverb and compression to distortion and synthesized voice doubling. (For the ultimate in processed vocals, listen to Cher on her hit, "Believe.")

Most of these effects are added by the engineer, but you may get the opportunity to participate in the creation of some effects and to listen to the results. Even with the most modest vocal processing, be prepared to hear your voice as something other than natural—and don't be shocked at what you hear! After all, your voice is just part of the total mix, so any processing you hear will be blended into the overall sound of the track.

Be Professional

Since the recording industry is a business, you should approach the studio just as a professional businessperson does his or her place of work. Don't just be prompt—be early. If the session starts at 10:00, don't show up at 10:00; be in place, warmed up, and ready to sing at 10:00. That means getting to the studio a good half-hour ahead of time. (This is also helpful if another musician doesn't show up—you may be asked to cover for them.)

In addition, it's important that you leave your artist persona at home. There's no place in the studio for bad attitudes. You're there to do a job, and you should do it—no matter what. Studio work can be extremely rewarding, both professionally and financially, but it demands the most professional attitude you can muster.

This is the music *business* we're talking about, after all.

The Least You Need to Know

- For both the stage and the studio, it's important to be well prepared before you sing the first note—and to learn to deal with any contingency that arises.
- When you're singing a traditional gig, less is more—keep the hand movements and between-songs patter to a minimum.
- Mastering the microphone is key to both stage and studio singing; learn how to hold and position the mic for the best possible sound.
- Studio singing is extremely demanding. Come prepared, be able to read new music, and don't get bored when you're asked to sing the same song a dozen times in a row.

Chapter 24

Follow Your Dreams

In This Chapter

- Discover the many different options available for serious singers
- Find out what you need to pursue a singing career
- Learn what to include on your demo CD
- Discover how to ace an audition

You've paid your dues. You've learned proper vocal technique, how to stand and how to breathe and how to project. You've learned how to read music and how to sight sing. You've listened to all the great singers and learned proper phrasing and diction. You've studied hard and practiced hard and now you're ready to make a name for yourself as a serious vocalist.

Just how do you do that?

Everything you've done up to this point has provided you with the foundation you need to enter the music business. But that's all—just the foundation. Now you have to do even *more* work—dedicated, physical work—to break into the business and, if all goes well, become a success.

Options for Serious Singers

Before you go knocking on doors, you have to determine which doors to knock on. If you want to make it as a singer in the music business, what options are available to you?

Karaoke

Don't laugh. Lots of semi-pro singers hone their skills at Karaoke bars. If you don't believe me, head out to a local Karaoke night and take a listen. In between the drunk businessmen and the big-haired housewives, you're likely to find some really fine singers plying their trade.

There are a number of reasons for this. First, it's an opportunity to rehearse with decent background musicians (on tape, of course) in front of a live audience. You don't have to pay for the musicians or for the rehearsal space; you even get a decent sound system to use for free.

Second, it's possible, just possible, that someone from the music industry will be in the crowd and hear you strut your stuff. I'm not saying that big-time A and R staff make a habit of hanging out at Karaoke bars, but it's not uncommon to find folks from local radio stations and recording studios, out for an evening of fun. If they're there and you catch their ear, all power to you.

Finally, many Karaoke bars hold "best singer" contests. You might even stumble onto a regional or national contest, as depicted in the movie *Duets*. Even if you're singing for a $50 prize in your local bar, it's real money—and it's generated from your singing. Good for you!

Talent Contests

The big brother of the Karaoke contest is the traditional talent search or contest. These things go all the way back to *Ted Mack's Amateur Hour*, and have helped to "discover" all manner of future superstars—from the Carpenters to Christina Aguilera. As this book is written, *American Idol* is one of the biggest hits on the small screen, and the venerable *Star Search* appears to be in the midst of a significant comeback.

> **Caution**
>
> Beware any talent search that charges a high "entrance fee" for your participation; these are likely to be run by rip-off artists. Instead, look for contests and searches associated with name institutions, such as music magazines, local radio stations, record labels, and the like.

Winning a talent contest is one of the easiest forms of garnering publicity. (Note that I didn't say it's a quick way to fame; getting noticed and becoming successful are two completely different things.) When you show off your talent onstage or on camera, you're reaching hundreds or thousands or even millions of potential fans. You're also getting your face and your voice in front of the people who really matter—the talent scouts and A and R men for the major record labels. You don't have to win the grand prize to get a recording contract; if a music scout likes what he hears, you could be on your way to a rewarding recording career.

Even if you don't reach anyone from the record labels, you still could get noticed by local recording engineers, advertising songwriters, music contractors, choir directors, and the like. A talent contest is the perfect place to promote your wares and reach all those people in the music industry who otherwise wouldn't return your calls.

While some talent contents and searches are run by disreputable folks with the sole goal of separating you from your money, there are a number of respectable, well-regarded opportunities out there. The best-known of these include:

- American Idol (www.idolonfox.com)
- Country Showdown (www.countryshowdown.com)
- George London Foundation Competitions (www.georgelondon.org)
- Octave Digital Excellence in Arts Competition (www.octavedigital.com)
- Pantene Pro-Voice Competition (www.pro-voice.com)

For an up-to-date list of all types of music competitions, go to the Indiana University School of Music Competitions page, at www.music.indiana.edu/som/placement/competitions.html. You can also find a list of competitions in *Classical Singer Magazine* (www.classicalsinger.com) and in the Concert Artists Guild's *Guide to Competitions* (www.concertartists.org).

Singing in Church

If you want to place to showcase your vocal talents, look no further than your local place of worship. Most churches have some sort of choir, and the bigger churches often feature vocal soloists on a regular basis. You probably want to shop for a church that features the type of music you like to sing—traditional Catholic or Protestant hymns, exuberant gospel, or something more contemporary.

When you look at some of the bigger churches, know that their top vocal talent sometimes gets paid. That's right, you can actually make money by singing in church! While this isn't necessarily the norm (especially among smaller congregations), there are a number of churches that try to make a name for themselves by the quality of their musical offerings—and offer some sort of compensation to attract the best singers in their community.

Community Choirs

Almost every city of medium size or larger has at least one community choir. Where I live, in Indianapolis, it's the Indianapolis Symphonic Choir, which rehearses weekly and performs several high-profile concerts a year—some of which are in conjunction with the Indianapolis Symphony Orchestra. (The artistic director of the Indianapolis Symphonic Choir, Dr. Eric Stark, was kind enough to help us fine-tune the content of this book—thanks, Eric!)

Tip

Many towns and cities have more than one community choir. Depending on your interests and inclinations, you may want to audition for the local woman's choir, gay men's choir, and the like. (Check out GALA Choruses, the Association of Gay and Lesbian Choruses, at www.galachoruses.org.)

These community choirs are wonderful opportunities for singers; not only do you get to sing quality repertoire on a regular basis, you also get to meet and network with the best vocalists in your area. It's not uncommon for community choir members to land other gigs as a result of their choir association; you can also learn a lot about the music industry in your town by talking with your fellow choir members.

Community Theater

Along the same lines, most towns and cities have one or more community theater operations. While you might not be an actor per se, community theaters just love to produce musicals—which is where you come in. Musicals need singers, both in the main roles and in the chorus.

When you participate in a community theater musical, you get to sing some of the best repertoire of the American musical theater. You also get to meet other singers and professional folk in your town; it's a perfect learning and networking environment. (Plus it's a lot of fun!)

Demo Sessions

Now we move from the stage to the studio—the recording studio, to be precise. Most towns and cities have several recording studios, which are used to record everything from local rock bands to radio and television commercials. If you can break into your local studio scene, you have a potentially lucrative career in front of you.

One of the biggest opportunities for studio singers is the recording of demo tracks. These are songs that local performers record to sell themselves to people in the music industry. Some bands might need a professional lead singer to make them sound good on tape; others might need background vocalists. Many songwriters need to record demos of their latest songs but aren't singers themselves; they'll pay for a professional singer to cut a demo of their songs.

If you're interested in demo work, you have to make yourself known in the local music community. It's especially useful to make friends with the folks in your local recording studios and with the music contractors who hire the musicians for these sessions.

Background Vocals

You don't have to be the lead vocalist to have a successful singing career. Many of the best singers of our generation make a living out of singing background vocals—and still others use background singing as a stepping stone to a lead position.

Think about it. Dionne Warwick got her start as a background singer, as did Sheryl Crow and Trisha Yearwood. Singers Rosemary Butler and Donna Davidson have made their entire careers singing background vocals, for artists like Jackson Browne, Bonnie Raitt, Linda Ronstadt, Whitney Houston, Michael Jackson, and Amy Grant. It's definitely a legitimate option for any aspiring singer.

Singing background vocals is an exciting challenge. Some artists provide detailed vocal arrangements, while others expect you to come up with your own parts on the spot. (This latter style is called a *head chart*.) That means you need to be a good sight reader *and* a good improviser—and you need to know your harmony and basic music theory.

Background singers need faultless pitch and the ability to blend with the other singers and instrumentalists—and, of course, the lead vocalist. You need to be able to change your voice and vibrato for specific musical situations. After all, the background vocals for Willie Nelson are going to be different from the background vocals for Steely Dan. You have to adapt your voice and style for the situation.

Equally important, you have to be a team player. Artists and producers want supporting musicians who fit in and get along; there's no room for prima donnas in the chorus. That might mean subordinating your personality to the rest of the group, but that's part and parcel of the job—and part of the challenge.

Jingles

Jingle singing is a lot like background singing—you need to fit into a specific musical situation, efficiently and effectively. When you walk into a jingle session, you're likely to find a specific written part, so you'll need to hone your sight singing skills. And you'll have to be quick about it; time is money in the advertising world, and you probably won't have time for too many takes.

A producer who hires you for jingle work assumes you can read the parts and sing the notes; that's the minimum required for admittance. What you add above and beyond those notes on paper determines whether you'll be called back for additional work. Even if you're just singing the praises of a local used car dealer, you can still add some personality and a subtlety of expression to make this jingle stand out from all the others on the radio. And, of course, you have to do it fast.

Note

A **jingle** is a song that accompanies a radio or television commercial.

If you're interested in jingle work, get to know the engineers at your local recording studios and the key creative staff at your local advertising agencies. It also doesn't hurt to get friendly with your local radio DJs; a lot of commercial work these days originates with the radio station, bypassing the advertising agency completely.

Singing in a Band

If singing in the background isn't your style, you're probably better suited to be a lead vocalist. Which means, of course, that you need to find a band.

Singing in a band is a lot of work, but it also can be a lot of fun. You have to learn to work with three or four or more other creative personalities; you have to coordinate schedules, musical tastes, and egos, none of which is easy. And you'll need to do a lot of practicing along with your performing, along with a fair share of promotion. (After you get the job, the band has to get some gigs!)

Performing in a band isn't all fun and giggles, either. You'll need to arrive at the gig early, help set up the P.A. system, do a sound check, and then get ready to perform. If you're playing in a local club, you'll probably do three or four forty-five minute sets each night, which is a *lot* of singing—especially if the club is hot and smoky. Then, when the gig's over (and you're ready for a good night's sleep), you have to help pack up all that equipment and make sure you get paid (perhaps the toughest chore of the evening) before you drive home, unwind, and hit the pillows. As you can see, singing is only part of the job.

There are lots of different types of bands you can sing with. If you're young and sufficiently alternative looking, look for an independent band playing punk or metal or whatever type of music you're into. If you're a little older, consider a cover band playing music of the past or present. Or if you're into a specific type of music—country, folk, French cabaret, you name it—look for a band that shares your musical interests.

For example, I have one friend who's in a vocal group that sings songs from the 1940s and 1950s (in period dress!) for corporate events, retirement parties, local festivals, and the like. They don't sing every weekend, but they get a lot more gigs than you might imagine, thanks to their unique repertoire and constant self-promotion.

You just have to look beyond the obvious nightclubs scene. Lots of bands find good work playing corporate events, high school reunions, proms, private parties, and the like. These types of events are great for all sorts of groups, from barbershop quartets to madrigal choirs—in addition to the standard cover band.

Pursuing a Singing Career

Once you've decided what kind of singing you want to pursue, how do you go about pursuing it? This is where the hard work comes in; you'll need to do a lot of e-mailing, make a lot of phone calls, and pound a lot of pavement.

Put Together a Resumé

Just as a job applicant needs a professional resumé, a musician needs an artistic resumé. Your resumé should be 1 to 2 pages in length (shorter is better) and contain the following information:

- Your name, address, phone number, and e-mail address.
- A brief description of your vocal abilities, including your vocal type, range, and style(s).
- Your birth date and other important historical information.
- A list of the teachers you've studied with and the (music) schools and master classes you've attended.
- A list of your most important artistic accomplishments. This should include competitions, recitals, recording dates, and other key performances.

Your resumé should look as professional as possible. That means using a nice-looking template in your favorite word processing program, making sure it's proofread and free of spelling and grammatical errors, and printing it on a good-quality paper.

Many singers will print their resumé on the back of an 8" x 10" photo of themselves. (This is called a *head shot.*) That way everyone who sees your face has your resumé, and vice versa; it's also one less piece of paper to manage.

In addition to your resumé, you should also create a list of all the songs in your repertoire. For consistency, use the same word processing template and paper you used for your resumé to print your repertoire list.

Tip

If you want a really professional-looking resumé, contact your local Kinko's or similar printing business. Most offer resumé-creation services, for a fee.

When you hand out your resumé, your repertoire list, and your head shot, you might want to put them all in a nice folder, the kind that opens like a book and has two pockets inside. If you really want to look professional, have someone design a simple logo and print the logo on the front of the folder. Use the same design and color scheme for all your material, for maximum visual impact.

Cut a Demo

Nobody's going to hire a singer because of his or her resumé. Before you can get the gig, that person has to hear you sing.

The first step to getting heard is to distribute a demo CD that showcases your vocal talents. While you can record your songs in the comfort of your living room with a cheap Radio Shack microphone and an old cassette tape recorder, you're better saving your money and buying time in a professional recording studio. After all, the more professional your demo sounds, the better you sound—and a real engineer in a real recording studio will know how to make you sound as good as possible.

> **Tip**
>
> Having a demo CD is particularly important if you're pursuing recording studio work. Anyone who hires you will want to know not only how well you sing, but also how well you *record*.

> **Tip**
>
> In the old days you made demo tapes; today, you make demo CDS. If you have a personal computer with a recordable CD drive (sometimes called a *CD burner*), it's relatively easy to burn your own demo CDs from the master CD you produce at the recording studio.

You don't have to spend a ton of money to cut your demo. If you're efficient, you can cut all your tracks in a matter of hours. Add in another hour or two to mix your tracks and master the CD, and you'll probably spend $500–$1000 to hold a professionally recorded CD in your hands.

Your demo should be no more than five minutes long, and should contain short snippets of a variety of material. The goal is to demonstrate that you can sing in different styles, that you can blend with other voices (if you're doing a demo for background or jingle work), and that you can phrase properly for different musical genres (pop, country, jazz, etc.). Include some lead vocals and some backgrounds, with you singing all the parts yourself. (Easy enough to do in a multi-track studio.) You can sing with professional musicians backing you up (costs more money) or to prerecorded background tracks.

Your demo CD should be professionally packaged, with bright colors and your name in big, eye-catching type. The inner sleeve should include your name, address, phone number, and e-mail address. (If you have a website, include that address, too.)

Market Yourself

The goal of assembling all these materials isn't to produce a big bundle of stuff to sit on your kitchen table; it's to help you market yourself to others in the music business. Here's what you need:

- Resumé
- Repertoire list
- Business card
- Any referrals or reviews
- Head shot (photograph)
- Demo CD

Once you have all these materials assembled, there's more work ahead of you. You'll want to send your packet of materials to as many people as you can think of. Send it to local and regional recording studios, record labels, radio stations, agents, managers, music publishers, and so on. Each packet you send out should be accompanied by a custom-tailored cover letter; depending on who receives the demo, you can be a background singer, a jingle singer, a blues singer, a pop singer, you name it.

After you send out a packet of materials, follow up by phone or e-mail. Ask the intended recipient, "Did you receive my materials?" *Never* ask "Did you listen to my demo?" You don't want to put the person on the spot; you only want to make sure they remember who you are.

In addition, you can find work by placing listings with local musician's referral services and bulletin boards. (You should find lots of "up and coming band needs lead singer" listings on these services, as well.) There are many local and national websites that help musicians find new gigs; for example, Harmony Central (www.harmony-central.com) has a Musician Wanted/Available service that lets you search for bands and other musicians by zip code.

To some degree, making a name for yourself in the music business is all about networking. Get to know the major players on the local music scene. Make acquaintances with other local singers, and ask them where the jobs are, who's hiring, who the best contractors are, and so on. You don't want to steal gigs from these folks; you just need their help in finding out where the gigs are.

You should also make contact with the local songwriting community. Many songwriters need professional singers to record demos of their songs; making a demo (even for free) will give you valuable studio experience and look good on your resumé. Contact the Songwriters Guild of America (www.songwriters.org) to find songwriters in your area.

Audition, Audition, Audition

If you're lucky (and you're good), working your network and sending out all those demos will eventually pay off, and you'll be called in to audition for a gig. I'll talk more about how to handle auditions in the next section; what I want to touch on here is the importance of taking all the auditions that present themselves to you.

To some extent, there's no such thing as a bad audition. Any audition can lead to a paying job; even if you don't win the audition, you might end up high on somebody's list for a future gig. To that end, you should search out as many auditions as you can find. If nothing else, an audition is great practice for performing in front of other people!

It's important, as well, not to turn down an audition—or to sign up for an audition and never show up. The more auditions you go on, the better your chances of getting chosen. If you blow off an audition, you'll never win that part.

In addition, if you blow off too many auditions, it can come back to haunt you. There's a good chance that most of the vocal contractors in your community know each other, and word gets around. If you develop a reputation for turning down or not showing up for auditions, then it's likely that the calls will dry up. An audition is an invitation-only party, and no one wants to invite someone who blows them off.

So you should *always* show up for your scheduled auditions. Even if you're under the weather. Even if you had something else planned. Even if you don't think there's a chance in hell you'll get the gig. Show up for the audition, give it your best shot, and display your most winning attitude. Someone will notice.

Caution

Always remember the old adage about counting unhatched chickens. Just because you have a demo CD and are starting to get audition calls doesn't mean you have a lock on a successful singing career. It's a really good idea to hang on to your day job until your singing activities are consistent enough to support you financially. Lots of vocalists work during the day and sing at night—which may be the only way to pay the bills!

Going Professional

If you're serious about embarking on a professional singing career, at some point you'll need to join the union. That means the American Federation of Musicians (www.afm.org) and, if you're interested in radio, television, or film work, the American Federation of Television and Radio Artists (www.aftra.org) and the Screen Actor's Guild (www.sag.org). Joining the musician's union is especially important if you're doing studio work, even as a background vocalist. Many studios won't hire non-union musicians, period.

Many singers think they need a manager or an agent to help them get those big gigs. They should think again; when you're just starting out, you'll probably be pounding the pavement on your own. In fact, having a manager or an agent isn't that important when you're first starting out. Let's face it; you don't need an agent to score a place in a church choir or land a role in a community musical. And if you specialize in recording work, managers and agents are virtually irrelevant, since the musician's union forbids them from taking a percent of your pay. (And no agent will work for free!)

It's when you start getting the big gigs that you should look for professional management. Talk to other local singers and see who they recommend—and who they don't. Make sure your agent or manager will earn their pay and get you jobs you wouldn't have gotten otherwise. You don't want someone leeching their percent off the top without doing any work for it!

Acing the Audition

When it's time to try out for a new gig, you have to prove that you're the right singer for the job. It's the same routine whether you're interested in a spot in the church choir, background vocals for a recording date, or singing lead in a Broadway play—you have to audition for the part.

To ace an audition, you have to have the right attitude. You can't be too shy or too cocky; you can't be overeager or disinterested. You have to be confident of your abilities and then walk the walk—prove that you have the stuff they're looking for.

How to Prepare

Before you walk into any audition, you need to ask yourself the following questions:

- Why do you want this audition? Will this part advance your career, or do you just need the money? Is this a project you will enjoy? Is this a part well suited for your abilities?
- Are you thoroughly prepared? Have you chosen and rehearsed an appropriate audition piece? If the contractor requests that you sing specific songs (or types of songs), have you prepared those songs? Is your voice in good shape? Do you have good "leave behind" materials—head shot, resumé, business card?
- Are you well rested? Did you refrain from partying (and drinking alcoholic beverages) the night before? Did you get a good night's sleep? Have you done your vocal warm-ups? Are you relaxed and confident?
- What kind of first impression will you make? How should you carry yourself? Should you smile or be serious? Do you project a good attitude? Do you appear confident—without being cocky?
- Are you dressed for success? Is your dress professional—yet still reflecting of your personality?

Only when you know *why* you're auditioning and *how* you're auditioning will you be ready for the audition. If you have the skills—and are confident of that—you can then spend your time on those theoretically superficial details that have more impact than you might imagine.

How to Dress

You'd think that someone looking for a singer would care more about how you sound than how you look—but that isn't always the case. As much as we might like to think otherwise, your appearance plays a very important role in the decision whether or not to hire you for a singing gig.

The main thing to remember, appearance-wise, is that you should dress appropriate to the project, with an emphasis on being as professional as possible. When it comes down to hiring a good-looking guy with a good voice or a bum with a good voice, the good-looking guy will get the gig every time.

Men should either wear business casual (perfectly acceptable for most auditions), a suit and tie, or similar professional dress. Make sure your clothes fit well, and that your shirt and pants are well ironed and wrinkle-free. Clean shaven is the best look; if you have a beard or mustache, make sure you're neatly trimmed. And get a haircut—straggly, unkempt hair is a big turn-off!

Women should dress simply, but professionally. That means a dress, blouse and skirt, or pantsuit, in black, gray, or another neutral color. Your skirt should be long or medium length; unless you're trying out for a Mariah Carey-like role, avoid mini-skirts and plunging necklines. You don't want your clothing to distract from your face and voice, which also means you should wear your hair out of your eyes and away from your face. Avoid distracting jewelry, too. Wear a nice pair of dress shoes, but without too high a heel. (High heels can throw off your posture.) And don't overdo it with the makeup.

What to Take

Here's what you should always take with you to an audition:

- Copies of the music you'll be performing—for you, for your accompanist, and for the auditors
- Music for additional songs, in case an auditor wants to hear alternative selections
- Copies of your demo CD
- Copies of your artistic resumé
- Copies of your repertoire list
- "Head shot" 8'' x 10'' photographs, with your name and contact information stamped or printed on the back
- Business cards

Put everything you'll hand to an auditor or contractor in a single folder or envelope. Make sure they have a nice takeaway that reminds them positively of you.

How to Enter

How you walk into the room can determine whether or not you'll win the audition. If you walk in shy and hesitant, the auditors might think you're underqualified for the gig. If you strut into the room all cocky like, they might think you're a showoff and a braggart and not a team player.

The right way to walk into the room is confident and self-assured. Walk with good posture, your back held straight, and a slight smile on your lips. Look the auditor or contractor directly in the eye, and give a firm (but not crushing) handshake. Speak in a clear, confident voice, but only when spoken to; don't try to start a conversation on your own. Answer any questions you're asked as directly as possible. Don't hem and haw—and if you don't know the answer to a question, say so.

Hand out your materials to the auditors and give a copy of your audition music to the pianist. Stand in your proper singing posture beside the piano, or where you're directed by the auditors to stand. Wait with your hands straight at your sides (*not* in your pockets!) until you're directed to sing.

Then it's show time.

How to Exit

When you've finished singing, remain in place until acknowledged by the auditors. You might be asked to perform another song or sing some scales or arpeggios. You may even be asked some additional questions; answer these to the best of your abilities.

After you've been dismissed, you should walk out of the audition the same way you walked in—with a smile and an air of confidence. It doesn't matter how well you did; even if you *know* you blew it, you should always act like a winner. (And if you know you did great, don't act cocky about it; raising your fists in the air and doing a little dance is definitely uncalled for!) So no matter how you think you did, keep your feelings to yourself and act (even if it is an act) completely self-assured. You never know who might be watching you!

Whether you win the audition or not, it should always be a learning experience. After you've left the room, examine your performance and ask yourself what you could have done better. What were your strong points—and your weak points? How did you compare to other singers at the audition? Were you well-enough prepared? Did *you* like your performance?

If you get the gig, congratulations! Act as gracious as possible, and accept the thanks of your fellow musicians. If you get the opportunity, thank the auditors with a handshake and a short, appreciative "thank you." Don't hug them, don't cry tears of gratitude, and don't send them fruit baskets afterward. It's all in a day's work, after all.

Finally, if you *don't* get the gig, don't be upset, don't obsess about it, and most definitely do not confront the contractor and ask "Why didn't you hire me?" (That's a sure way to ensure that that person won't hire you in the future, either.) Just accept it and move on. It's just one audition, after all.

Stay Focused—and Become the Singer You Know You Can Be

Now we've come to the end of this book, and the beginning of your life as a singer. Remember, the most important thing you need to be a singer is a desire to sing. If you have the desire, you can—you *will*—be a singer. Let your desire fuel your discipline, and keep studying and singing, no matter what obstacles you encounter.

If your heart is in it, you *will* succeed!

The Least You Need to Know

- There are many different outlets for your singing talents—from Karaoke contests to church choirs to recording studio work.
- To promote yourself as a singer, you need an artistic resumé, a repertoire list, an 8" x 10" head shot, a business card, and a demo CD.
- Your demo CD should be no more than five minutes long and include snippets of songs in a variety of styles.
- Treat an audition as professionally as possible; dress appropriately, act confident, and sing your heart out!
- Don't take rejections *too* seriously—learn from them and keep on auditioning.

Appendix

The Complete Idiot's Vocal Music Glossary

a cappella Vocal music, without instrumental accompaniment.

a tempo Return to the previous tempo.

accelerando Gradually speed up. (Abbreviated as *accel.*)

accidental A marking used to raise and lower the indicated pitch; sharps raise the note a half step, flats lower the note a half-step, and naturals return the note to the original pitch.

allegro Tempo marking for a fast, cheerful tempo.

alto The lowest female voice.

aria A solo song performed in an opera or oratorio.

arpeggio A chord that is broken up and played one note at a time.

art music Music written by a trained composer and passed on in written form.

articulation The manner in which notes are struck, sustained, and released. One indicates articulation by the use of markings such as legato, staccato, tenuto, and so on.

attack The beginning part of a sound.

bar line The vertical line placed on the staff between measures.

baritone A male voice category between bass and tenor voices; not always isolated in choral music.

bass The lowest male voice.

bass clef A clef, used by lower-pitched voices and instruments, that places middle C on the first ledger line above the staff.

beat Any pulsing unit of musical time.

bel canto Literally "beautiful singing;" Italian vocal style characterized by flowing melodic lines delivered by voices of great agility, smoothness, and purity of tone.

belting A style of singing that uses heavy or forced tones throughout the vocal range.

blend (1) The combination of voices in group singing so that individual performers are indistinguishable.

blend (2) Smooth transitions between the registers of the singing voice.

blue note A slight drop of pitch on the third, fifth, or seventh tone of the scale, common in blues and jazz. Also called a "bent" pitch.

call and response Performance style with a singing leader who is imitated by a chorus of followers. Also called responsorial singing; commonly heard in spiritual or gospel music.

cambiata voice Some composers and choir directors refer to this as the changing young man's voice.

cantabile Italian term meaning "in a singing style," i.e., with the melody smoothly articulated.

cantata Vocal genre for solo singers, chorus, and instrumentalists based on a lyric or dramatic poetic narrative. It generally consists of several movements including recitatives, arias, and ensemble numbers.

castrato A male singer who was castrated during boyhood to preserve the soprano or alto vocal register. This practice was prominent in the seventeenth and early eighteenth century.

chamber choir Small group of up to about 24 singers, who usually perform a cappella or with piano accompaniment.

chart Colloquial term for a score or arrangement; used frequently by jazz musicians.

choir A group of singers who perform together, usually in parts, with several singers on each part; often associated with church singing.

chorale Baroque congregational hymn of the German Lutheran church. The term is often used interchangeably with choir to describe a singing group.

chord Three or more notes played simultaneously.

chord progression A series of chords over a number of measures.

chorus (1) Fairly large group of singers who perform together, usually with several on each part.

chorus (2) In jazz, a single statement of the melodic-harmonic pattern.

chromatic scale A scale containing 12 equal divisions of the octave—all the white keys and black keys within an octave.

Coda Ending section of a piece of music.

coloratura A soprano voice who can sing the florid passages either written into an aria or inserted by the singer to show the singer's dexterity and skill. (Also refers to the aria passages themselves.)

common time The 4/4 time signature.

covering The technique of "darkening" the tone (increasing pharyngeal space), especially at register transition points.

crescendo Gradually louder.

crooning A style of singing popular during the big band era (1920s–1940s) characterized by a smooth tone that is light in intensity. A crooner depends upon a microphone for projection, and sometimes scoops or slides into pitches when singing.

cut time The 2/2 time signature.

D.C. al Coda Navigation marking meaning to go back to the beginning and play to the Coda sign and then skip to the Coda section.

D.C. al Fine Navigation marking meaning to go back to the beginning and play through to the fine marking.

D.S. al Coda Navigation marking meaning to go back to the sign and play to the Coda sign; then skip to the Coda section.

D.S. al Fine Navigation marking meaning to go back to the sign and play through to the end.

decrescendo Gradually softer.

dissonance A combination of tones that sounds discordant and unstable, in need of resolution to a more pleasing and stable harmony.

dynamics Varying degrees of loud and soft.

embellishment Melodic decoration, either improvised or indicated through ornamentation signs in the music.

falsetto Vocal technique whereby men can sing above their normal range, producing a lighter, higher sound.

fermata Symbol used to indicate that a note should be held indefinitely; sometimes called a "bird's eye."

focused tone A singing tone that is acoustically efficient and without audible air in the tone.

folk music Music of the peasantry or common folk created by unknown or untrained composers and typically passed on orally from person to person.

form The structure or shape of a musical work, based on repetition, contrast, and variation; the organizing principle in music.

forte Loud. (Abbreviated as *f*.)

fortissimo Very loud. (Abbreviated as *ff*.)

frequency A scientific measurement of how fast the molecules of air are vibrating; the faster the vibrations, the higher the *pitch*.

glottal attack The onset of phonation produced by excessive tension in the closure of the vocal cords.

gospel music Twentieth-century sacred music style associated with the Protestant African American church.

grace note One or more notes, played lightly and quickly, that precede a main note.

half step The smallest distance between two pitches in Western music.

harmony The sound of tones in combination; also used to refer to the accompanying parts behind the main melody.

head register A vocal adjustment producing light, flute-like tones, conducive to soft and high singing. Also called head tone or head voice.

improvisation Creation of a musical composition while it is being performed.

interval The distance between two pitches or notes.

jingle A song that accompanies a radio or television commercial.

key The relationship of tones with a common center or tonic. (Also a lever on a keyboard or woodwind instrument.)

key signature The sharps or flats that are placed at the beginning of a staff to indicate the key of the music.

larynx Often called the Adam's apple, it sits in the front of the throat and can be felt moving up and down when you swallow.

leading tone The note that is a half step below the tonic of the scale; thus leads up to the tonic. "Ti" of the Solfeggio scale.

legato Notes sung or played smoothly together, for the full rhythmic value of each note. (From the Italian, meaning "bound" or "tied.")

libretto The text of an opera or oratorio. (Literally, "little book.")

lied German for "song;" most commonly associated with the solo art song of the nineteenth century, usually accompanied by piano.

lieder Plural of lied.

madrigal Secular work for voices, originating in Renaissance Italy (but also popular in England), set to a short, lyric love poem. A madrigal can be either with or without instruments.

madrigal choir Small vocal ensemble that specializes in a cappella secular works such as madrigals.

major The most common mode, consisting of the following intervals: whole-whole-half-whole-whole-whole-half.

mass A choral composition set to the text of the central service of the Roman Catholic Church.

measure A group of beats, indicated by the placement of bar lines on the staff.

melody The combination of tone and rhythm in a logical sequence.

meter The organization of beats and their divisions.

mezzo Short for *mezzo soprano.*

mezzo forte Medium loud. (Abbreviated as *mf.*)

mezzo piano Medium soft. (Abbreviated as *mp.*)

mezzo soprano A woman's voice slightly lower in range and (usually) darker in tone than a soprano.

minor A non-major scale or mode, with a flatted third of the scale.

mode A set of scales, based on centuries-old church music that preceded today's major and minor scales.

moderato Tempo marking for a moderate pace.

modulation A change of key.

musical The genre of twentieth century musical theater, especially popular in the United States and Great Britain; characterized by spoken dialogue, dramatic plot interspersed with songs, ensemble numbers, and dancing.

nonsecular music Music that is sacred in nature.

notation The art of writing musical notes on paper.

note A *symbol* used to indicate the duration and pitch of a sound, as in whole notes, half notes, and quarter notes.

octave Two pitches, with the same name, located 12 half steps apart.

opera A musical drama that is generally sung throughout, combining vocal and instrumental music with dramatic acting, scenery, and costumes.

oratorio Large-scale dramatic choral work originating in the Baroque period, based on a text of religious or serious character, performed by solo voices, chorus, and orchestra; similar to opera but without scenery, costumes, or action. One of the most famous oratorios is Handel's *Messiah.*

otolaryngologist A physician specializing in problems of the ears, nose and throat.

passagio The part of the pitch range of a singer's voice ("the passage") that is transitional between registers, especially the transition to the "head voice."

perfect pitch The ability to hear absolute pitches in your head, without any outside assistance.

phonation The production of voiced sound by means of vocal fold vibration.

phrase Within a piece of music, a segment that is unified by rhythms, melodies, or harmonies and that comes to some sort of closure; typically composed in groups of 2, 4, 8, 16, or 32 measures.

pianissimo Very soft. (Abbreviated as *pp.*)

piano Soft. (Abbreviate as *p.*)

pitch The highness or lowness of a tone. (In scientific terms, a specific frequency.)

placement A technique of singing guided by sensations of vibrations in the face, behind the teeth, in the nose, i.e., "forward placement."

polyphony Music with many interwoven parts.

rallentando Gradually slow down. (Abbreviated as *rall.*)

range The distance between the lowest and highest tones of a melody, instrument, or voice. This span is typically described as narrow, medium, or wide.

recitative A solo vocal declamation that follows the inflections of the text rather than the melody. A vocal passage that is more recited than sung; found in opera, cantata, and oratorio.

register A series of tones that are produced by similar vocal fold vibration and placement, resulting in similar tone quality (i.e., chest register or head register).

relative keys Keys that share the same key signature but not the same root. For example, A minor and C Major are relative keys.

relative pitch The ability to identify relationships between notes of a scale without knowing the actual pitch names.

resonance The intensification of sound by sympathetic vibration.

rest A symbol used to denote silence or not playing a particular note.

rhythm The organization of sound in time; the arrangement of beats and accents in music.

rhythm and blues Popular African-American music style of the 1940s through 1960s featuring a solo singer accompanied by a small instrumental ensemble (piano, guitar, bass, drums, tenor saxophone), driving rhythms, and blues and pop song forms.

ritard The Italian musical term for slowing down the tempo. See *ritardando.*

ritardando Gradually slow down. (Abbreviated as *rit.* or *ritard.*)

root The lowest note of an interval, chord, or scale.

rubato "Borrowed time," common in Romantic music, where the performer either hesitates or rushes through certain notes imparting flexibility to the written note values.

sacred music Religious or spiritual music, for church or devotional use. Also called *nonsecular music.*

SATB Shorthand for soprano, alto, tenor, and bass. (Choral scores are sometimes called SATB scores.)

scale A sequence of related pitches, arranged in ascending or descending order.

scat singing A jazz style that sets syllables without meaning to an improvised vocal line.

scoop An undesirable singing habit of beginning a note beneath the desired pitch, then sliding up to that pitch.

score The written depiction of all the individual parts sung or played by each of the voices or instruments in an ensemble.

secular music Music that is nonreligious in nature.

song cycle Group of songs, usually lieder, that are unified musically or through their texts.

song form The structure of a short piece of music. Usually diagramed as AABA.

soprano The highest female voice.

sostenuto Sustained singing; long, rather slow phrases that the singer is capable of singing on one breath. Considered one of the hallmarks of bel canto singing.

sotto voce In a soft voice.

speech pathology The study of abnormalities of speech and voice. A speech pathologist is a specialist in speech, language, and voice disorders.

spread tone A vocal tone that is unfocused or airy.

staff An assemblage of horizontal lines and spaces that represent different pitches.

style A characteristic manner of presentation of musical elements such as melody, harmony, rhythm, or dynamics.

swing A style of music, typically associated with jazz, where eighth notes are played in a triplet rhythm.

syncopation An accent on an unexpected beat—or the lack of an accent on an expected beat.

tempo The rate of speed at which beats are played in a song.

tenor The highest male voice.

tessitura The portion of a singer's range where production is easiest and most beautiful.

throaty tone A singing tone that sounds swallowed, tight, or dark. Produced by excessive pharyngeal tension.

tie A curved line over or under two or more notes that "ties" the two notes together into one.

timbre Tone quality or tone color. (Pronounced "tambor.")

time signature A symbol with two numbers, one on top of the other (like a fraction), that indicates the basic meter of a song. The upper number indicates how many beats are in a measure; the bottom number indicates the type of note that receives one beat.

tonal center The key in which the music is written; another term for the Solfeggio Do.

tonality The organization of musical notes around a tonic, or home pitch, based on a major or minor scale or mode.

tonic The first note of a scale ("Do" in Solfeggio), which serves as the home base.

treble clef A clef, used by higher-pitched voices and instruments, that places middle C on the first ledger line below the staff.

tremolo Any vocal vibrato that is undesirable; a vibrato that is uncontrolled and either too fast or too slow, producing a wobble in the voice.

trill Melodic ornament consisting of the rapid alternation between one tone and the next above it.

tritone An interval consisting of three whole steps; sometimes called "the Devil's interval." An augmented fourth or a diminished fifth.

tutti "All," the opposite of solo.

unison Two notes of the same pitch; voices singing "in unison" all sing the same pitch.

upbeat The last beat of a measure as conducted; a weak beat which anticipates the downbeat (the first beat of the next measure).

vamp A short passage with simple repeated rhythm and harmony that introduces a soloist.

variation A technique in which some aspects of the music are altered but the original is still recognizable.

vibrato Small fluctuation of pitch used as an expressive device to intensify a sound.

vocal fatigue The deterioration of the vocal quality due to prolonged use; may be the result of vocal misuse or abuse, or may be indicative of a pathological condition.

vocal nodes Thickenings at the junction of the anterior and middle thirds of the vocal folds (sometimes called nodules), resulting from vocal misuse or abuse.

vocalese Jazz-style scatting to an existing melody or solo.

vocalise A textless vocal melody, as in an exercise or concert piece.

vocalize To exercise the voice.

voice Melodic lines of music.

voice breaks The sudden abnormal shifts of pitch during singing or speaking.

voice leading The motion of a single voice.

vowel modification Adjustments in the usual pronunciation of vowels for more favorable resonance throughout the singing range.

whole step An interval equal to two half steps.

The Complete Idiot's Pronunciation Reference

Use this appendix to discover the correct pronunciation for pieces with Italian or Latin lyrics.

Italian Pronunciation Guide

Vowels

Vowel	Pronunciation	Examples
a	as in *father*	*pasta*
e	as in *pet* (open) or *gate* (closed)	*polenta*, *mette*
i	as in *machine*	*primo*, *spaghetti*
o	as in *pot* (open) or *post* (closed)	*appoggiare*, *colto*
u	as in *cool* or *boot*	*numero*, *duomo*

Consonants

Consonant	Pronunciation	Examples
c (before e and i)	as in *church*	*cinque*, *focaccia*, *ciao*
c (before a, o, and u)	as in *cake*	*casa*, *calamari*
g (before e or i)	as in *general*	*gelato*, *formaggio*
g (before a, o, u)	hard, as in *goat*	*gamba*, *prego*
gl (before e or i) equivalent to the *l* sound in *familiar* or *million*	forms a palatal sound	*figlio*, *inglese*
gn (before all vowels)	like the *ni* in *onion*	*gnocchi*, *cigno*, *agnello*
h	always silent, except when used with *c* or *g*, when it produces the hard *k* sound	*Abbacchio*, *Chianti*

continues

Consonants (continued)

Consonant	Pronunciation	Examples
l	as in English, but placed more forward in the mouth	*lungo, palazzo*
q (grouped with u)	takes the sound of *qw*, as in *quick*	*Quello, quando*
r	as in English, but with more of a flip of the tongue against the hard palate, or trilled when doubled or the initial letter of a word	*Roma, marroni*
s	initial *s* before vowels and unvoiced consonants (c, f, p, q, s, t) is pronounced like the *s* in sun	*Varese, sapere*
z	takes the sound of *ds* (as in *maids*) if initial, or *ts* (as in *rats*) if doubled	*zabaglione, zero,* (both *ds*); *pizza, mezzo* (both *ts*)

All other consonants are pronounced as in English.

Pronunciation Tips

More advice for singing Italian lyrics:

- Italian is known as a musical language because every vowel and most consonants are pronounced clearly and precisely. The language is spoken with a lifted soft palate and lots of expression and inflection, or lilt.
- It's quite easy to switch from speaking Italian to singing Italian, which is probably why so many Italians seem to be blessed with "natural" singing voices. Italian speakers place the vowels in a forward position and almost sing when they speak. Although syllables and words are linked together, they never lose their fundamental and individual vowel sound.
- Italian is a phonetic language, which means that it is spoken the way it is written. Italian and English share the Latin alphabet, but the sounds represented by the letters often differ considerably in the two languages.
- In most cases, it's the next-to-last syllable that is accented. If an accent mark falls on the last syllable, it should be pronounced as in *piu*. (The *u* is accented and will sound more like the English "pew.") There are exceptions to this rule that must be learned.
- When an *i* comes before a, o, u, or c, the sound of the *i* becomes subordinate to the following vowel. This is common in names such as Giovanni, Giuseppe, and Gianna. Thus, Giovanni is not pronounced as if spelled "gee-oh-van-nee," but instead is pronounced as if spelled "joe-van-nee."
- The letter *p* is pronounced as it is in English, but without the aspiration that sometimes is heard in English.
- The letter *t* is pronounced approximately the same as in English, but there is no escaping of breath when pronounced in Italian.

Latin Pronunciation Guide

Vowels

Vowel	Pronunciation	Examples
a	as in *am*	*amen, pax, mater*
e	as the *a* in *fate*	*me, credo*

Vowel	Pronunciation	Examples
i	as in *machine*	*qui, kyrie, spiritui*
o	as in *or*	*domine, nobis*
u	as in *tutor*	*cum, dominum*

Diphthongs

Diphthong	Pronunciation	Examples
ae	as the *a* in *fate*	*saeculorum*
oe	as the *a* in *fate*	*coelum*
au	as in *out*	*aut, lauda*

Consonants

Consonant	Pronunciation	Examples
c (before *e* or *i*)	as in *church*	*certus, cibus*
ch	as in *ache* (hard *k*)	*christus*
g (before *e* or *i*)	as in *gentle*	*gens, agit*
g (before other letters)	as in *go*	*gratis, gloria*
gn	*ny* as in *canyon*	*agnus, signor*
j (or consonant *i*)	as in *yes*	*jesus, justus*
s	as in *sing* (never as *z*)	*passus*
sc (before *a*, *o*, *u* or a consonant) as in *scope*	*vobiscum, schola*	
sc (before *e* and *i)*	as in *shall*	*ascendit, suscipe*
th	as in *ten*	*catholicam*
ti (when followed by a vowel and preceded by any letter except *s*, *t*, or *x*)	as *tsee*	*gratias*
x (in words beginning with *ex* followed by a *vowel* or by *h*)	as *egz*	*examine*
x (in words beginning *ex* and followed by *s*)	as *eks*	*exsilium*
x (when the prefix *ex* is followed by a soft *c*)	*as exsh*	*excelsis*

All other consonants are pronounced as in English.

Pronunciation Tips

More advice for singing Latin lyrics:

- Consonants must be articulated with a certain crispness; otherwise, the singing becomes unintelligible.
- The letter *h* is pronounced *k* in only two words: *nihil* and *mihi* (pronounced nee-keel and mee-kee); in all other cases *h* is silent. (For example, *hosannah* is pronounced o-sah-nah.)
- The letter *j*, often written as *i*, is treated as *y*, forming one sound with the following vowel. (For example, *alleluia* is pronounced as al-le-lóo-ya; *major* is pronounced as ma-yor.)
- When the letter *r* appears with another consonant, it should be slightly rolled on the tongue, as in the word *carnis*. Care must be taken not to modify the quality of the vowel in the syllable preceding the *r*. (For example, the word *kyrie* is pronounced kée-ree-e, *not* kear-ee-e.)
- In Latin, the letter *y* is considered a vowel and sounds like *i*.
- The letter *z* is pronounced *dz*. (For example, the word *lazarus* is pronounced la-dza-roos.)

Appendix C

Troubleshooting Vocal Problems

Problem	Probable Causes	Remedies
Breathy tone (too much air in the tone)	Weak and insufficient muscular involvement; uncontrolled exhalation; possible tightness in the throat; faulty tonal imagery	Review Chapter 8; review Chapter 9; revisit breath support exercises 5.1, 5.2, and 5.3
Harsh, forced tone	Tight, constricted muscles in torso and/or throat; overuse of chest voice; possible hyper-inhalation; faulty tonal imagery	Relax and open the throat; elevate the voice into the head; don't rely on chest voice or belting for emotional impact; reduce volume levels; form the mouth around the vowels and make them more vertical (covered) at higher pitches; involve breath support muscles (rather than the throat) for volume; review Chapter 9
Nasal tone	Lazy (low) soft palate; mouth too closed; tongue is too high or too far back; faulty tonal imagery	Raise the soft palate to the beginning sensation of a yawn; check in a mirror to see if your tongue is arched or too high in the mouth; repeat study of the "hung-ah" exercises (5.6 and 5.7) to refresh your memory of the difference in the closed and open airway where the tongue and the soft palate come together
"Swallowed" tone (throaty, covered, or "hooty" tone)	Exaggerated opening of the throat; forced lowered tongue; overzealous attempt to produce a resonant tone; singing out of your comfortable range; faulty tonal imagery	Only open the throat to the natural position of the beginning of a yawn; make sure not to overexaggerate the idea of the open throat, to the point of tension; don't strive for a big, deep sound—keep it light and in the head; review Chapter 9 and think more of your voice as being in your face, or in your eyes, rather than in your throat; if you're a male, review falsetto singing

continues

continued

Problem	Probable Causes	Remedies
Singing under pitch (flat)	Lack of breath support and focus; droopy facial posture; forcing the tone; singing out of comfortable range; general fatigue; weather conditions; lack of careful listening and self monitoring; music written in inappropriate key for your voice	Use better breath support; review Chapters 7 and 8; think of approaching pitch from above rather than below; keep your head and neck in alignment (raised chins cause straining and flatting on high pitches); avoid singing when fatigued; consider performing the song in another key; energize yourself with a little exercise; carefully monitor yourself—listen!
Singing above pitch (sharp)	Tension in the breath support muscle group; tension in the throat; excitement, "nerves," or stage fright; tightly set jaw; lack of careful listening and self monitoring; weather conditions	Relax your body and your tone; don't force the voice into extreme, unnatural focus; look out for tension in the jaw—keep it loose and free with lots of space in the mouth; warm or cover the high vowels; think vertical rather than horizontal mouth position; do some breathing exercises for control (and also for relaxation); listen carefully and monitor yourself
Glottal attack of words (particularly vowels)	Tension in the throat upon phonation; hyper-inhalation followed by constriction of breathing muscles; tightness in the jaw; lazy velum; improper stylistic concept or application	Swallow several times (or drink some water) to relax the larynx; review "sighing" sensation exercises; strive to retain the open yawn sensation as you begin to phonate; use a slight hint of "h" in the initial vowels, to sense the natural flow of air over the vocal cords; revisit exercises 5.9 and 5.10 ("Ha-ha" and "Ho-ho")
Sliding or swooping from note to note	Uncontrolled exhalation; faulty pitch imagery; lack of focus; lazy diction practices; faulty stylistic concept or application	Work to improve breath support with particular attention to controlled and steady exhalation (Chapter 8); practice singing your vocalises in a staccato (separated) fashion—do this with your songs, too, until you begin to appreciate the integrity of each note in the phrase; avoid overuse of ornamentation/improvisation; emphasize consonant clarity
Lyrics can't be understood	Lazy tongue or improper tongue position; too much tension in tongue; overly breathy tone; improper speech patterns carried over into singing; tight jaw restricting mouth and tongue movement; lack of consonant articulation; faulty execution of diphthongs	Review Chapter 13; do exercises that relax the tongue and increase its flexibility; open the mouth sufficiently and relax the jaw; form words in the front of your mouth, being very conscious of the roles of the teeth, tongue, and lips in the formation of consonant sounds; give special attention to internal consonant sounds, as they are often the most ignored

Appendix 

Practice Checklist

On the next page, you'll find a reproducible checklist you can use as your own personal practice log or journal. This checklist will help you develop a regular, disciplined routine that will minimize your practice time and maximize your results.

This checklist is based on a practice session of 40 minutes—a reasonable time for even the most busy schedules. Make adjustments to the schedule as necessary, but remember that abbreviated daily practice is far more beneficial than once-a-week marathon sessions!

Date:____________________

Practice began at ________________ **and ended at** ______________

Goals:

____

____

____

It's very important to have a plan, even if it's only to do breathing exercises for 15 minutes, or memorizing a single piece of music. Whatever your goals, they should be spelled out clearly and in writing before you ever begin to practice.

Physical warm-ups:

____

____

____

List specific exercises that you do during this session. These should include stretching and breathing exercises. ***10 minutes***

Vocal Exercises:

____

____

____

List specific warm-ups and exercises for range extension, flexibility, vowel purity, or dynamic control[md]even interval recognition and sight singing practice. ***10 minutes***

Repertoire Work:

____

____

____

This is where you zero in on a particular piece or, better yet, an isolated section of a piece you are learning. Remember that it's better to concentrate on short passages than to sing a piece "straight through." ***20 minutes***

Notes for your next practice session:

____

____

____

This is where you can make a note of what worked or what didn't seem to work in your last session, as well as things done or left undone (as a place to start in your next session).

Bonus time:

____

____

____

List any "extra listening you did during the day, singers who caught your ear, songs you heard and liked. This is also a place to record any related musical practice you may have done, such as score study, theory exercises, or keyboard practice.

Appendix E

CD Tracks

The audio CD bound into the back of this book includes examples of material presented in the text, performed by professional vocalists. Use the Next Track and Previous Track controls on your CD player to advance from track-to-track on the CD.

1. Exercise 2.1: Yoo-Hoo!
2. Exercise 2.2: Ah-Ha!
3. Exercise 2.3: Whee!
4. Exercise 2.4: Oh, No!
5. Exercise 2.5: Hey, Ray
6. Exercise 2.6: Singing the Alphabet
7. Vocal Ranges
8. Exercise 5.1: Hiss Like a Snake
9. Exercise 5.2: Hissy Doodle
10. Exercise 5.3: Sing the Alphabet—In a Single Breath
11. Exercise 5.4: Don't Get Hung Up!
12. Exercise 5.5: Humming a Tone
13. Exercise 5.6: Finding Your Focus
14. Exercise 5.7: More Vowels
15. Exercise 5.8: Nee Neh Nah Noh Noo
16. Exercise 5.9: Ho-Ho!
17. Exercise 5.10: Ha-Ha!
18. Exercise 8.5: Sing a Scale
19. Exercise 9.3: Falsetto to Full
20. The intervals of the natural minor scale
21. "Twinkle, Twinkle Little Star" in Solfeggio
22. The G Major scale in Solfeggio
23. Ascending intervals
24. Descending intervals
25. Exercise 12.1: Prime (unison) intervals
26. Exercise 12.2: Major and minor seconds
27. Exercise 12.3: Major and minor thirds
28. Exercise 12.4: Perfect and augmented fourths
29. Exercise 12.5: Perfect and diminished fifths
30. Exercise 12.6: Major and minor sixths
31. Exercise 12.7: Major and minor sevenths
32. Exercise 12.8: Octaves
33. Exercise 12.9: "Twinkle, Twinkle Little Star"
34. Exercise 12.10: "Frere Jacques" in G
35. Exercise 12.11a: "Frere Jacques" in D
36. Exercise 12.11b: "Amazing Grace"
37. Exercise 12.12: "Go Tell Aunt Rhody"
38. Speaking whole notes
39. Speaking half notes
40. Speaking quarter notes
41. Speaking eighth notes
42. Speaking sixteenth notes
43. Exercise 12.13: Reading Rhythms
44. Exercise 12.14: Reading Rhythms
45. Exercise 12.15: Reading Rhythms
46. Exercise 12.16: Reading Rhythms
47. Exercise 12.17: Reading Rhythms
48. Exercise 12.18: Reading Rhythms
49. Exercise 12.19: Reading Rhythms
50. Exercise 12.20: Reading Rhythms

51. Exercise 12.21: Reading Rhythms
52. Exercise 12.22: Putting Pitches and Rhythms Together
53. Exercise 12.23: Name That Tune
54. Exercise 12.24: "Poor Wayfaring Stranger"
55. Exercise 12.25: "Erie Canal"
56. Exercise 12.26: Sight Singing
57. Exercise 12.27: Sight Singing
58. Exercise 12.28: Sight Singing
59. Exercise 12.29: Sight Singing
60. Exercise 12.30: Sight Singing
61. Exercise 12.31: Sight Singing
62. Exercise 12.32: Sight Singing
63. Exercise 12.33: Sight Singing
64. Long vowels and pronunciations
65. Short vowels and pronunciations
66. "I Ain't Got Nobody (And Nobody Cares for Me)" sung straight and syncopated
67. "Shenandoah" (vocals by Brad Brock)
68. Choral: "Kyrie" (vocals by Stephanie Mitchell, Phyllis Fulford, Joe Brown, and Brad Brock)
69. Lieder: "Below in the Valley" (vocals by Dr. Mitzi Westra)
70. Lieder: "Below in the Valley" (piano only)
71. Pop: "The Water Is Wide" (vocals by Joe Brown)
72. Pop: "The Water Is Wide" (instruments and background vocals only)
73. Jazz: "I Ain't Got Nobody (And Nobody Cares for Me)" (vocals by Phyllis Fulford)
74. Jazz: "I Ain't Got Nobody (And Nobody Cares for Me)" (jazz trio only)
75. Gospel: "Amazing Grace" (vocals by Mary Moss)
76. Gospel: "Amazing Grace (piano only)

Vocal Credits

Brad Brock (baritone, solo on "Shenandoah") is a junior at Butler University, where he is majoring in music.

Joe Brown (tenor, solo on "The Water is Wide") holds a B.M. from DePauw University. He has performed commercial jingles, operas, and musicals on the East Coast, Florida, and Indiana. Joe currently sings with the Indianapolis Symphonic Choir and a variety of other musical groups throughout the central Indiana region.

Phyllis Fulford (alto, solo on "I Ain't Got Nobody")

Stephanie Mitchell (soprano) is a senior at Ben Davis High School in Indianapolis and hopes to pursue a professional singing career.

Mary Moss (solo on "Amazing Grace") is a respected member of the central Indiana jazz scene, having performed with a number of different groups and musicians over the past several decades. In 2002, Mary was inducted into the Indianapolis Jazz Foundation Hall of Fame; she currently performs with other local musicians in the group Mary Moss & Women Kickin' It.

Dr. Mitzi Westra (mezzo-soprano, solo on "Below in the Valley") is an active soloist and chamber musician who currently teaches voice and music theory at both the University of Indianapolis and Wabash College in Indiana. She sings with several chamber ensembles in the Indianapolis area and spends her summers performing with the Santa Fe Desert Chorale, a professional choral group in New Mexico.

Instrumental Credits

William Barnhardt (electric and acoustic bass) began his studies on bass at nine. He holds a Bachelor's degree in Music from Butler University and currently performs in several jazz, classical, and rock groups in the central Indiana area.

Ken Fary (jazz and gospel piano) is a highly respected jazz musician and teacher in the Indianapolis area. He performs both solo and with various local jazz groups.

Phyllis Fulford (piano and synthesizers)

Doug Henthorn (acoustic and electric guitar) got his first guitar at age 11; his first teacher was one of the authors of this book, Phyllis Fulford. Doug is a classically trained musician with a degree from Butler University, and is currently guitarist and vocalist with the group Healing Sixes (www.healingsixes.com). Their CD, *Enormosound*, is available from CoraZong Records in Canada and Europe.

Michael Miller (drums)

Recording Credits

Recorded, mixed, and mastered at The Lodge Recording Studios, Indianapolis, Indiana. Recording and mixing engineer: Michael Graham.

Produced by Phyllis Fulford and Michael Miller

Index

C

D

J

K-L

M

N-O

P

Q–R

S

T

U-V

W-X-Y-Z